WANDERING

Duke University Press   Durham and London   2014

WAN DER ING

Philosophical Performances of Racial and Sexual Freedom

Sarah Jane Cervenak

© 2014 DUKE UNIVERSITY PRESS

DESIGNED BY NATALIE F. SMITH

TYPESET IN GARAMOND PREMIER PRO BY COPPERLINE

Cover art: Carrie Mae Weems, *All That Passes Before You*, 2006.
© Carrie Mae Weems. Courtesy of the artist and Jack Shainman Gallery, NY.

LIBRARY OF CONGRESS CATALOGING-IN-PUBLICATION DATA

CERVENAK, SARAH JANE, 1975–

Wandering : philosophical performances of racial and sexual freedom / Sarah Jane Cervenak.
pages cm   Includes bibliographical references and index.

ISBN 978-0-8223-5715-5 (CLOTH : ALK. PAPER)

ISBN 978-0-8223-5727-8 (PBK. : ALK. PAPER)

1. RACE—PHILOSOPHY.   2. FEMINIST THEORY.   I. TITLE.

HT1523.C47 2014   305.801—DC23   2014006867

for Edison

CONTENTS

ACKNOWLEDGMENTS

This book has been and continues to be a long trip. Inasmuch as it is a product of private roaming, it is also a site where many have traveled. It is those travelers whom I thank here.

To begin, the book wouldn't be what it is without the loving support of my dissertation advisor, Fred Moten. Fred has been with and for this project from the beginning; in fact, I recall sharing my initial fragments of an idea with him in his office at NYU. Even though I didn't know what *Wandering* would become, what it would care about and what it would leave alone, Fred's faith in the work stayed constant throughout the duration of the project. I have learned what it means to teach from that faith. Indeed, I have benefited from Fred's model, as a teacher, scholar, and ethical person. I love this guy and am tremendously thankful for his presence in my life. I am also deeply blessed to know his wife, Laura Harris, and to have met his awesome kids.

Also during my graduate work at NYU, I am thankful to have learned from professors such as May Joseph, André Lepecki, the late and deeply missed José Muñoz, Kobena Mercer, and Barbara Browning, and from my fellow graduate students as well. They include Alexandra Vazquez, Christine Bacareza Balance, Hypatia Vourloumis, Ayanna Lee, Lauren Cooper, Shane Vogel, Ricardo Montez, Arin Mason, Jennifer Chan, Jo Novelli, Danielle Goldman, Tony Perucci, Cristof Migone, and Sara Jane Bailes. Also, I'm happy to have traveled with some of my old Rutgers comrades at that time as well—Edgar Rivera Colón and Jeremy Glick.

After NYU I continued work on the dissertation as a visiting scholar in the Ethnic Studies Department at UC Berkeley. I thank Jahleezah Eskew,

Norma Alarcón, Rani Neutil, and Karina Cespedes for their support of me and the project during my stay there. I wandered back home and then on to Stanford for a postdoctoral fellowship, and I thank the friends and colleagues I made there: Alice Rayner, Erin Ferris, Mark Sander, Magdalena Barrera, Jenny Barker, Uzma Rivzi, Michael Feola, Michael Hunter, Renu Cappelli, and Nadine Schibile. Kathryn Mathers, in particular, is a good friend I made at Stanford and someone whose kindness fills this book and my life.

Since the postdoctoral fellowship, I've been lucky to move to North Carolina to join the faculties of African American Studies and Women's and Gender Studies at the University of North Carolina, Greensboro. I thank the following people for their support of me and the project: Kathy Jamieson, Leila Villaverde, Gwen Hunnicut, Mark Rifkin, Bill Hart, Shelley Brown-Jeffy, Omar Ali, Tara Green, Frank Woods, Michael Cauthen, Robert Randolph, Demetrius Noble, Sally Deutsch, Logie Meachum, Beth Walker, Carole Lindsey Potter, and Bruce Holland. My colleague Danielle Bouchard has read this book more times than she'd probably care to admit, and it wouldn't be where it is without her commitment, her genius, and her love.

Thanks to Seth Moglen for his rigorous engagement with chapter 2. I also thank Fred Moten, Mercy Romero, and Kathryn Mathers for reading the whole manuscript and for being genuinely awesome.

At Duke University Press, I thank my editor, Courtney Berger, and her assistants, Deborah Guterman and Erin Hanas. Courtney's constant encouragement and guidance has helped my thinking enormously. I also thank the anonymous readers who took the time to read the manuscript and provide rigorous feedback.

Recently I've had the privilege of joining and participating in the Black Performance Theory working group. I've been blessed to meet and learn from Koritha Mitchell, Hershini Bhana, Jayna Brown, Uri McMillian, Rashida Braggs, Christina Knight, Jeffrey McCune, N. Fadeke Castor, Yolanda Covington, Stephanie Batiste, Matt Richardson, Omi Osun Jones, and Tommy DeFrantz.

I also want to acknowledge all of my students at these various institutions. Their genius and good energy make the job worthwhile, and I'm tremendously honored to know them.

Lastly, my family. I begin by thanking someone who might as well be family, my best friend, Mercy Romero. Mercy and I share a brain and heart;

her wisdom and love have helped me be the kind of person and writer I want to be, and for that I'm truly thankful. To my sisters, Maryellen and Lizzie, I love you more than anything and thank you for putting up with my craziness. Also, thanks for smiling and making fun of my nerdiness when I talked about the project. Thanks to my dad, who reminds me not to burn the candle at both ends every time we talk. Finally, thanks to my mother, my best friend, the person who saves my life on a daily basis and reminds me who I am and can be every day.

In the end, I close by thanking the two halves of my heart. To my love, Marc Derro, thank you for being the kindest, most supportive person in town and for loving me the way you do. Oh, and for agonizing (along with me) over that first paragraph of my introduction. And to my baby son, Edison, who is named after the town in New Jersey that I'm from. You are the love of my life and the reason I write. Your kicks and giggles are all over this book, making you in some ways its coauthor. I love you forever and more.

An earlier version of chapter 2 was published in *Palimpsest: Women, Gender, and the Black International* 1, no 1 (2012). An earlier version of chapter 4 was published in Lovalerie King and Linda Selzer's *New Essays on the African American Novel: From Hurston and Ellison to Morrison and Whitehead* (Palgrave, 2008). An earlier version of the conclusion was published in *Spectator* 30, no. 2 (Fall 2010).

Finally, thanks to the artists Carrie Mae Weems, Yinka Shonibare, William Pope.L, and Adrian Piper for letting me feature their art.

INTRODUCTION

I leaned against the seat and closed my eyes. Then, suddenly, it was like I was remembering
something out of a long past. I was a child, drowsy, thinking I was sleeping or dreaming.

GAYL JONES, *CORREGIDORA*

Ursa's bus ride inspired this book. The bus ride transpires quietly in the
middle of Gayl Jones's *Corregidora* (1975), a story about the haunted life of
a Southern blues singer. It is during this ride that Ursa Corregidora wanders to recover a lost privacy and, with it, a grip on a landscape that cannot
be encroached: a locale where she might roam without surveillance, out
of harm's way.

The novel indeed begins in harm's way and shuttles between private
pain and public trespass. It starts with Ursa's hospitalization. While fight-
ing with her husband, he pushes Ursa down the stairs; she suffers a mis-
carriage and eventual hysterectomy as a result. The novel tells that story,
of private harm and recovery. The sips of chicken soup and nightly singing that bring her through. At the same time, Ursa's private story suffers
from endless trespass. The novel moves quickly from a single-occupancy
hospital room to an overcrowded main character. As Ursa slowly heals,
the voices of family and lovers form a noisy traffic that she must amble
through. This traffic consists of stories of Old Man Corregidora, her family's Portuguese slave owner, now deceased, alongside familial injunctions
to reproduce, to pass down, and to not forget what he did. Joining this
traffic too are the needs of lovers, impatient with the time and form of
Ursa's return. All of which result in a heavily encroached upon main char-

acter. She is someone who rarely gets to move by herself, as she is subjected to racial slavery's enduring whims and the confining scripts of its survivors.

Against these competing scripts and choreographies, Ursa's yearning for anonymous and solitary comportment takes form; fleeting drifts of philosophical possibility hover in the opaque terrain next to the visible word. Such drifts can happen on bus rides. The bus ride in *Corregidora* is a tiny moment at the end of a chapter. It follows the scene where Ursa asks her mother about the other past, the one not shredded by Old Man Corregidora's phantasmatic wandering. In *Corregidora* such questions and their answers are thick with individual and collective need, making unremarkable bus rides (un)remarkable. It's on the bus that Ursa finally achieves some privacy, a rare occasion to wander and dream without interruption. To imagine the possibilities for her "own life," beyond the push and pull of other people's memories, other people's desires.[1]

This is where my idea for this book came from: my elusive recollection of Ursa's ride. A ride without narration, where the main character drifts off someplace else, just beneath the text, and off its page. A rare moment of privacy for someone whose experience of the world is never free from the trespassive enactments of others. Even though the voices of a man and woman come to her in a dream, Ursa wakes up and shifts to thinking about something else; the details of that dream are never disclosed. Further, while the broken speech of the man and woman lingers on a readable surface, Ursa contemplates "what [she had] done about [her] own life."[2] The traveling engendered by such an inquiry also remains unnarrated—the philosophical meaning and nature of that life are not contingent upon its availability to prose.

This absence of description doesn't necessarily indicate an absence of movement. More broadly, wandering—daydreaming, mental and rhetorical ramblings—offers new pathways for the enactment of black female philosophical desire. Because a scene of unremarkable travel, a barely described philosophical movement, inspired this book, I begin by inquiring into whether such movement should be engaged at all. This is not to say that what happens on the bus for Ursa isn't important, but its importance is not contingent on its interpretation (or interpretative availability) as such.

In many ways such contingencies form a troubling tendency within performance studies, where the presumed philosophical capacities of performances and gestures are inextricable from their readability. What is more, as a scholar trained in this field, I also struggle with the discipline's tendency to privilege the philosophical capacities of purportedly legible acts over unseen drifts and dreams. For example, in a textbook on the field, *Performance Studies: An Introduction* (2002), Richard Schechner argues that "performance studies scholars are able to 'read' popular culture."[3] In another major performance studies anthology, *Critical Theory and Performance* (2007), the editors Joseph Roach and Janelle Reinelt advance the notion that "performance can be articulated in terms of politics."[4] Considering these assumptions, I ask, what would it mean to leave alone that which cannot be read or that which resists the epistemological urgencies at the heart of such readability and knowability? What if Ursa's daydreams are philosophical in ways that have nothing to do with the their availability to external meaning or their ability to *articulate* anything at all?

These questions index dual ethical interests that are at once conjoined and seemingly opposed. On the one hand, *Wandering* is not interested in interrupting anybody's bus ride, let alone Ursa's. Jones's reclusiveness moves alongside her characters' own longing for unfettered movement. In some ways the worlds made by Jones are better off when left alone. Still, even as this book is an exercise in learning from Jones, *Wandering* seemingly undermines that learning in its own movement. More precisely, unlike Jones's novels, *Wandering*'s assertion that enactments of philosophical desire are possible despite and because of their resistance to verifiability is troubled by its own tendency to make much of that possibility. While making much of infuses the kinds of analytic tendencies I otherwise critique—those that shift the philosophical from the private domain of its making to the public mode of its decryption—I want to express a different relation to this procedure. In my engagement with diverse aesthetic and historical scenes, then, I advance the possibility of philosophical abundance against racist, sexist, classist, spatial, ableist, logocentric, homophobic, and ocularcentric assumptions that presume both its impossibility and absence. In this way, making much of is an attempt to attend to the violence of such erasures while understanding that only much can really be made by the author or artist, daydreamer or bus rider.

This ethical complexity moves *Wandering* and celebrates the fact that the book both is and isn't about what it says its about, both can and can't be about wandering. What is powerful about wandering, I think, is its potential to resist this book's enclosures—to be not only a mutant form of enunciation, articulation, and textuality but also an enactment that signals the refusal of all three qualities.[5] Because wandering is as much an interior as it is an exterior activity, it at once resists decryption and sustains an unavailable landscape of philosophical desire. In Jones's *Corregidora*, for example, Ursa's private wisdom wanders as song: "My voice was dancing, slow and blue, my voice was dancing but I was saying nothing. I dreamed with my eyes open."[6] While the private "slow and blue" voice moves undetectably in the ether underneath and around "nothing" said, the visible and ostensibly public movements of the body aren't necessarily *articulating* a *readable* story either.

In my musings on wandering, however, I had a hard time finding work that didn't aggregate wandering with exterior kinesis (specifically walking) and, more problematically, corporeal readability, enunciativity, and agentic possibility. For example, Michel de Certeau argues that walking enacts a

> triple "enunciative" function: it is a process of *appropriation* of the topographical system on the part of the pedestrian (just as the speaker appropriates and takes on the language); it is a spatial acting-out of the place (just as the speech act is an acoustic acting-out of language); and it implies *relations* among differentiated positions, that is, among pragmatic "contracts" in the form of movements (just as verbal enunciation is an "allocution," "posits another opposite" the speaker and puts contracts between interlocutors into action). It thus seems possible to give a preliminary definition of walking as a space of enunciation.[7]

Drawing parallels between walking and speech, using the language of enunciation, implies a shared quality of discursive availability and rests on the presumption of the walker as agent. In the spirit of Certeau, the dance studies scholar Susan Leigh Foster also employs a literary term to describe the walker's "swerve [as] a trope" that illuminates and resists state apparatuses of control.[8] Both models presume a notion of human agency that is readable as exterior kinesis. Still, if to be an agent means having "intention, which is variously glossed as 'plan,' 'awareness,' 'willfulness,' 'directedness,' or 'desire,'" then what is at stake for those whose pedestrian "acting out(s)" are always already surveilled?[9] What if state surveillance gets oddly replicated in tropological readings of the body's movement? Finally, what happens if the exercise of agency as exterior kinesis resists reading, or rather becomes agentic in its unreadability?

Crucially, scholars engaged with black performance, feminisms, and critical theory have advanced the notion that terrains of movement thrive beyond the discursive, epistemological, and empirical. For example, Jayna

Brown and André Lepecki's scholarship attends to the agentic qualities of corporeal unreadability and the exterior, kinetic bias of the post-
Enlightenment's idealized subject, respectively. In her important work
on early twentieth-century black female performers, *Babylon Girls: Black
Women Performers and the Shaping of the Modern* (2008), Brown contends that "racialized bodies wriggle through, around, with, and against . . .
claims" that read them as discourse or discursive effects.[10] Reimagining
the black body as active in ways that exceed or resist discourse is crucial
as the body's presumed discursivity often facilitates the most vicious of
constraints. For example, before it was determined to be unconstitutional,
California penal code section 647(e) rendered illegal the act of loitering
or "wandering upon the streets or from place to place without apparent
reason or business."[11] In the early 1980s, Edward Lawson, a black man who
enjoyed late-night walks, refused to disclose his identity to authorities
when out and about and was arrested under this penal code.

Arguably, Lawson was arrested because his exercise of kinetic agency
was discursively troubling to the state and, further, incommensurate with
racialized and classed post-Enlightenment logics of the idealized moving
subject. According to the philosopher Denise Ferreira da Silva, late eigh-
teenth- and nineteenth-century (normative, sanctioned, recognized) post-
Enlightenment logics of subjectivity continue to hold powerful sway: "The
subject of transparency, for whom universal reason is an interior guide [, is
still associated with white Europeanness, while] subjects of affectability,
for whom universal reason remains an exterior ruler," are still racialized
and figured as Europe's outside.[12] What these post-Enlightenment logics
presume is a notion of racialized, gendered subjectivity that is incapable of
philosophical production though nonetheless subjected to the violation
of being philosophically produced (recall Brown's critique). Put another
way and in the context of Lawson and Ursa, black movement is, more often than not, *read* as disruptive physicality, a philosophical problem to be
solved as opposed to that which resolves philosophical problems.

Moreover, this figuration of blackness is key to the racial consolidation
of post-Enlightenment subjectivity. Along with da Silva, Lepecki argues
that a key feature and privilege of post-Enlightenment subjectivity is (exterior) kinesis, the illusion of a normative body that enjoys and regulates
his or her own "autonomous, self-motivated, endless, spectacular movement."[13] I would add here that because external kinesis is given as either
the sign of one's reason or its absence, critical theories of bodily readability

and discursivity limit black wandering's radicalism.[14] We need a new way to think about wandering as philosophical performance, one not contingent on its availability to discourse or to analytics of bodily enunciativity, exterior-oriented narratives of kinesis, and individual agency. In the scene from Jones's *Corregidora*, for example, bus riding makes a world to which the novel's readers have no access.

Powerfully, these elusive philosophical worlds engendered by daydreams and prayers subvert the aforementioned, confining rhetoric of subjectivity held over from the Enlightenment. People move in ways that are invisible, along the grooves of their own mind, in the motion of a rambling tongue, outside the range of an administrative and purportedly enlightened gaze. Dealing with the legacy of the Enlightenment, then, is essential to this argument in that its theories of the normative subject thrive and continue to be shaped at the intersections of race, sexuality, and the logics of legibly rational philosophical comportment. As da Silva and Lepecki demonstrate, for example, the rational, self-same, self-possessed, and self-mobilizing subject, invented and revised by recognized European and American Enlightenment philosophers from the seventeenth through nineteenth centuries, still pervades state thinking about appropriate public (read: visible) kinesis and inspires an antiwandering ethos targeted particularly at the nonnormative. Concerning Lawson, according to Dan Stormer and Paul Bernstein, the police called him "the Walkman. . . . He liked to walk whenever possible—especially in white neighborhoods late at night. While in San Diego on business between 1975 and 1977, Edward Lawson was stopped fifteen times by police. . . . Later the officers offered a variety of explanations for stopping Lawson that fell far short of the reasonable cause requirement read into section 647 (e) by the courts. One officer thought that Lawson's behavior, which he described as 'dancing around,' might lead to someone's injury."[15]

The presumption that "dancing around might lead to someone's injury" indexes a larger belief system that figures blackness as incapable of rational comportment. Lawson's wandering was criminalized precisely because of its performative figuration as injurious and disorderly. What is more, because his "dancing" appeared recklessly unchoreographed, the state moved in to impose or solicit a script. Lawson refused and was arrested. Even though Lawson's subsequent lawsuit against the state resulted in a declaration of the unconstitutionality of section 647(e), police officers can still request a "suspicious" wanderer's legal identification. In fact, "stop and identify" statutes are on the books in twenty-four states and affect "minority communities disproportionately."[16]

Again, following da Silva, the state's criminalization of black walkers resonates with the post-Enlightenment's figuration of people of color as guided by an illegitimate, unlawful outside. Ironically, however, according to Lepecki, "*all* subjectivity that finds itself as a total 'being-toward-movement' must draw its energy from some [outside] source."[17] The scene of eighteenth- and nineteenth-century white European Enlightenment philosophy, in particular, was often animated and constituted by a vampiric cruising, with the "ground of modernity [being] the colonized, flattened, bulldozed terrain where the fantasy of endless and self-sufficient motility [took] place."[18] In fact, the Enlightenment's supposedly straight text or choreographic script—where *straight* refers to the putatively disinterested investments in reason, morality, and justice—was frequently written through wandering: sidesteps into Otherness that forged the Enlightenment's racialized, gendered, and sexualized energetic conditions of possibility. These conditions of a simultaneously disinterested and ecstatic racial and sexual kinesis often tragically resulted in the evacuation of life from the Enlightenment's objects. Like vampires, the subject of the Enlightenment errantly moved under the cover of light, reducing others' lives—either through the pen or the gun—to sustain the subject's own.

In his discussion of nineteenth-century colonial travelogues, Johannes Fabian addresses this vampirism by arguing that explorers, in their collision with "unfamiliar cultures," resolved the "moral puzzles and conflicting demands" by "stepping outside, and sometimes existing for long periods outside, the rationalized frames of exploration, be they faith, knowledge, profit, or domination."[19] Methodologically speaking, the condition of possibility for the repeated consolidation of the hegemonic, sovereign subject of the Enlightenment (who da Silva names the subject of transparency) was an anthropological-explorationist project that required man to "step outside," diverge from, or run astray of his own fixed threshold. Even as, according to Sankar Muthu, the Enlightenment philosopher Denis Diderot argues that errant movement, particularly the "unchecked passions . . . unleashed among crusading voyagers," was a betrayal of an Enlightenment ethic of universal humanity, I maintain that errant movement itself shaped the uneven enactment of such ethics.[20] Indeed, Michel Foucault speaks to this "fundamental arrangement" between anthropology and philosophy when he writes that "anthropology constitutes perhaps the fundamental arrangement that has governed and controlled the path of philosophical thought from Kant until our own day."[21]

The opening that made possible the fundamental interplay between philosophy and anthropology animated and was (de)formed by the emissaries of imperialism's own "affectable" movement. Moreover, as the philosopher Sylvia Wynter observes, those humans who endured the violence of imperialists' inherent affectability described such movements accordingly, as drunk or under an outside influence. Quoting from the Cenu Indians' response to the Spanish Requisition of 1492, whereby Spain was given land (or "the new world") that didn't belong to it, Wynter connects the Cenus' perception of imperial drunkenness to a larger set of irrational procedures. That is, the condition of possibility for the Requisition itself rested on a paradoxically restrictive notion of the human, one that passed itself off as "natural, supracultural and isomorphic with the human species" but that in actuality foregrounded white Europeanness and a monotheistic belief system as its raison d'être.[22] The exercise of humanity was nothing if not trespassive, where Europe's meandering "identitarian land claim[s]" overruled all others.[23]

Still, these philosophers advanced Enlightenment humanism as self-determined, unaffected, and teleological mobility. In doing so, wandering became pathologized even as it remained methodologically necessary. Discerning such movement requires that we recognize that while Europeans' finitude was tested and transgressed in the interest of its definition, the bodies and minds that provided the anthropological and epistemological occasions—figured as the scene and embodiment of affectability—as well as the conditions of possibility of such exploration suffered the severe constraints of forced (im)mobilization.

In the context of colonial exploration and the transatlantic slave trade, this often manifested, time and again, in a quasi-spiritual transcendence for the subjects of the Enlightenment and a brutally material death for the Enlightenment's objects. In other words, affectability, being moved by an outside force or "dangerously unproductive will," in da Silva's words, was an experience, a vacation from reason that was also reason's very condition.[24] These vacations from reason, however, were "perilous passages," both for the recognized subject whose very descent into affectability meant his temporary loss of transparent self-determination and independent mobilization as well as for the objects of (un)reason whose imbrication with affectability resulted in their endless trespassive violation and containment.[25] What is more, the danger experienced by the subject of the Enlightenment was often resolved through the homicidal eradication of its objects. As Wynter argues, "We have lived the millennium of Man in the last five hundred years; and as the West is inventing Man, the slave plantation is a central part of the entire mechanism by means of which that logic is working its way out."[26]

To be sure, the endless roaming of the purportedly enlightened emissaries of imperialism, and with it a promiscuous and increasingly narrow understanding of the human, required the energetic hijacking of someone else's will. African slaves in the Americas and their descendants, through their very politico-economic, racial, sexual, and ontological inscription as chattel, according to Hortense Spillers, experienced the unimaginable violation of being radically severed "from [their] motive will."[27] Slaves were "perceived as the essence of stillness (an early version of 'ethnicity'), or of an undynamic human state, fixed in time and space. . . . 'Slaves [were] deemed, sold, taken, reputed and adjudged in law to be *chattels personal*, in the hands of their owners and possessors, and their executors, administrators, and assigns, to all intents, constructions, and purposes whatsoever."[28] Temporally fixed in a hierarchical historical geography, slaves were also defined by their fundamental disposability, affectability, movability, and alienability.

The radical fracture of the captive self's being from its motive will, in conjunction with the slave's status as stock and as necessarily stock-still, produced a series of violent choreographic effects. Namely, while regarded as the "essence of stillness," slaves endured the racial, sexual, and philosophical *whims*—the economic, political, sexual, aesthetic, and epistemological desires—of the master. Saidiya Hartman observes, "[E]njoyment [in the context of antebellum slavery] is virtually unimaginable without recourse to the black body and the subjection of the captive, the diversion engendered by the dispossession of the enslaved, or the fantasies launched by the myriad uses of the black body."[29] Such crookedly whimsical *flights* of fancy enlarged the performative scope of whiteness while consolidating a vicious state of black unfreedom.

In response to this violently paradoxical crisis of unfreedom—where unfreedom meant, among other things, being ontologically codified as the nowhere, the detour, the backyard, and the movable and material sign of white diversion—black people philosophized, moved. As Wynter writes, "[The] slave plot on which the slave grew food for his/her subsistence, carried over a millennially *other* conception of the human to that of Man's."[30] Indeed, it was often not just the plot itself but how one moved through it that shaped these alternative "genres of the human," in the words of Alexander G. Weheliye.[31] On the one hand, the set of performances associated with the drive toward anticaptivity bespeaks a powerful philosophical claim associating black humanity with self-possession, determination, and, for some, the fulfillment of Enlightenment ideals. Further, self-possession and self-determination in the antebellum era involved a set of philosophical performances characterized as moving for oneself. This self-mobilization refers to a range of physical and rhetorical transgressions, according to Hartman, such as "movement without a pass to visit a loved one, stealing, unpermitted gatherings," slave revolts, and published polemics against slavery.[32]

On the other hand, while self-direction and self-mobilization were key to antislavery consolidations of humanness, other modalities of movement across the plot were just as important. That is, the plot also became the ground for diverting the pursuit of others, and, in that way, respatializing the terrain of freedom. An aesthetics of diversion is arguably at work in the slave narrative. Powerfully, (anti)slave narration's informational withholding and aleatory prose corresponds to tactics practiced by those who worked and traveled on the Underground Railroad. This has all contributed to the protection of black humanity from the trespassive encroachments of the slave catcher and abolitionist reader, both exemplary products of recognized European and American Enlightenment traditions. Just as the emissaries of the imperial Enlightenment immobilized (by fixing and rendering transparent) black life in their attempts to know it, the slave catcher and abolitionist reader performed similar, albeit politically distinct, labors. This is not to say that all abolitionists operated in the spirit of Enlightenment-as-pornotropic-trespass but that some tendencies reveal an ugly, energetically comparable trace. According to the contemporary scholars Deborah Garfield and Carol Lasser, an emphasis on sexual violence, what Garfield refers to as an "impassioned speech," formed a troubling early tendency of nineteenth-century abolitionism.[33] While this tendency was one of many and should not be conflated with the rich and complicated abolitionist movement itself, I query this problematic violation of black people's right to privacy and why it was necessary for the achievement of so-called real Enlightenment freedom.

Moreover, in the context of racial slavery, black privacy figured as dangerous, a highly pursued philosophical scene of potential insurrection and unreadable desire. Curiously, in the context of antislavery, black privacy sometimes suffered a similar fate, albeit motivated by different political and ethical intentions. In *Incidents in the Life of a Slave Girl* (1861), for example, Harriet Jacobs's narrative oscillates between an interior (private) kinesis—an embrace of wandering manifested through recklessness, prayer, and daydreaming—and a strategic rhetorical commitment to transparent, enlightened, and self-regulated comportment.[34] This oscillation, or, for some (including Jacobs), waywardness, proved crucial for her enactment of black female enlightenment. That is, just as some white female antislavery activists required Jacobs to renounce her right to privacy as a condition for her inclusion in their enlightenment project, her strategic information withholdings (particularly with respect to sexual violence) along with other unnarrated sojourns elsewhere expressed her philosophical desire while subverting theirs.

Similar to Lawson's dangerous dancing and Ursa's bus riding, Jacobs's trips into undisclosed locales refused the pull of someone else's script. This is not to say that such movements remained unpoliced or unscripted; all three movements negotiated the kinetic constraints engendered by others' anxious readings. Rather, because wandering exceeds the terrains of the visible and the physical and because it's not possible to *know* and legislate the private ambulations of the spirit, antiwandering laws and acts don't spell the end of black freedom. In fact, historically speaking, against the state's figuration of black wandering as disruptively criminal (and trespassive) physicality, black artist and activist philosophers have expanded black wandering's kinetic meaning and philosophical potential.

Significantly, black feminist theory informs my engagement with wandering's complexity and radical possibility. To begin, black feminists have been at the forefront of theorizing the limits of the Enlightenment and post-Enlightenment as racial, patriarchal projects by interrogating the fictitious mind-body split (Audre Lorde and Barbara Christian) and by defamiliarizing the imperial, epistemological processes of nonconsensually naming, codifying, and immobilizing the movements of black women (Spillers).[35] Lorde, in particular, powerfully critiques the constraints on black women's movement as a legacy of the Enlightenment. More precisely, her work defamiliarizes and deconstructs key features of post-

Enlightenment society, among them the mind-body split, the devaluation of the nonrational, and the fraudulent normativity of white, heterosexual, bourgeois, able-bodied subjects.[36]

For Lorde these Enlightenment inheritances have historically denied racialized, gendered, and classed bodies the right to wander along the limits of their own desires. Moreover, because of the pervasiveness of the post-Enlightenment's continued rejection of ecstasy and embodiment, particularly for racialized and gendered bodies, Lorde argues that "when we live away from those erotic guides from within ourselves, then our lives are limited by external and alien forms, and we conform to the needs of a structure that is not based on human need, let alone an individual's. But when we begin to live from within outward, in touch with the power of the erotic within ourselves, and allowing that power to inform and illuminate our actions upon the world around us, then we begin to be responsible to ourselves in the deepest sense."[37]

While the embrace of the erotic is a crucial maneuver for subjects historically disentitled from desire, it is important to realize that the erotic was a key condition of possibility for the Enlightenment and for post-Enlightenment subjectivity. Still, because desire often upsets the illusion of rational self-determination, desire was and is figured as antithetical to reason, belonging to the unwieldy, pathological domain of the racialized, classed, and gendered: a physicalized domain sanctioning the most vicious of state constraints. As Sharon Patricia Holland argues,

> [the] focus on desire—the erotic of Lorde and [Simone de] Beauvoir, to some extent—is important in the process of orientation under colonialism, as desire (longing) marks the place of colonial access, thus turning the desired one into a kind of melancholic digestif. You can incorporate *it* all you want to, but the thing you want will remain forever elusive, so you try to capture it in other ways—fixing it through law (the condition of the child shall follow the condition of the mother in the United States context) and custom (the overall perception that the idea of a "neighborhood" reflects cultural ebb and flow rather than racist practice).[38]

For Holland, Lorde's "Uses of the Erotic" raises important questions about "desire's [radical and philosophical] autonomy," particularly in the face of histories that figure that autonomy as impossible.[39] Moreover, Lorde's critique of the Enlightenment's dephilosophization of the erotic evokes other meditations about black women's relation to desire more specifically; this is a relation historically wounded by the trespassive regulations of racist and sexist inscription. Put another way, for the objects of colonialism whose continued figuration as "affectable" endangers their right to walk down the street, the use of the erotic is criminal.

But, as both Lorde and Holland argue, the state's illusory attempts to police the erotic, to guide and shape its expression, are always already subverted by the erotic's private exercise. Indeed, for some black feminist philosophers (e.g., Lorde and Holland), such mobilization "from within ourselves" is advanced as essential to their project. For example, whereas Farah Griffin argues that a "focus on the interior grows out of a black feminist project," Mae Henderson identifies the "intimate, private, inspired utterances" as a key feature of black women's writing.[40] Moreover, M. Jacqui Alexander figures African-diasporic engagements with spirituality (the felt but unseen) as essential to any radical feminist politics. For Alexander, the sacred, like Lorde's erotic, facilitates "the alignment of mind, body, and Spirit" in ways that subvert the straightening out violences of "social practices of alienation."[41]

While it would be problematic to reduce black feminisms to a specific set of political and ethical interests, there is an important tradition instantiated by figures such as Sojourner Truth and Lorde that regards the interior as a philosophical site of radical desire, guidance, errant performativity, and healing. This line of black feminist criticism, which imagines the world-making potential of spirit, the erotic, desire, and the private, simultaneously disrupts illusions of bodily readability and discursive availability at the heart of hegemonically sanctioned, post-Enlightenment constructions of black female subjectivity. Further, the philosophically generative act of phantasmatic travel engendered by the unpredictability of spirit and desire questions racialist logics that presume that bodies of color can only be moved by an outside force and not from within. As the black feminist critic Katherine McKittrick argues, such movement from within agitates against a dominant geographic logic that figures black women as locked outside space and time, at once terminally dispossessed and fundamentally ungeographic. As demonstrated in the case of Jacobs, what is hidden from view—the attic and garret where she hid from slavery—is also a "concealed sense of place [that] looks outward, offering a different perspective through which slavery can be mapped."[42]

Significantly, the philosophical movements of nineteenth-, twentieth-, and twenty-first-century black wanderers amble within and sometimes out from "a concealed sense of place," troubling philosophical, artistic, and literary orthodoxies that aggregate freedom with transparency. Tragically, though, because these figures have often been dismissed as incomprehensible, hard to follow, and psychotic, they remain marginal in conversations on (legitimate) freedom. What their critics sadly miss are the ways that a resistance to understanding is the site of radicalism. Daphne Brooks's and Fred Moten's works are crucial in my thinking here and model, as do the work of Lepecki and Brown, the kind of ethical performance studies project that I'm interested in.

More specifically, Moten and Brooks advocate a performance studies project that celebrates the "resistance of the object."[43] Moten, for example, troubles the assumption within performance studies that acts and movements in the world easily lend themselves to philosophical and analytic codification. He argues that objects not only resist the gaze of the spectator but also undermine the empirical, epistemological desire at the heart of such spectatorship. Similarly, Brooks discusses the ways that black women resist objecthood through eccentric, untraceable, and radical artistic and literary practice. In her engagement with black artists in the late nineteenth and early twentieth centuries, Brooks observes that "the opaque performances of marginalized cultural figures call attention to the skill of the performer who, through gestures and speech as well as material props and visual technologies, is able to confound and disrupt conventional constructions of the racialized and gendered body. In what we may refer to as a 'spectacular opacity,' this cultural phenomenon emerges at varying times as a product of the performer's will, at other times as a visual obstacle erupting as a result of a hostile spectator's epistemological resistance to reading alternative racial and gender representations."[44]

The opacity in the spectacular is the undetectable place of an errant movement, an interior kinesis that resists forces attempting to trace, follow, and read. In *Wandering* I take care not to replicate the very same epistemological impulse I otherwise critique. I do this by refusing to offer totalizing readings or diagnoses of that which resists a reading. This is not to say that the crooked enactment of racial, sexual, and imperial desire should not be read. Such unethical movement must be read and thereby immobilized in the interest of freedom. But my reading gesture is only meant to usher in other modes of engaging with the philosophical performances of black wanderers and to do so in ways that untether justice from its entrapment in understanding. Presented differently, wandering aligns with the free at precisely those moments when it bends away from forces that attempt to translate or read. In that way we must interrogate epistemological maneuvers and histories that seek to decipher, diagnose, and criminalize black movement precisely because of its resistance to being followed and understood.

Indeed, as the postcolonial philosophers Denise Ferreira da Silva, Gayatri Spivak, and others argue, the consolidation of the white male Enlightenment subject as rationally self-determined required the epistemological localization of racial and gendered Others, particularly in pathological impulsivity. Quite literally, they remained radically outside the straight and upright course advanced by Enlightenment philosophers, and therefore were paradoxically able to be trespassed. *Wandering* continues in chapter 1 to interrogate the performative contradictions at the heart of the recognized Enlightenment and the ways that those contradictions are racialized and gendered. Further developing this argumentation is important as I share the belief held by some postcolonial philosophers that this Enlightenment model of subjectivity still persists today and provides the rationale for various forms of racist and sexist restraint.

In chapter 1, "Losing Their Heads: Race, Sexuality, and the Perverse Moves of the European Enlightenment," I argue that the epistemological and moral disinterestedness said to characterize the Enlightenment was formed through an ecstatic, erotic existence, or wandering off the straight and narrow path. Engaging with some of the seminal work of the recognized Enlightenment philosophers Immanuel Kant and Jean-Jacques Rousseau, I think about how their encounters with racial and sexual difference undermined the requisite disinterestedness of the Enlightenment itself. Put another way, the straight path of reason was always already troubled by its impossible reach, the promiscuous maneuvers of an "epistemic model that takes as its model the colonization of the world (of experience)," according to Willi Goetschel.[45] If it is the case, for example, that Kant is largely responsible for the "first theory of race," then it is crucial to understand that such a theory was predicated on a straying from reason's teleological ground.[46] In fact, the racist and biologically deterministic musings of Kant are, given his own analytic of reason, illegitimate and impossible.

Unlike the straight and narrow course advanced by Kant and others, the invention of race depended on a violent wandering. Similarly, race and racial difference energize the straying of one of Kant's key influences, Jean-

Jacques Rousseau. Like Kant, Rousseau betrayed an ethical principle at the heart of his universally minded *social* contract by advancing the right to freedom as particular. Such particularity emerged as a condition and effect of his wandering and was deeply shaped by racialized and sexualized narratives of the right to (private) freedom. For both philosophers wandering is a self-interested straying from the ethical—a straying that, as with the colonial method it was inspired by, devastates all in its path. As David Scott argues, in dialogue with Wynter, such straying again expresses Western humanism's own errancy: "Humanism and colonialism inhabit the same cognitive-political universe inasmuch as Europe's discovery of its Self is simultaneous with its discovery of its Others."[47]

Tragically, for the objects of the Enlightenment, the force of such an encounter resulted in the radical disavowal of subjectivity, of philosophical and geographic desire. But this denial of philosophical and geographic desire is not to be confused with its absence. Rather, black resistance to the waywardness of European reason was the scene of profound, vexed, and complicated philosophical insight, and in many ways an originary site for reason's radical enactment. Still, while black philosophers critiqued the waywardness of colonial reason and often did so through a deregulated openness to the twists and turns of interior guidance, the "appositional" expression of black enlightenment often replicated the recognized Enlightenment's stifling modes of (imperial and masculinist) comportment.[48] According to Hartman, the "equality of rights to be extended to freedmen depended upon the transformation of former slaves into responsible and reasonable men. As would be expected, the norms at issue were masculinity, rationality, and restraint."[49]

Indeed, before and after legislative emancipation, black people's capacity for self-control figured as essential in the acquisition of freedom. This definition did emerge out of a white-supremacist fiction and fear of black recklessness (or unenlightenment), but, more profoundly, it worked to shape and constrain some performances of freedom advocated by black philosophers themselves. Chapter 2, "Crooked Ways and Weak Pens: The Enactment of Enlightenment against Slavery," examines the ways that the antislavery activists David Walker, Martin Delany, and, in a more subversive manner, Jacobs, contrasted their focused movement, moral uplift, and refinement with acts ideologically imagined as wayward, nonsensical, unenlightened, and offtrack. Strikingly, the secondary set of performances was often gendered and classed in ways that suggest a powerful group of as-

sociations (forged in Revolutionary War–era, white American Enlightenment philosophy) between blackness, (the absence of) manhood, poverty,
slavery, and unenlightenment. For example, though Walker critiqued the
racist underpinnings of European and American Enlightenment projects,
he at the same time believed in what Seth Moglen and David Kazanjian
call, after Moten, appositional, "black enlightenment."[50]

This political and philosophical undertaking worked to realize the
very universal ideas of liberty and natural right otherwise neglected by
the racisms of recognized Enlightenment philosophers. This is not to say
that black enlightenment was merely a corrective philosophical project.
Rather, in many ways, it rewrote the story of the Enlightenment as one
where what is invisible—the mythic, the private, and the spiritual—was
not to be overcome but instead radically engaged. Moreover, what is invisible—what Wynter calls a "millennially other conception of the human
to that of Man's"—became the place for an alternative geographic desire.[51]
Once again, as McKittrick argues, if it's the case that the European Enlightenment and its particular understanding of humanity required "the
profitable [and drunken and mad] erasure and objectification of subaltern
subjectivities, stories, and lands," then the aim was to render black people
ungeographic.[52] Nonetheless, despite and in the face of dispossession and
of being disentitled from material landscape, black philosophers made terrain through wandering. At the place where Walker exulted the heavens,
Jacobs drifted off, and Truth prayed, black philosophers' wanderings created ground for a different kind of movement.

In some ways, the drifts in tone and pitch, the unnarrated reveries, and
the private musings disrupted the requirement of rational self-determination
and transparency at the heart of the racial Enlightenment's idealized subject. As such, other theorizations of the human "unburdened by shackles
of Man," in Weheliye's words, became possible.[53] Put another way, unrestrained theorizations of the human and freedom occurred in the "liminal precincts" poised between legible, rational words and actions, in the
place where movement drifted away from all external devices designed to
map and read.[54] Arguably, the antislavery philosophy I engage was partially made on the "demonic" grounds engendered by wandering—terrains
outside the recognized Enlightenment's "governing system of meaning," as
Wynter says.[55]

However, at the same time, as with the exclusionary tradition to which
they often responded, black philosophers sometimes expressed hostility

toward those other places, those privately inspired modes of comportment discerned as unenlightened, nonstraight, upright, unrestrained, and, by paradoxical implication, less free. In particular, one's relationship with slavery—its private impact on public performance—became the measure of one's capacity for transparently straight, enlightened comportment. In other words, for some black Enlightenment philosophers, slavery's trace emerged at the level of moral, intellectual rectitude and formal literacy. Plainly stated, slavery made the difference between crooked and backward movement, or between wandering and straight progressive movement. Moreover, black women and men who were associated with the *place* of slavery—residing in the South (or being read as Southern), lacking formal literacy and middle-class respectability, or who were born enslaved—were often associated with a set of movements said to characterize unenlightenment: wandering, waywardness, and being off the straight and narrow. Sojourner Truth's illiteracy, for example, tied her to slavery and, with it, unenlightenment; as a result, her rhetorical and bodily enactments of freedom were often reduced to a form of racialized, intellectual caricature. Even though Truth offered a philosophy of liberation, the racial, economic, and sexual logics of supposedly enlightened embodiment (dis)missed the profundity of her revolutionary movement.

In the tradition of Truth, the artists that I engage in the second half of the book agitate against the straight and narrow constraints of hegemonic and counterhegemonic post-Enlightenment subjectivity. By hegemonic I mean state-sanctioned, white, male, heterosexual, able-bodied subjectivities and their (imagined) modes of upright comportment. Counterhegemonic post-Enlightenment subjectivity is a similar enactment of upright comportment but by those who otherwise interrogate the state's racist, sexist, heteronormative, or able-bodied kinetic constraints. For example, such expressions of uprightness (in the spirit of the nineteenth-century figures discussed in chapter 2) emerge as a regulative gesture in relation to artist-philosophers whose expressions of identity are putatively incompatible with counterhegemonic narratives of freedom. Moreover, anxieties around these artists' (resistance to) readability and uprightness reveal an antiwandering ethos. Crucially, however, through wandering these figures disaggregate freedom from the empirical measures presumed to assess that capacity for upright comportment and freedom and do so through privately choreographed philosophical performances. In doing so, these figures claim the place of freedom, not by "material ownership and black repossession but rather by a grammar of liberation, through which ethical *human*-geographies can be recognized and expressed."[56]

In chapter 3, "Writing under a Spell: Adrienne Kennedy's Theater," I consider how the playwright's use of surrealist aesthetics is a wandering: a fundamentally nonstraight, twisted, and hard-to-follow storytelling that extends a tradition of black feminist anticaptivity inaugurated by Truth's own privately guided "incomprehensible" movement. In the plays *Funnyhouse of a Negro* (1964) and *The Owl Answers* (1965), Kennedy's black female characters daydream, speak with ghosts, and talk to themselves in empty apartments and bustling subways. Because of the complicated polyvocality and nonlinear, elusive nature of Kennedy's storytelling, many critics dismissed her work as psychotic. Further, her characters' supposed psychosis is sometimes read as a by-product of an internalized racism; interestingly, such political backwardness, as with the nineteenth-century philosophers who were imaginatively associated with slavery's trace and place, expresses a pathologically crooked relationship to freedom. But what gets missed in their analysis are the ways that a certain unscriptable speech and movement powerfully interrupt the pursuit and epistemological and geographical regulation of black female desire at the heart of post-Enlightenment subject production.

Similarly, in chapter 4, "'I Am an African American Novel': Wandering as Noncompliance in Gayl Jones's *Mosquito*," I think about how Jones also resists epistemological desire by making reading hard. Indeed, a reader of Jones must stop reading and start listening precisely for that which eludes capture. In Jones's novel *Mosquito* (2000), capture is evaded through plotlines that meander off the page and a black female narrator who, in the spirit of the Underground Railroad, refuses to tell you the whole story. Still, critics cite Jones's rambling storytelling—that contains within it acknowledged and unacknowledged ellipses—as cause for their negative reviews.[57] Because Jones's *Mosquito* formally and conceptually subverts the regulative moves at the heart of hegemonic and counterhegemonic *visions* of freedom and (post-)Enlightenment—for instance, her critiques of the U.S. border patrol are told through a wandering, non-law-abiding (unstraightforward) prose—critics dismiss the book as bad writing.

But maybe bad writing is what is necessary to heal from modernity's violence. As de Certeau observes, travel stories are often forged at the meeting ground of text and antitext. In some ways, they're always partial, "punched and torn open by ellipses, drifts, and leaks of meaning."[58] *Mos-*

quito is a traveler's tale. The movement through space is a drifting through history, memory, and desire. What is more, the improvisatory twists and turns of the book's multiracial and multigendered political meditations on freedom, along with its refusal to abide by post-Enlightenment modes of efficient storytelling (linear narratives with beginnings, middles, and ends), produces "possibilities of moving into other landscapes, like cellars and bushes."[59] Landscapes that are unbound and cannot be surveilled.

Indeed, formally speaking, the improvisatory character of Jones's and Kennedy's writing—the continual shuttling back and forth of time, image, and space—opens up portals for other kinds of errant, nonenunciative, unreadable movement. Moreover, by disrupting the epistemological impulse to know (and understand) the full story, Jones's and Kennedy's art extends the tradition of information refusals at the heart of antislavery writing. Their respective philosophical crafts enlarge a critique of captivity to include those readers who equate the ability to discern, follow, and politically cognize a story (and its narrator) with its success. Further, Jones, as much as Kennedy, indicts the violence of following as a frequent trope in her novels as well as an oppressive desire to heed. Similar to their predecessors—a group that includes Kant and Rousseau as well as Truth and Walker—Kennedy and Jones produce characters that wander in and as the production of their own philosophies of freedom to the meeting ground of performance and philosophy, the place where privately shaped resistance flows. But unlike Kant and Rousseau, their wandering is an ethical, harm-free embodiment of self-interest—a recuperative, deregulated, interior kinesis that agitates against others' *visions* of the Enlightenment and freedom from subjection.

What is more, these resistant philosophies push the question of black freedom, desire, and possibility beyond the world of the material, the discursive, and the physical, of readable words and actions. In Kennedy's theater, for example, resistance often manifests itself as existential renunciation, evidenced by her most famous character's, the Negro Sarah, desire "not to be."[60] Not only does Sarah ramble and daydream, messing with the plot and the reader's own sense-making protocols, but she expresses a desire to hide from the lay world and not be found. Similar to Ursa, all Sarah wants is to be left alone slouching on the bus (of her own thoughts).

Often critics do not engage lines such as "I want not to be" in this spirit of antisurveillance or as formal and conceptual strategies that thwart facile understanding. These lines are instead *read* as evidence of the main character's supposed internalized racism. In my chapter on Kennedy, however, I argue that Sarah's desire of nonlocalizability works alongside narratological manipulations to radically self-humanize and upset what Brooks calls the "tyranny of stillness" at the heart of "racial and gender epistemologies."[61] In other words, "I want not to be" is not necessarily a refusal of blackness, but an affirmation of its kinesthetic constraints in reality as we know it. Consider the following line from Sarah in *Funnyhouse*: "My white friends like myself will be shrewd, intellectual and anxious for death."[62] While critics sometimes read this type of line as an expression of black self-hatred, what gets missed are the ways in which death does not always already imply a terminal absence. In fact, I think the association here between intellectualism and death implies something like an existentialist crisis, resolved only through a flight from the subjective trappings of modernity.

According to Donna Haraway, a legacy of the Enlightenment involves a notion of the subject "endowed with inner coherence and rational clarity."[63] Indeed, this configuration of the subject has always been suffocating, both for the subjects and objects of the Enlightenment alike. "In their collision with unfamiliar cultures," for example, explorers resolved "the moral puzzles and conflicting demands" by "stepping outside, and sometimes existing for long periods outside, the rationalized frames of exploration, be they faith, knowledge, profit, or domination," according to Fabian.[64] In many ways, this "stepping outside" staged an encounter with death as a temporary loss of subjectivity in and as (racialized and gendered) transcendence—a loss of subjectivity reconciled through the subsequent homicidal operations of empire.

The momentary renunciation of claims to self and subjectivity, made possible through a peripatetic "stepping outside," enabled a freedom from the moral and rationalist hazing of the hegemonic Enlightenment. This repudiation of claims to self, which has meant (among other things) taking a reprieve from reality, life, is not only akin to death but has historically been predicated on racial and gender privilege. In other words, white men (explorers and Sarah's "friends" alike) could surpass the limits of self and achieve momentary transcendence, because they were not bound by the constraints of spectacular Otherness. In the context of the post-Enlightenment, what would it mean for black people whose bodies are already imagined to be dead and unlivable to reimagine the "horizon of death" as instantiating another deregulated plane of mobility, an unsurveillable terrain of wandering, transgression, and trespass?

I am using da Silva's concept "horizon of death" here, by which she refers to a racialized, gendered domain of unlivability distinct in its spatiotemporal difference from the space inhabited by the idealized post-Enlightenment subject.[65] Against the confinement and localization at work in these murderous spaces (stages), I argue that the figure of the absent, dead, surplus, black subject dances, roams, daydreams, and rambles back from that unlivable space and does so in a manner that, in Holland's words, "gnaws away at any established center by removing the focus on *unicentered* to a *multicentered* discourse, thus creating a place that is destabilized and liminal, a margin that has a myriad of interpretative possibilities and a host of unruly subjects."[66]

As Holland argues, the dead don't just stay put. They are disorderly and occupy a highly trespassed domain all the while trespassing upon the living themselves; the dead and death index "a cultural and national phenomenon or discourse, . . . a figurative silencing or process of erasure, and . . . an embodied entity capable . . . of transgression."[67] This space is devastating, as the association of racial and gendered difference with unlivability and a deadly absence of reason often result, for example, in the state's devaluation of black female life. Paradoxically, however, for the subject of the imperial (post-)Enlightenment, an encounter with death holds new possibilities for life. As I argue in chapter 1, imperial-minded philosophers of the Enlightenment and civilization frequently wandered away from the horizon of life instantiated by the tyranny of "universal reason"—the domain of livability formed through the illusion of self-possession and control—only to dance (without a script) at the horizon of death.[68] In the context of idealized post-Enlightenment subjectivity, whiteness also wanders to reinstantiate and overcome itself. If this wandering meant and means transcendence and transgression for the white (post-)Enlightenment subject, then could it ever mean the same for those incarcerated and killed off by those movements?[69]

I conclude *Wandering*, in "Before I Was 'Straightened Out,'" with a turn toward the work of the artists Adrian Piper, Carrie Mae Weems, and William Pope.L, and I think about how their sacred and sublime reimaginings of the beyond—what hovers on the other side of post-Enlightenment horizons of life and light—signal an undisclosed terrain of philosophical desire. Both Piper and Pope.L, in her Everything series (2003) and his *Thunderbird Immolation* (1978) performance, evoke scenes of racialized, classed, and sexual devastation, figured by state-sanctioned post-Enlightenment logics as the unlivable horizon of death, to suggest the possibility of unrestrained movement, "more humanly workable geographies," beyond the brutally empirical, epistemological, and material, bulldozing motility of this world.[70] In Piper's work the devastation lies in and underneath images of trauma—the bulldozed landscape of a post-Katrina New Orleans, the faded countenances of assassinated antiracist activists, and the barely *readable* news story about the racialized, sexualized torture of a black woman in West Virginia. For Pope.L, the scene of devastation is visible on the ground upon which he sits. On a yellow mat placed on the sidewalk outside an art gallery in New York City, the artist surrounded himself with matches and a fortified wine; the wine, Thunderbird, was specifically targeted toward low-income communities in the 1970s.

For Piper and Pope.L, the elusive movement of black life swirls around the stagnant scenes of death, occurring on another plane. So too does Weems's Roaming (2006) series figure an abundance of movement, sublime and sacred, on the other side of dwarfed agentic possibilities and narrow *visions* of freedom. Staged in various Italian cities, Roaming queries the nature of free movement in everyday life. More particularly, Roaming formed out of Weems's interest in the interaction between real and phantasmatic architectures of power and the bodies who wander within and around them. Significantly, the activity of roaming frames images of public strolling and private gazes at the ocean. Like the art of Piper and Pope.L, the wandering in Weems's work exceeds even while constrained by the roaming shadow of the state.

In all of these artists' works, daydream, fantasy, rambling and meandering, meditation and prayer, privately inspired philosophical acts, and revelations recover the broken-down body and as Eric Stanley writes, "vitality is worked otherwise."[71] Free black worlds become possible on the edge of bus-ride ruminations and in stares at the sea. Free black worlds become possible in wandering.

ONE

Losing Their Heads

Race, Sexuality, and the Perverse Moves

of the European Enlightenment

In 2008 the British-born Nigerian artist Yinka Shonibare put the European Enlightenment on display. Dressing headless mannequins in Victorian-era costumes made from Dutch wax (otherwise loosely known as "African") fabrics, Shonibare resurrected famous white philosophers and assigned them physical disabilities. The political economist Adam Smith has a hunchback; the chemist Antoine Lavoisier sits in a wheelchair; the mathematician Gabrielle Émilie Le Tonnelier de Breteuil misses a foot; the philosopher Jean le Rond d'Alembert leans on crutches; and Immanuel Kant lacks legs to move upon. As the curator Rachel Kent observes, "Shonibare's alterations to these historical figures . . . make rare autobiographical reference to the artist's own physical disability—he was left partially paralyzed after contracting a virus at the age of 19—and interrogate our concepts of reason and unreason within the present."[1]

Shonibare's Age of Enlightenment installation is a display of disfigurement, deformity, and compromised mobility. In it we see headless, disabled philosophers engaged in the production of reason—for example, Kant writes at a desk while holding a globe (see figure 1.1).

Moreover, these decapitated bodies are cloaked in so-called African fabric, suggesting a relation between race, travel, mindlessness, and nonupright comportment at the heart of reason. What Shonibare reveals is, in fact, the Age of Enlightenment's hegemonic conceit. That is to say, even though the performative conditions of the Enlightenment's philosophy and attendant notions of the subject were deformed and amputated by

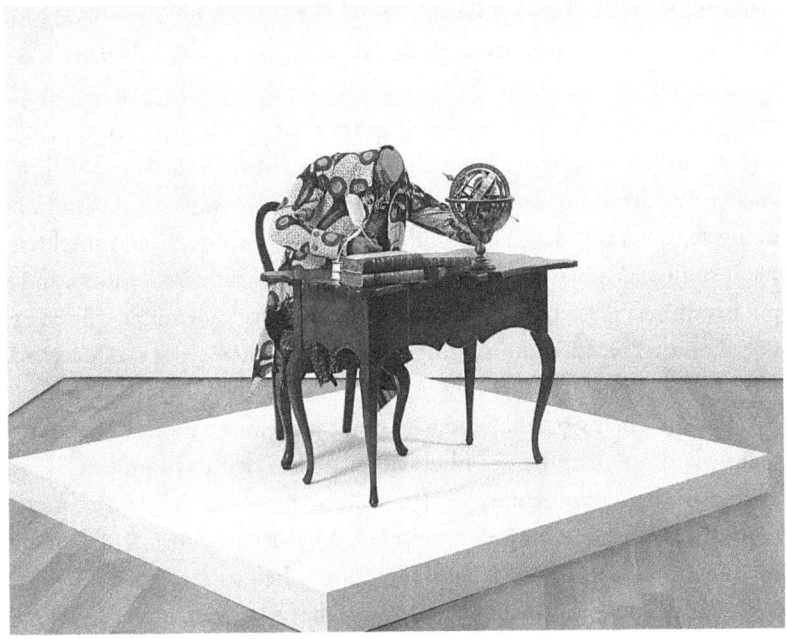

1.1 Yinka Shonibare, MBE, The Age of Enlightenment-Immanuel Kant, 2008.
© Yinka Shonibare, MBE. All Rights Reserved, DACS 2013. Collection: Milwaukee
Art Museum. Image courtesy of James Cohan Gallery, New York/Shanghai.

these relations, the illusion of self-determination, given as intact heads and
otherwise normative (able) embodiment, was nonetheless advanced.

As such, the maintenance of this performative illusion required other
bodies to bear the unruly, disabled, "outer-determined" consciousness previously disavowed.[2] People of color, in particular, figured as the embodiments of this unruliness and always already movable by forces outside their
control. Even today, as Denise Ferreira da Silva argues, such performative
assumptions tragically persist in animating post-Enlightenment's hegemonic disciplinary operations—operations that sanction the regulation
of, among other things, public black kinesis. For da Silva the devaluation
of black life is bound up with the "violent gesture[s] necessary to sustain
the post-Enlightenment version of the [white, male, heterosexual, able-
bodied, and bourgeoisie] Subject as the sole self-determined thing."[3]

This chapter's task is, in part, to elucidate the inherent affectability
of such violent enactments of white (European) self-determination. More
precisely, while this idealized mode of self-determination imagines itself
as guided and regulated by "universal reason" from within, it asserts this

ground by way of a deregulated, affectable trespassing.[4] To be sure, this was a reckless roaming outwardly determined and mobilized by myths of racial and sexual difference. Moreover, because these performative contradictions, as Shonibare illustrates, originated along with the seventeenth- and eighteenth-century Enlightenment concepts of self-determination, reason, and freedom, we must return to these originary theorizations. In doing so, the fraudulence of an inherent association between Enlightenment subjectivity, whiteness, male gender identity, able-bodiedness, and a putatively unaffected and self-directed *straight* comportment will be exposed and will lead to an interrogation of its contemporary, unchecked, illusory reenactments.

To begin, being straight and narrow is the idealized mode of comportment for those invested in enlightened subjectivity and signifies a kind of transparent, morally upright, law-abiding movement. By straight and narrow, I mean something akin to Robert McRuer's definition of compulsory heterosexuality. For McRuer compulsory heterosexuality constitutes a regulative apparatus invented to police "the disorderly array of possible human desires and embodiments."[5] Significantly, in McRuer's definition, the reach of said apparatus exceeds the sexual in its regulation of all "possible" expressions of wayward desire; in that way compulsory heterosexuality attempts to reform (straighten out) the errancy of queerness and the queerness of errancy. Unruly bodies. Unruly desires. However, because the errant exceeds its reach, straightness must continually reinvent itself in order to sanction its own impossible movement. Put another way, in the interest of its definition, straightness crookedly moves by way of the very disorderliness to which it is otherwise said to respond. That said, while I want to valorize this disorderly, out-of-step, and antiregulative interior kinesis at the heart of wandering, I also want to make a distinction between that valorization and a critique of the crookedness at the heart of the Enlightenment's straight philosophy. On the one hand, what is interesting about wandering is that its opening up of desire alongside its resistance to bodily and intellectual management enables a "contingent universalization of queerness/disability."[6] However, because such movement, integral to the functioning of reason itself, was figured as that which corroded idealized comportment, the force of such a disavowal took crooked form. The liberatory divergence from Enlightenment ideals was, by definition, crooked when it morphed from wandering into trespass. As Shonibare so insightfully illustrates, European philosophers often stumbled through the world without their heads, and such constitutive stumbling was violently trespassive. For the victims of these trespasses, the crooked expression of reason meant epistemological or actual dismemberment. Joan Dayan's discussion of René Descartes's vampiric fantasies powerfully anticipates Shonibare's exposure:

> The thinker of Descartes' *Meditations* in 1640 sets the stage for the 1685 edict of Louis XIV: the making of enlightenment man led to the demolition of the unenlightened brute. The thinking mind's dismembering or generative proclivities dominated a passive nature or servile body. Descartes sits by the fire. He dismembers himself. He can play with asking what remains if he takes off his ears, his arms, and removes all his senses in his urgency to know what constitutes his identity: "Although the whole mind seems to be united to the whole body, I recognize that if a foot or arm or any other part of the body is cut off, nothing has thereby been taken away from the mind." The mutilation only aggrandizes this "I" that needs *no* senses and *no* body. Listen to Descartes's elation of discovery: "Thinking? At last I have discovered it—thought; this alone is inseparable from me. . . . I am, then, in the strict sense only a thing that thinks; that is, I am a mind, or intelligence, or intellect, or reason. . . . I am a thing which is real. . . . But what kind of a thing? . . .—a thinking thing."[7]

As Dayan continues to argue, Descartes's self-dissection, albeit imagined, was essential for the consolidation of the "white universal [Enlightenment] subject," for whom the body was said to be superfluous.[8] Tragically, however, such dissection was also literally carried out against black bodies, under such bloody measures as the Code Noir (Black Code).[9] Again, the hegemonic labor of recognized Enlightenment was, in keeping with the scene with Descartes, a mutilating expression of a methodological disavowal. Further, the reckless dismembering reverie at the heart of reason foregrounded a transcendent white subject as author while consolidating black people's status as objects to be written, beings for whom the mind was said to not be the governing principle.

In fact, in the face of slave insurrections, most notably the Haitian Revolution, slaves were *read* as having a perverted will.[10] This notion of a perverse will at once depoliticized and dephilosophized black rage and desire, but it also missed the ways that the enactment of racist, sexist enlightenment itself was inherently perverse. If to be perverse means "*to turn* away from that which is good, right or true," then the enactment of hateful reason was exemplary.[11] As I argued by way of Shonibare, the racialized and sexualized particularization of the Enlightenment depended on a perverse, errant, (im)possible movement despite its pretense to an undifferentiated straight and upright comportment. These were its performative contradictions as a certain kind of nonstraight and nonteleological movement (Descartes's dream, the Code Noir) was at once essential and unsound for the production of reason.

At the same time, this is a dream whose murderous course has been met by the philosophical interventions and rehabilitations of those trampled upon. As David Scott, Paul Miller, Sylvia Wynter, and C. L. R. James (among others) argue, the actual fulfillment of Enlightenment ideals was achieved not by its idealized subject but on behalf of its pathologized objects.[12] While this contradiction is not without its own contradictions, it is important to acknowledge, for example, that the "universal human right of liberty [was] to be found in the Haitian Revolution" and not within either Kant's categorical imperative or Jean-Jacques Rousseau's social contract.[13]

Still, the presumption of the absence of black will, or the imbrication of blackness itself with perversion and a perverse kinesis, was key to the racist consolidation of the Enlightenment subject. Further, even if theorized otherwise, the hegemonic discourse of race and sexuality as performatively perverse facilitated the Enlightenment's idealized subject's propertization of rational subjectivity while errantly sustaining its mythical conditions. This can be observed in the invention of race in the eighteenth century. Kant, the recognized Enlightenment philosopher, according to Robert Bernasconi, was the author of the "first theory of race worthy of the name"—a theory that scientifically figured race as a purposive differentiation.[14] Significantly, such a theory formed out of a reading of explorers', missionaries', and settlers' travel reports (or more broadly, tales of intrusive wanderings). This leads me to ask: if it's the case that Kant invented a theory of race and that such a theory emerged from a methodological crookedness, what would it mean to think about race as corporeal trespass?

This is an interesting question considering that Kant once "claimed that people from Africa and India lack a 'drive to activity,' . . . never becoming anything more than drifters."[15] But if anyone is a drifter, someone with a promiscuous relationship to space, place, and principle, then Kant is exemplary. What an encounter with racial and sexual difference in Kant's writing produces is a kind of drifting—an intrusive itinerancy induced by the "terrible struggle between imagination and reason."[16] Gilles Deleuze describes this "illegitimate use of the faculties" in Kant accordingly.[17]

> In many ways, understanding and reason are deeply tormented by the ambition to make things in themselves known to us. Kant constantly returns to this theme that there are *internal illusions* and *illegitimate uses* of faculties. The imagination sometimes dreams rather than schematizes. Moreover, instead of applying itself exclusively to phenomena ("experimental employment") the understanding sometimes claims to apply its concepts to things as they are in themselves ("transcendental employment"). But this is still not the most serious problem. Instead of applying itself to the concepts of the understanding ("immanent or regulative employment"), reason may claim to be directly applicable to objects, and wish to legislate in the domain of knowledge ("transcendent or constitutive employment"). Why is this the most serious problem? The transcendental employment of the understanding presupposes only that it abstracts itself from its relation to the imagination. Now, this imagination would have only negative effects were the understanding not pushed by reason, which gives it the illusion of a positive domain to conquer outside experience.[18]

This conquering outside experience, essential in the production of myths about civilization and barbarity, rational comportment and impulsivity, reveals the ways that the struggle among reason, understanding, and the imagination was not only terrible but also, for many, tragic. Paradoxically, this conquering outside experience prompted Kant's writing the *Critique of Pure Reason* (1781) in the first place.

Indeed, Kant's critical philosophy emerged because of his refusal, according to Deleuze, to abide by a dogmatic rationalist "theory of knowledge founded on the idea of a correspondence between subject and object, of an *accord* between the order of ideas and the order of things."[19] In opposition to this tendency, which Kant perceives as a crisis in philosophical thinking generally and a crisis in metaphysics specifically, he proposes his own Copernican Revolution. Kant's Copernican Revolution involves "substituting the principle of a *necessary* submission of object to subject for the idea of a harmony between subject and object (*final* accord). The essential discovery is that the faculty of knowledge is legislative, or more precisely, that there is something which legislates in the faculty of knowledge[.]"[20] For Kant "we," not God, "are the legislators of Nature."[21] Kant demonstrates this in his calling for the "tribunal" of reason, asking: what is reason and what is it capable of knowing about itself? How is the tribunal of reason the ethical scene of the Enlightenment?

Nevertheless, even while the tribunal itself importantly questioned an "epistemic model that takes as its model the colonization of the world (of experience)," the enactment of reason's colonizational roaming continually undermined the tribunal's ethical value.[22] Arguably, Kant's wandering transported him from a critique of reason's epistemic promiscuity toward a wobbly, trespassive invention of race. The performative betrayal of reason's limits, as Kant makes clear, is its methodological condition. Through an engagement with some of his precritical and critical writings, I explore the ways that ideas of race and gender perversely enact the very mythical scene and unregulated performances which the Age of Enlightenment was said to straighten out.

According to Miller, after Theodor W. Adorno and Max Horkheimer, the mythic was the anti-Enlightenment, "a 'time', when the will was subordinate to the world."[23] Because the mythos of racial and sexual difference instantiated a "lost plenitude" into which Kant dangerously wandered, he advanced the inherent whiteness of self-determination (of a non-drifting, if you will) to sustain the notion of Europe "being philosophically identical with itself."[24] The illegitimate, affectable movement key to enlightened subjectivity, as da Silva, Gayatri Spivak, and others have shown, became externalized and figured as the kinetic (and fundamentally nonphilosophical and unenlightened) essence of the racialized and gendered.

In *Observations on the Feeling of the Beautiful and Sublime* (1764), for example, Kant's encounter with the "Negro" is nothing short of an empirical and epistemological wandering, where blackness is illegitimately and trespassively linked to stupidity. In the decades that followed the *Observations on the Feeling of the Beautiful and Sublime*, Kant's thinking moved more "critically" to consider reason's relationship to dogmatic illusions, a relationship that demonstrates the fundamental discord between subject and object. Kant's critical philosophy, in fact, involved an interrogation of these ethically bankrupt relations, aspiring toward a system, as Curtis Bowman says, of "human freedom, both in theoretical and practical matters . . . [where] the enlightened person is [at once] rational and autonomous, accepting nothing without a reason, never acting without a reason, always pursuing his or her freedom and the freedom of others."[25]

The person largely responsible for Kant's ethical reevaluation of the Enlightenment was Rousseau.

If Kant is the first author of a theory on race, then one might say that Rousseau prefigures the ethical waywardness of such a theory in his philosophizations of free comportment. In Rousseau we "agree to give ourselves up to the direction of the general will[;] . . .[however,] we sometimes fail to follow its dictates because our private will, present in us as individuals, conflicts with our general will, present in us as citizens. This conflict comes about largely through our inability to curb our desires and instincts."[26] This tension between the general will (shared agreement, through laws, of appropriate public kinesis) and private will (the refusal of such kinetic constraint) animates Rousseau's philosophy. Rousseau, like Kant, was often moved by desire, straying from the straight-and-narrow course of his political and moral philosophy and wandering along the racialized and sexualized interests of his private will.

Indeed, Rousseau's complicated ties to the Enlightenment move in his grappling with the nexus of disembodiment, self-understanding, and self-determination central to the work of reason and freedom. Whereas Rousseau, in *The Social Contract* (1762), advocates the suppression of the private in favor of the general will, Kant's *Observations on the Feeling of the Beautiful and Sublime* suggests that the "principled" enlightened man is often "moved at the same time by a secret impulse [while] tak[ing] a standpoint outside himself, in thought, in order to judge the outward propriety of his behavior as it seems in the eyes of the onlooker."[27] While Kant and Rousseau agree that self-determination is only possible through alienation, both concede the essential though dangerous presence of a "secret impulse" that agitates against that disembodied estrangement at every turn.

As previously mentioned, the problem with Rousseau is that the inhabitation of the secret impulse becomes the occasion of an ethical breach. Indeed, the secret impulse at once endangers the ethical, and presumably universally minded, imperative of the general will and, in Rousseau's and Kant's cases, portends the erasure of the other's right to philosophical subjectivity and kinesis. Moreover, what happens outside of the general will, outside of a self-determined and restrained moral philosophy, is a drifting into what da Silva terms "affectability."[28] Because affectability—being moved by the outside—was and continues to be antithetical to enlightened subjectivity, it remains attached to racialized and gendered bodies instead of to the headless philosophers in question. In this examination of Rousseau's writings, then, I consider the long history of this paradox and how the unpredictable kinesis engendered by the secret impulse became permissible and unpunishable for bodies otherwise presumed to be innately self-determined. For bodies and ontologies said to lack such capacity, any unrestrained movement, or wandering, was paradoxically figured as at once impossible, injurious, and criminal.

The Social Contract

Beginning with Rousseau's *The Social Contract* is crucial because it lays the groundwork for his political investment in self-regulation. It is precisely in this document that freedom emerges not only as circumscribed and particular but as inextricably tied to self-abnegation. As such, in many ways, this document agitates against any private embrace of desire and the wandering that such an embrace potentiates. In fact, it is only after Rousseau's eventual break with the contract that such an embrace becomes possible—a move riddled with conflict and deeply shaped by racialized, sexualized, and ontological notions regarding not only who is a part of the contract but who has the right to wander against it.

The Social Contract begins with Rousseau's tortured musings over why it is that "man was born free, and [yet] he is everywhere in chains."[29] These chains are symbolic and not actual, in that black bodies were, as a matter of fact, born unfree in galleys and on ships at the time of his writing. As Susan Buck-Morss observes, "No human condition appears more offensive to his heart or to his reason than slavery. And yet even Rousseau, patron saint of the French Revolution, represses from consciousness the millions of really existing, European-owned slaves, as he relentlessly condemns the institution." This unspoken, racialized, and sexualized contradiction moves Rousseau's political philosophy, illuminating most powerfully the ways that the social contract is, following Charles Mills, a "racial contract."[30]

This is clear in the fundamental assumption of the contract: for Rousseau, men come into the world free, become unfree as members of a family, and then rearticulate their relationship to freedom as they reach "the age of reason."[31] Part of Rousseau's project is to imagine a successful governmental system that supports man's freedom even as it necessitates his alienation from that freedom. The assumption that men are born free and not contracted themselves racializes the document and, with it, the distinction between general and private will. More particularly, freedom itself moves by way of an unspoken racialization and gendering of self-interest. Consider the following two quotations from Rousseau:

> To renounce freedom is to renounce one's humanity, one's rights as a man and equally one's duties. There is no possible *quid pro quo* for one who renounces everything; indeed such renunciation is contrary to man's very nature; for if you take away all freedom of the will, you strip a man's actions of moral significance. . . . If everything he has belongs to me, his right is my right, and it would be nonsense to speak of my having a right *against* myself.[32]

> Immediately, in place of the individual person of each contracting party, this act of association creates an artificial and collective body composed of as many members as there are voters in the assembly, and by this same act that body acquires its unity, its common *ego*, its life and its will.[33]

In the first quotation, enslavement emerges not as trope but as material condition. As the philosopher argues, to commit such acts of unfreedom is to betray the very essence of mankind. To enslave another, as Rousseau contends, is to unlawfully assume the rights and will of another. Enslavement is as immoral as it is illusory.

The second quotation, however, argues that the existence of a republic requires "the total alienation by each associate of himself and all his rights to the whole community."[34] This state-sanctioned alienation is given as necessary, but it is also "unconditional." The reasons for the unconditionality are tied to Rousseau's beliefs that men share similar understandings of (and, by implication, relationships to) freedom, and that freedom is tantamount to self-preservation. For Rousseau, by rescinding one's rights to self (or private will), the state can function and eventually restore to the citizenry the freedom and rights sacrificed earlier (general will).

I wonder about this sudden ambivalence toward freedom. Why is it that freedom can and should easily slide into unfreedom in order for a reconfigured freedom to emerge as part of a moral and equitable society? As Kant later warns, "If freedom were determined in accordance with laws, it would not be freedom," a moral principle to which Kant and Rousseau were in continual and, perhaps for them, necessary violation.[35] The ambivalence, however, that facilitates the slide toward unfreedom may bespeak an anxiety around an imagined, racialized lawlessness, embodied in some ways by the "savage."[36] Maurice Cranston, a Rousseau historian and translator, argues that the need to make a distinction between man and his purportedly barbaric counterpart is bound up with an urgent desire to defend the moral imperative of governance.[37]

Along these lines, Rousseau's contradictory relationship with nature and its chief resident, the savage, is reason alone for republican governance and its requisite sacrifice of freedom. Indeed, even as Rousseau comes to embrace nature and self-interest, he worries about the freedoms that come with staying and straying too long outside the city, a straying that compromises his desire to stay "straight" and "upright." Cranston argues that, for Rousseau,

> It is partly because of this intimate connection between liberty and law that the freedom of man in a state of nature is inferior. The freedom of the savage is no more than independence; although Rousseau speaks of the savage being subject to natural law, he also suggests that the savage has no consciousness of natural law; thus Rousseau can speak of a man being "transformed" as a result of his entry into civil society from a brutish into a human, moral being. A moral being is, or can be, free in another sense than the political; if, instead of being a slave of his passions, he lives according to conscience, lives according to rules he imposes on himself, then he has a liberty which only a moral being can enjoy. The savage has no sense of this; for one thing, the passions only begin to develop with society, which explains why society can mark the beginning of a change for the worse as well as the beginning of a change for the better.[38]

Implicitly, the idea that consciousness evolves from one's immersion into city, civic life presupposes that nature is not conducive to appropriate exercises in self-determination, moral rectitude, and freedom. According to *The Social Contract*, to be in nature is to live a degraded and precarious existence. Interestingly, such codification corresponds to what Mills would call "the moralization of space," where "the journey" away from "the outposts of civilization into native territory—acquires deep symbolic significance."[39]

In some ways this spatial moralization in Rousseau persists as a structuring tension. Whereas in the republic (the city) the idealized citizen-subject enjoys a circumscribed freedom, in nature (outside the city) freedom is morally bankrupt. Concerning the former state of existence, while this notion of freedom, as the condition of possibility for any encounter with one's passions and desires, appears liberatory, it is bound by the kinetic constraints of the social contract; in the republic, freedom (paradoxically) takes the form of laws, as "registers of what we ourselves desire."[40] How one moves through the world is shaped not by the unbound ambulations of private desire but by an ethos of self-restraint and antiwandering key to civic order.

Still, this state formation is figured as a kind of freedom from enslavement, where man is no longer subordinate to the will of other entities, such as nature or the ruling class. It is here where racism is both enacted and critiqued. At the time of Rousseau's writing, enslavement (an exemplary state of subordination) existed as a trope in European Enlightenment scholarship and characterized a set of material conditions for black and brown peoples. Because there is a general lack of precision in defining the contours of enslavement's meaning in *The Social Contract*, its radical potential as an antislavery document is foreclosed. Buck-Morss says, "Even when theoretical claims of freedom were transformed into revolutionary action on the political stage, it was possible for the slave-driven colonial economy that functioned behind the scenes to be kept in darkness."[41]

Moreover, the anxiety around a lawless desire, metaphorically embodied by the savage in nature and perhaps literally embodied by the contract-breaking and reforming black Jacobins themselves, racializes the relationship between Rousseau and civic desire (the general will). These racialized contradictions within *The Social Contract* complicate Rousseau's position on freedom, and it isn't until his traumatic exile that he reevaluates the meaning of freedom and desire—the performative tensions between private and general will and unbound and bound kinesis, respectively—apart from Enlightenment scripts. What we'll see more particularly in *The Confessions* is the beginnings of an embrace of private desire and, with it, an openness to wandering. But as with the racially and sexually circumscribed conception of freedom in *The Social Contract*, the embrace of private interest cannot be generalized. Plainly put, not everyone gets to roam freely; in fact, even as Rousseau wanders away from Enlightenment scripts of acceptable comportment, such movement is figured as problematic for racialized and gendered bodies. In this way, to wander is a privilege for those said to have already arrived at enlightenment. The unbound movement of all others figures as crime and pathology.

The Confessions

The Confessions (1782), Rousseau's autobiography, attends to wandering's inability to be generalized and the right to private desire. The text does this by particularizing the relation between freedom and wandering, using the language of anecdote and autobiography to do so. In lieu of an explicit critique of the contract, for example, Rousseau describes his childhood dissatisfaction with "filial" and economic dependence, lamenting, "I should have passed a calm and peaceful life in the security of my faith, in my own country, among my family and friends. . . . I should have been a good Christian, a good citizen, a good father, a good friend, a good workman, a good man in every way."[42] But Rousseau wasn't happy abiding by the civic, social, and economic expectations of the liberal citizen-subject. In fact, after accidentally missing the city's curfew and being shut outside the city's gates, Rousseau decides to sever his material relationships in Paris and roam physically: "The only thought in my mind was the independence I believed I had won. Now that I was free and my own master, I supposed that I could do anything, achieve anything. I only had to take one leap, and I could rise and fly through the air."[43]

From that point on, Rousseau wanders through the cities and countryside of France and Switzerland, benefiting from the kindness of strangers who feed him and give him shelter. In Geneva, he introduces himself to a famous Catholic priest, M. de Pontverre, who receives Rousseau into his home and sets up an encounter with a woman, Mme de Warens, who would later become a pivotal character in Rousseau's life. This encounter is marked by feelings of enrapture and love at first sight. Mme de Warens eventually becomes Rousseau's true love.

At once his soul mate and symbolic mother—he affectionately refers to her as "Mamma"—Mme de Warens quickly takes the young Rousseau under her wing. She coordinates employment opportunities for him with wealthy Parisians who pay him for companionship. He works in this capacity for some time while simultaneously continuing local apprenticeships with engravers and watchmakers. Significantly though, while living with Mme de Warens and M. de Pontverre, Rousseau recognizes (as do his temporary guardians) that he has yet to cultivate a strong sense of self. After being abandoned by his father at a very young age, he spends his early years wandering, being taken in and instructed by well-meaning older citizens in how to live his life. Such unattached and philosophically open comportment along with physical wandering figure as the cause for the absence of self-determination.

As such, Mme de Warens and M. de Pontverre decide that lessons on the catechism might help the young Rousseau in realizing the end of affectability. Paradoxically though, at this moment in *The Confessions*, the young Rousseau's religious instruction unleashes the (dis)abling forces of desire and freedom, which upset the straight and self-determined interest at the heart of such schooling. A homoerotic encounter, for example, between Rousseau and an anonymous "Moor" at the seminary occurs during a break after the first religious lesson and a week before Rousseau's official baptism by the church:

> There is no soul so vile, no heart so barbarous as to be insusceptible to some sort of affection, and one of the two cut-throats who called themselves Moors took a fancy to me. He was fond of coming up to me and gossiping in his queer jargon. He did me little services, sometimes giving me some of his food at table, and he frequently kissed me with an ardour, which I found most displeasing. But, frightened though I naturally was by his dusky face, which was beautified by a long scar, and by his passionate glances, which seemed to me more savage than affectionate, I put up with his kisses, saying to myself, "The poor man has conceived a warm friendship for me it would be wrong to repulse him." But he passed by degrees to more unseemly conduct, and sometimes made me such strange suggestions that I thought he was wrong in the head. One night he wanted to share my bed, but I objected on the plea that it was too narrow. He then pressed me to come into his. I still refused, however, for the poor devil was so dirty and smelt so strongly of the tobacco he chewed that he made me feel ill.
>
> Next day, very early in the morning, we were alone together in the assembly hall. He resumed his caresses, but with such violence that I was frightened. Finally he tried to work up to the most revolting liberties, and by guiding my hand, to make me take the same liberties with him. I broke wildly away with a cry and leaped backwards, but without displaying indignation and anger, for I had not the slightest idea what it was all about. But I showed my surprise and disgust to such effect that he then left me alone. But as he gave up the struggle I saw something whitish and sticky shoot toward the fireplace and fall on the ground. My stomach turned over, and I rushed on to the bal-

cony, more upset, more troubled and more frightened as well, than ever I had been in my life. I was almost sick.

I could not understand what was the matter with the poor man. I thought he was having a fit of epilepsy or some other seizure even more terrible. And really I know of no more hideous sight for a man in cold blood than such foul and obscene behavior, nothing more revolting than a terrifying face on fire with the most brutal lust. I have never seen another man in that state; but if we appear like that to women, they must indeed be fascinated not to find us repulsive. . . .

This adventure put me on my guard for the future against the attentions of the pederasts. And the sight of men with that reputation, by reminding me of the looks and behaviour of my frightful Moor, has always so horrified me that I have found it difficult to hide my disgust. Women, on the other hand, acquired a greater value for me, by way of contrast. I seemed to owe them a reparation for the offences of my sex, that could only be paid by the most delicate affection and personal homage. My memories of that self-styled African transformed the plainest of sluts into an object of adoration.[44]

During the week following the unwanted sexual advance by the "self-styled African," Rousseau is baptized. It is upon his reintroduction into the world as a "good Christian" that Rousseau leaves the seminary and resumes his wandering around the city (this time Sardinia): "The first thing I did was to satisfy my curiosity, or perhaps to celebrate my liberty."[45] What I want to signal again is Rousseau's repeated citation and refashioning of freedom—in this case, *liberty*. Subjected to the homosexual advances made by the "queer" moor, Rousseau feels physically repulsed by what he identifies as the African's "most revolting liberties." Liberty here is an indictment, a pathology, and a problematic effect of one Moor's pathologically errant roaming into sexual and racial freedom. The encounter also becomes the occasion for a general denunciation of manhood, the exercise of a free, unrestrained, cross-racial, and "unproductive" sexuality momentarily (dis)ables the kinetic conditions of enlightened subjectivity. Rousseau "leap[s] backwards."

Freedom is a contradictory state, and for Rousseau sexual freedom is permitted if and only if the specters of racial difference and racial freedom have been vanquished. "The plainest sluts" now are "objects of adoration." In this way, according to Spivak, "the freedom of desire is the condition of possibility of the concept of freedom."[46] But, given that in Rousseau's

Confessions the freedom of desire is realized in (an often sexual) wandering and that such unbound movement is pathological for racialized and
gendered bodies, the concept of freedom is applicable only to the Enlightenment subject. For Rousseau, after having traversed the racialized, queer
threat of desire—the illegitimate roaming of the Other—he takes the "self-
interested step" and leaves the seminary.

Rousseau's wandering is said to resume only after he departs from the
church. But arguably the erotic encounters inside the church facilitate a
kinetic reprieve, or wandering away, from the choreographic constraints
of reason. Still, in the end, the self-interested step, which paradoxically also
initiates unrestrained comportment, takes precedence over other kinds
of illegitimate movement—unanticipated drifts resulting from a young
philosopher's momentary enchantment with another man's scar along
with that other man's return of gaze. This tension at the heart of *The
Confessions*—of legitimate and illegitimate wandering's (self-directed or
otherwise) relationship to reason—expresses the performative contradictions at the heart of his philosophy. He describes the tenor of this struggle
accordingly:

> In me are united two almost irreconcilable characteristics, though in
> what way I cannot imagine. I have a passionate temperament, and lively
> and headstrong emotions. Yet my thoughts arise slowly and con-
> fusedly, and are never ready till too late. It is as if my heart and my
> brain did not belong to the same person. Feelings come quicker than
> lightning and fill my soul, but they bring me no illumination, they
> burn me and dazzle me. . . . During this stir of emotion I can see noth-
> ing quickly, and cannot write a word; I have to wait. Insensibly all this
> tumult grows quiet, the chaos subsides, and everything falls into place,
> but slowly, and after long and confused perturbations. Have you ever
> been to the opera in Italy?[47]

Rousseau reveals here how his passions "dazzle" more than they illuminate,
making the kind of writing he wants to do hard. Being dazzled and stirred
gets in the way of cognitive, disembodied enlightenment.

The "two almost irreconcilable characteristics" of a passionate temper-
ament and a desire for order are what complicate Rousseau's relationship
to legitimized, enlightened comportment. Here is a self-professed wanderer who argues for the regulation of freedom, a philosopher interested
in order but troubled by passion's tendency to mess up and move astray.

These tensions in Rousseau have everything to do with the conflict between private and general will, what the philosopher himself desires and
what he is taught to desire by others. But at the same time, these tensions
between a private and general will are shaped by some deeply racialized
and sexualized beliefs about wandering and governance. Those imagined
as already enlightened and on track can move off course while the wandering of the ungovernable figures as excessive and pathological. In his final
work, *Reveries of a Solitary Walker* (1782), Rousseau again legitimatizes
his wandering and right to freedom and does so through a reidealization
of nature. But nature's inability to be governed presents a crisis for the
philosopher precisely at the moment when his roaming crosses with the
unruly gait of the Other.

What we see in Rousseau is the simultaneous identification with and
renunciation of enlightened self-determination. As we saw in *The Confessions*, for Rousseau wandering sustains an openness to the undetermined
and unpredictable. But while he admits that this openness and the "thousand different passions that [keep him] in a state of constant agitation" are
crucial to his philosophy, it also spells the end of his claim to enlightened
subjectivity.[48] This becomes clear in his doubled understanding of the nature that embodies this indeterminacy and that also provides the backdrop
for his *Reveries of a Solitary Walker*.

Rousseau interprets nature in two ways. On the one hand, nature is the
assemblage of woods, plant life, and flowers that accessorize his wandering.
On the other hand, nature is the end of man; in *The Social Contract*, this
end is racially embodied by the savage. In *Reveries of a Solitary Walker*, the
end evokes a metaphysical locale, the final landing place for a philosopher
who has nothing left: "Everything is finished for me on this earth. Neither
good nor evil can be done to me by any man. I have nothing left in the
world to fear or hope for, and this leaves me in peace at the bottom of
the abyss, a poor unfortunate mortal, but as unmoved as God himself."[49]
In both scenarios nature is the terrain on the outskirts of man, a place of
deregulated passion and wandering's embrace. Instructively, it is also the
place for an encounter with God. Just on the other side of the moralized
spaces key to Enlightenment subjectivity—the city and the secular—
nature becomes the idyllic locale for Rousseau's end-of-days wanderings.
In some ways, nature provides the condition of possibility for a renunciation of enlightened subjectivity. However, once the roaming of the Other
threatens Rousseau's unbound travels, the assertion of that subjectivity, as

we saw in *The Confessions*, occurs by way of a deeply antiwandering ethos. The Second Walk exemplifies this collision in Rousseau's wandering.

On October 24, 1776, Rousseau takes an after-dinner stroll around the Boulevard Beaumarchais. He carefully examines the plant life that swarms the countryside, reflecting, "I saw myself at the close of an innocent and unhappy life, with a soul still full of intense feelings and a mind still adorned with a few flowers, even if they were already blighted by sadness and withered by care."[50] Immersed in nature and his feelings of depression and isolation, Rousseau wanders sadly. He is remorseful about not having fully lived, commenting that his life is nothing more than a set of misfortunes and disappointments. Eventually the reverie changes from sadness to pleasure as Rousseau reflects on his current state of unbridled meditation and daydreaming. This free and limitless rumination, however, is soon dramatically interrupted by the unforeseen onrush of a Great Dane. Rousseau describes the accident and subsequent paralysis:

> At about six in the evening I was on the hill leading down from Ménilmontant, almost opposite the Jolly Gardener, when some people walking in front of me suddenly stepped aside and I saw a Great Dane rushing at full tilt toward me, followed by a carriage. It saw me too late to be able to check its speed or change its course. I judged that my only hope of avoiding being knocked down was to leap into the air at precisely the right moment to allow the dog to pass underneath me. This lightning plan of action, which I had no time either to examine or to put into practice, was my last thought before I went down. I felt neither the impact nor my fall, nor indeed anything else until I came to. . . .
>
> Night was coming on. I saw the sky, some stars, and a few leaves. This first sensation was a moment of delight. I was conscious of nothing else. In this instance I was being born again, and it seemed as if all I perceived was filled with my frail existence. Entirely taken up by the present, I could remember nothing; I had no distinct notion of myself as a person, nor had I the least idea of what had just happened to me. I did not know who I was, nor where I was; I felt neither pain, fear, nor anxiety. I watched my blood flowing as I might have watched a stream, without even thinking that the blood had anything to do with me. I felt throughout my whole being such a wonderful calm, that whenever I recall this feeling I can find nothing to compare with it in all the pleasures that stir our lives.[51]

The dog's collision with the philosopher produces a (dis)abling severing of consciousness from reflexivity. He is violently thrust into a present and is born again; the shock of the collision sends him into the radically new state. Being unable to anticipate the Other's errant insurgency forces Rousseau to "recompose all of [his] relations of speed and slowness, all of [his] affects, and to rearrange the overall assemblage."[52] There is no time to change the plan, and as a result a new plane of consciousness emerged. Further, this consciousness by accident (which is also a consciousness by surprise) produces a recombination of affect: "I felt throughout my whole being such a wonderful calm, that whenever I recall this feeling I can find nothing to compare with it in all the pleasures that stir our lives." With this giddy recombination, new and important ontological questions concerning Rousseau's relationship with the outside (world) emerge.

At the same time, Rousseau's rebirth and subsequent amnesia actively forget that an animal was involved in the collision. All we know, at the close of the accident, is that Rousseau survives. Akira Lippitt says, "Animals are deprived of futures. Thus, in Rousseau's contribution to the thought of animal being, the animal is confined to a perpetual presence that never advances in being or time, since the animal can never anticipate the arrival of what is unperceived, or unimagined."[53] Despite his compromised faculties (recall Shonibare's series), Rousseau remains the reasoning subject and author of the Enlightenment. For the object of the Enlightenment, who is figured as its interruption and cause of disability—in this case, the animal and in the earlier case the "self-styled African" (both of whom, in the context of Enlightenment racist thought, share ontological status as well as an imbrication with nature)—such capacity is rendered impossible and illegitimate.[54]

Once again, the discord between freedom and desire along with an aggressively straight comportment result in the ambivalent imagining of wandering as the enactment or paralysis of reason. In some ways Rousseau's wandering, the exercise of his private will, is the end of the Enlightenment. Rousseau's interaction with the private desire of the Other threatened to move him off course, resulting in his crooked deployment of reason as racism, sexism, and homophobia. In this scenario Rousseau rejects freedom and the right to private desire. However, freedom and the exercise of private will is permissible once outside the domain of "man," in landscapes figured as beyond "this earth." To be even more precise, straight white male identities (figured always as the antithesis of savagery) get to move promiscuously from town to country, from the republic to nature, from general to private will. It is this promiscuity of movement, permissible within the gendered, sexualized, and ableist expression of whiteness alone, that makes Rousseau's Enlightenment possible. As we move to Kant, we will again observe the trace of Rousseau's ethical waywardness and, in particular, the ways that race and sexuality figure in reason's crooked and (dis)abling desire to wander against the private will of the Other.

Immanuel Kant

Such crookedly unethical deployments of reason are indeed visible in Shonibare's piece *Age of Enlightenment-Immanuel Kant* (2008). The piece features Kant as a headless and legless mannequin at a desk, writing with one hand and holding a globe in the other. The unethical moves in an imperial gaze where the Other's right to self-definition and self-determination— the premise of Rousseau's general will and Kant's categorical imperative— collapses under Kant's hand. Part of what Shonibare's piece does in pulling together disability, philosophical production, and imperialism is express the performative antagonism at the heart of Kant's philosophy—that is, reason's self-imposed constraints are surpassed by its uncontrollable, colonially shaped kinetic desire to "conquer [or trample] outside experience."[55] Beginning with an exemplary text from his "precritical" period, *Observations on the Feeling of the Beautiful and the Sublime* (1764), and ending with the "critical" "On the Use of Teleological Principles in Philosophy" (1788), I consider the methodological centrality of this colonialist wandering in Kantian philosophy. Further, I argue that despite the antiwandering ethos of the *Observations on the Feeling of the Beautiful and the Sublime*, *Critique of Pure Reason* (1787, second edition), and "On the Use of Teleological Principles in Philosophy," Kant authorizes such errant and impossible movement as reason's very condition. His awareness of these performative contradictions is clearest in the *Critique of Pure Reason*, but they nonetheless uncritically energize his obsession with defining race.

Kant's precritical investment, according to Martin Schönfield, in the "unification of natural science and metaphysics" gave way to a faith in anthropology's ability to provide knowledge about humanity.[56] In many ways Kant relied on anthropology, and the (trans)national wanderings it required, to make conclusions about the racial and sexual requirements for enlightenment. The observations in the *Observations on the Feeling of the Beautiful and Sublime* are, in fact, a product of Kant's reading of travel reports and the "stories of the visits of savages to civilization."[57]

I start with the *Observations on the Feeling of the Beautiful and Sublime* for two reasons. It clearly establishes Kant's simultaneous critique and idealization of the empirical as guarantor of racialized and sexualized metaphysical insight. Second, the text was deeply influenced by Rousseau's inherently wayward ethical philosophy, motivating Kant to, as John Zammito writes, "establish what men were actually like before going forward to a consideration of what they should be."[58] Problematically, however, the purported straightness at the heart of his ethical commitment depended on an inherently wayward methodological principle, the empirical. In the *Observations on the Feeling of the Beautiful and Sublime*, Kant crookedly uses the empirical to make metaphysical claims about racialized and gendered bodies' supposed unenlightened status. In this way he legislates his own colonialist wandering and, in so doing, renders the work a (dis)abling unethical scene of trespassive movement.

Kant's Dandy

In the *Observations on the Feeling of the Beautiful and Sublime*, Kant makes the self-conscious shift from philosopher to *beobachter* (observer). Significantly, the anthropological nature of this shift was inspired by a Rousseauian ethical commitment to establish and secure "the rights of man . . . by teaching others how to live," as Susan Shell says.[59] Kant's translator John Goldthwait writes, "Whereas the *Critique* discusses faculties, the *Observations* describes people. The *Critique* is concerned with cognition alone; the *Observations* is addressed to cognition as integrated with the feelings and manifested in conduct."[60] In this way, while the *Critique of Pure Reason* cautions against the illegitimate use of the faculties in positing knowledge of objects in themselves, the *Observations on the Feeling of the Beautiful and Sublime* sanctions reason's trespassive movement as an expression of a moral commitment. By crookedly activating reason's colonial desire to wander beyond experience, Kant undermines the categorical imperative he otherwise seeks to advance. These links are most explicit in his engagement with racial and sexual difference—a performative engagement that upsets the putative straightness (and nonerrancy) of Kant's idealized moral subject.

Even though Kant's translator, John Goldthwait, connects the categorical imperative, the bridge between individual desire and the common good, to the critical philosophy, it is posited as central to the *Observations on the Feeling of the Beautiful and Sublime*.[61] For example, just as the sublime and the beautiful describe the different impressions made by objects and experiences, they also prescribe moral codes of conduct—that is, understanding is sublime, as is the "subduing of one's passions through principles."[62] The sublime is also the place where the subdued passions and fear are in communion, at times regulating each other. For Kant the sublime is the reserve of the elderly; it is at this stage of life that the subduing of one's passions is mastered. However, "if age does not perhaps diminish his [the elderly man's] vivacity or bestow more understanding upon him, he is in danger of becoming an old dandy."[63]

The old dandy misbehaves, and the purportedly "trifling," "dawdling," and "childish" nature of his character and behavior figures as feminized excess.[64] He is "without principles" and is easily swayed; in this way, the old dandy fails at the straight, principled comportment required by Kant's Enlightenment project.[65] More precisely, lacking principles is precisely that which distances the old dandy from having "a reasonable feeling for the beautiful and the sublime"; such principles otherwise enable someone to be moved while taking "*a standpoint outside himself* in thought, in order to judge the outward propriety of his behavior as it seems in the eyes of the onlooker."[66] Paradoxically speaking, however, despite realizing that one's capacity for self-reflexivity differentiates the idealized moral subject from the "old dandy," the absence of such self-reflexivity in Kant enables the precritical fiction of an accord between subject and object as reason's methodological premise. As with Rousseau's assessment of the "self-styled African," the presumption of philosophical undevelopment is arrived at by way of an unprincipled movement.[67] Put another way, akin to the old dandy, Kant's reason is just as easily swayed.

This essential though dangerous errancy—which has everything to do with the waywardness of reason and desire, reason as desire—becomes explicit in the third and fourth sections, "Of the Distinction of the Beautiful and the Sublime in the Interrelations of the Two Sexes" and "Of National Characteristics." Indeed, if we hold Kant to his own moral compass (the categorical imperative), we see how profoundly he has moved off his own beaten path. The categorical imperative holds that love of self is and should be commensurate with the common good. But what happens when the teleology of the categorical imperative is rendered crooked by erroneous, unprincipled, and skewed impressions? Or when, in Rousseau's terms, the exercise of private desire, or wandering, erodes the Other's right to unfettered movement? What we find in sections 3 and 4 is that this errant, nonteleological movement occurs in Kant's trespassive encounter with racial and sexual difference.

In section 3, Kant argues that the fair sex, whose proper point is the beautiful, is unprincipled and irrational.[68] Her lack of principles causes her, like the old dandy, to "love pleasantry" and be "entertained by trivialities."[69] She is easily moved, charmed, and swayed; this makes *her* resistant to enlightenment. Still, the supposedly disinterested philosopher nonetheless finds himself vulnerable to her "secret magic" and is careful not to concern himself with "impressions that relate too closely to the sex impulse[,] . . . the sensual illusion[,] . . . because it lies outside the compass of finer taste."[70] What is instructive here is this notion that the sensual illusion presents a crisis for the moral disinterestedness said to characterize the Enlightenment proper. But here I also ask, isn't the sensual illusion the source of Kant's aesthetic and ethical judgments? In fact, Kant concedes in his discussion of obscenities and polite conversation that "judgment according to moral strictness does not belong here, because what I have to observe and explain in the sensing of the beautiful is only the appearances."[71] In recognizing that an observation of appearances disables moral evaluation, Kant undermines his own epistemic conceit. In that way, by creating a category of those resistant to enlightenment based on appearance alone, Kant roams past his own ethical mandate. This again reveals reason's inherent errancy, its desire for unbound movement despite severing its own legs.

In many ways reason moves by way of sensory illusions, and this coupled with its inherent colonial aspirations lead to section 4, "Of National Characteristics." Writing with one hand and holding a globe in the other, Kant racially divides the world into zones of affective intensity.[72] Affective intensity is identified here as the capability among first- and third-world peoples for feeling what is beautiful and sublime. For Kant the Italians and the French are more likely to be acutely aware of what is beautiful; the Germans, English, and Spanish are better observers of the sublime.[73] By contrast, Europe's colonies are critiqued for their wayward conduct. In particular, he highlights the "Oriental" man's so-called "degenera[tion] . . . into the adventurous."[74] For Kant the "adventurous" is the end of a kind of backward kinesis and is responsible for the simultaneous embrace of the wondrous and grotesque.[75] It is the movement of an unenlightenment, an opening that undermines any capacity for "finer feeling."[76] But again a contradiction shores up: if the expression of the adventurous is predicated on an "inflamed imagination [that] presents things [in] unnatural images," then Kant himself is an exemplary adventurer.[77]

On the "Negroes" of Africa, Kant makes the following leap:

> The Negroes of Africa have by nature no feeling that rises above the trifling. . . . Mr. Hume challenges anyone to cite a single example in which a Negro has shown talents, and asserts that among the hundreds of thousands of Blacks who are transported elsewhere from their countries, although many of them have even been set free, still not a single one was ever found who presented anything great in art or science or any other praiseworthy quality, even though among the whites some continually rise aloft from the lowest rabble, and through superior gifts earn respect in the world. . . . The blacks are very vain but in the Negro's way, and so talkative that they must be driven apart from each other with thrashings. . . . All these savages have little feeling for the beautiful in moral understanding, and the generous forgiveness of an injury, which is at once noble and beautiful, is completely unknown as a virtue among the savages, but rather is disdained as a miserable cowardice. . . . And it might be that there was something which perhaps deserved to be considered; but in short *this fellow was quite Black from head to foot, a clear proof that what he said was stupid.*[78]

Methodologically speaking, these claims emerge as a function of an adventurous movement, what Mills calls "a paradigm example of impure reason."[79] Similar to the "old dandy," whose reason is compromised by his vulnerability to "haphazard impressions," Kant is likewise affected.[80] His philosophy, despite its pretense to the opposite, is energized by the very "inflamed imagination" he otherwise critiques. In regarding the "Negro" as an image of what is conceptually regarded as stupidity, for example, Kant's adventures are nothing short of trespasses.

These trespasses anticipate and perform the very critique of reason soon to follow. Akin to the "higgedly piggedly" furniture in Rousseau's inner theater, Kant's racism was a product of the faculties' own dizzied arrangements.[81] More precisely, similar to Rousseau's opera, Kant's imagination gets stuck in the impressions of the moment, and from there reason sets off to wander. The observations on the fair sex, her wretched black counterpart, and the hopelessly dumb "Negroes" of Africa, for example, illuminate the essentially wayward and illusory desire of reason to know things in themselves. As we move to Kant's critical philosophy, we see this trespassive tendency critiqued. This is crucial and carries with it an Enlightenment potential to critique empire. But at the same time, this radicalism is undone by reason's adventurous spirit—a spirit that reinstantiates trespass as its very condition.

Kant and the Ocean

As Kant moved to the critical philosophy, he also arguably moved from the position of beobachter back to philosopher. Adorno might say that this move was necessary for the *Critique of Pure Reason*, which was "an encounter of philosophy with itself."[82] Philosophy's encounter with itself, among other things, enabled the self-reflexivity advanced and ignored by the precritical Kant. In the *Critique of Pure Reason*, it is reason that is self-reflexive, asking: What is reason and what is it capable of knowing about itself? What are the limits of reason in its claim to know the world? Or, posed another way, does reason cease to be reason once it wanders past its own limits?

Responding to these inquiries, for Kant, requires a simultaneous critique and incorporation of empiricism (which claims that "all ideas originate in sense and perception") and rationalism (which believes that "knowledge derives from the intellect . . . [and] may be hindered by sense perception").[83] With the empiricists Kant shares the belief in experience as epistemically valuable, while affirming, along with the rationalists, the notion that there exist principles outside of experience that make knowledge possible. In Kant's examination, Deleuze writes, the "ends or interests of reason cannot be justified in terms of experience."[84] As such, reason depends on knowledge conditions that exist outside of experience. Among other a priori conditions, for example, Kant says there exists a general concept of space as the "form of all appearances of outer sense."[85] Time also exists as a transcendental ideal characterized by serial points and instants that are successive and, unlike space, not simultaneous.

When subjected to the sensorial consciousness of the reasoning subject, contradictions emerge within these figurations of space and time. Kant writes that the same object might have different "contradictorily opposed predicates[,] . . . for instance, the being and the not-being of one and the same thing in one and the same place."[86] Kant attributes this problem to the limitations of space as a transcendental condition. Because space is restricted to "outer appearances," it lacks access to the "determinations of mind" essential for the total perception of objects.[87] Time, however, supplants the perceptual limitations of space, by being an "a priori condition of all appearance whatsoever," and mediates between "inner states" and "outer intuition."[88]

For Kant time is an important, if not the most important, transcendental condition for the dialectic of reason. What becomes problematic, however, is the assumption that time is infallible as a perceptual condition. Deleuze observes, "[Our] form of interiority means not only that time is internal to us, but that our interiority constantly divides us from ourselves, splits us in two; a splitting in two which never runs its course, since time has no end. A giddiness, an oscillation which constitutes time."[89] The dizzying nature of the ego's interaction with time is a fundamental metaphysical feature of the path toward reason. In fact, the dizzying, off-centered movements of the ego in space-time are arguably essential though dangerous for the work of enlightenment. While the a priori transcendental conditions of space and time are purportedly the grounds of reason's objectivity, space and time are embodied in the forms of "outer" sensibility and "inner states," respectively. Such convergence of sensibility and judgment not only undermines that objectivity but also presents the ethical crisis observed and enacted by the precritical Kant. This ethical crisis, to which the *Critique of Pure Reason* is said to respond, involves the idealized reasoning subject's enactment of self-determination over and against the object of reason's right to self-definition and private desire. In Rousseau this manifests as an indictment against the "queer" Moor's exercise in sexual freedom, and in Kant an antiwandering ethos is directed at the purportedly unprincipled, adventurous movements of racialized and feminized bodies. And all of this takes place in that expansive terrain between inner and outer states—an expansive terrain engaged through egoically driven wandering.

Indeed, in the *Critique of Pure Reason*, this crookedness at the heart of reason is acknowledged by Kant. In his elaboration of the faculties, for example, Kant acknowledges this expansive terrain between states but argues for its regulation by way of an "objective reality in the subject."[90] This objectivity emerges in the rhetoric of the transcendental deduction whereby the object must connect with a preexisting concept for cognition in order to be assimilated by the senses into consciousness. Once it does so and the bridge between appearance and consciousness is complete, the object is perceived. The object, as perception, becomes assimilated into consciousness via its affirmation of the tenets of the concept, and from there the object becomes incorporated into the subject's categories of knowledge. It can be thought. But in order to be thought, the object must first pass through the empirical exercise of the understanding:

> In all knowledge of an object, there is unity of concept which may be entitled qualitative unity, so far as we think by it only the unity in the combination of the manifold of our knowledge, as, for example, the unity of the theme in a play, a speech, or a story.... The impressions of the senses supplying the first stimulus, the whole faculty of knowledge opens out to them, and experience is brought into existence.... But a deduction of the pure a priori concepts can never be obtained in this manner; it is not to be looked for in any such direction. For in view of their subsequent employment, which has to be entirely independent of experience, they must be in a position to show a certificate of birth quite other than that of descent from experiences.[91]

The identification of an object set's theme or the relationship between a single object and its representative concept establishes a manifold of cognition; Kant calls such a manifold a schema. But even as a rhetoric of regulation moves through this elaboration of the faculties, Kant admits that what the schematizing of data requires is the highly disciplined and cautious deployment of a potentially volatile faculty of reason, the imagination. The imagination, as "a faculty of representing an intuition of an object that is not itself present," produces the condition of possibility for making synthetic judgments about the status of the object's meaning in relation to space and time.[92] But, the imagination also introduces the specter of an anti-Enlightenment movement—wandering—that is both reason's condition and absolute threat.

Working in tandem with the schema, the blind faculty (the imagination) paradoxically produces an image for a concept. In doing so, the blind faculty enables the work of reason's other faculty, the understanding. But how does a blind faculty perform the requisite labor of forming an image of a concept through the association of appearances? Kant writes,

> There must therefore exist in us an active faculty for the synthesis of this manifold. To this faculty I give the title, the imagination. Its ac-

tion, when immediately directed upon perceptions, I entitle apprehension. Since imagination has to bring the manifold of intuition into the form of an image, it must previously have taken the impressions up into its activity, that is, have apprehended them.

But it is clear that even this apprehension of the manifold would not by itself produce an image and a connection of the impressions were it not that there exists a subjective ground which leads the mind to reinstate a preceding perception alongside the subsequent perception to which it has passed, and so to form whole series of perceptions.[93]

If the objective ground of reason is steadied through the transcendental deployment of the understanding, it is at the same time vulnerable to the tremors of a reckless mind. The imagination, as a deregulated, subjectively constituted faculty, troubles the objectivity said to characterize reason proper. In this way, the straightness of the path guaranteed by the transcendental deduction is deformed by its very conditions, as the "field of pure reason" is never not the scene of "manifold wanderings" and blind proceedings.[94]

Still, it is precisely with the initial promise of reason that the threat of exceeding its limits is insinuated in the first place, a fact clearly demonstrated in the work of the imagination and the understanding. In many ways the faculties of imagination, understanding, and reason are "deeply tormented by the ambition to make things in themselves known to us."[95] Deleuze observes that "the transcendental employment of the understanding derives simply from the fact that it neglects its own limits, whilst the transcendent employment of reason enjoins us to exceed the bounds of the understanding."[96] Kant writes,

This domain (reason) is an island, enclosed by nature within unalterable limits. It is the land of truth—enchanting name!—surrounded by a wide and stormy ocean, the native home of illusion, where many a fog bank and many a swiftly melting iceberg give the deceptive appearance of farther shores, deluding the adventurous seafarer ever anew with empty hopes, and engaging him in enterprises which he can never abandon and yet is unable to carry to completion. Before we venture on this sea, to explore it in all directions, and to obtain assurance whether there be any ground for such hopes, it will be well to begin by casting a glance upon the map of the land which we are about to leave, and to enquire, first, whether we cannot in any case be satisfied with what it contains—are not; indeed under compulsion to be satisfied, inasmuch as there may be no other territory upon which we can settle; and secondly by what title we possess even this domain, and can consider ourselves as secured against all opposing claims.[97]

If the oceanic produces a crisis for the teleological work of reason in making otherwise secure claims to reason (as land of enchantment) untenable, then why does it get resituated by Kant as the absolute space of reason's possibility? In other words, the ocean—which, in the context of the Enlightenment age, is arguably metonymic with the space of the transatlantic slave trade and the unconscious—becomes the unruly environment for reason's colonial kinesis. As such, colonialism appears methodologically justified here even as reason asserts an antiwandering ethos to curb such movement.

According to Kant, before one can engage in the crooked movements of rational deduction, one must consult the map of reason's delimited ground. Such consultation is necessary before blind travel and provides an important ethical injunction against reason's colonial desire. In this way, reason is moved by an ethos of wandering and antiwandering; even as reason ethically struggles against the very desire that provides its condition of possibility, phantasmatic transoceanic travel (like the map) is an expression of reason's very exercise. At this juncture, then, it is not only important to recognize this duality but to ask who the travelers are and who embodies the soon-to-be-staked-upon "farther shores."

Tellingly, two other critics of civilization ask these same questions and do so in the middle of the ocean: Sigmund Freud and Hortense Spillers. Concerning the subject of the Enlightenment, Freud argues that, within the psyches of great men, there exists a "discrepancy" between civilized and civilizing actions and what he refers to as "the diversity of wishful impulses"[98]:

> One of these exceptional few calls himself my friend in his letters to me. I had sent him my small book that treats religion as an illusion, and he answered that he entirely agreed with my judgment upon religion, but that he was sorry I had not properly appreciated the true source of religious sentiments. This, he says, consists in a peculiar feeling, which he himself is never without, which he finds confirmed by many others, and which he may suppose is present in millions of people. *It is a feeling which he would like to call a sensation of eternity, a*

feeling as of something limitless, unbounded—as it were oceanic. . . . The views expressed by the friend whom I so much honor, and who himself once praised the magic of illusion in a poem, caused me no small difficulty. I cannot discover this "oceanic" feeling in myself. It is not easy to deal scientifically with feelings. One can attempt to describe their physiological signs. Where this is not possible and I am afraid that the oceanic feeling too will defy this kind of characterization—nothing remains but to fall back on the ideational content which is most readily associated with the feeling.[99]

The oceanic is the site of an illusion, the poetic, and the worrisome promise of emotion's insight. The oceanic's material effects are gestured toward and momentarily foreclosed by Freud's admitting that he has not *discovered* the oceanic in himself. Interestingly, this tension between the possibility and impossibility of discovery is also at the heart of reason's kinetic ambivalence—that is, its desire to stake claims beyond its delimited ground. Nonetheless, in Kant's formulation, the ground is privileged; even as the ocean enables reason's exercise, it must be forgotten once the land is in sight.

Spillers is also attuned to this quality of the ocean and the oceanic as it operated in the pornotropic unnaming and misnaming of black Africans aboard slave ships bound for the New World. Departing from Freud's writing on the oceanic, Spillers argues for the ocean's continued relevance in thinking the psychoanalytic implications of the transatlantic abduction:

> Those African persons in "Middle Passage" were literally suspended in the "oceanic," if we think of the latter in its Freudian orientation as an analogy for undifferentiated identity: removed from the indigenous land and culture, and not-yet "American" either, these captive persons, without names that their captors would recognize, were in movement across the Atlantic, but they were also *nowhere* at all. Inasmuch as, on any given day, we might imagine, the captive personality did not know where s/he was, we could say that they were the culturally "unmade," thrown in the midst of a figurative darkness that "exposed" their destinies to an unknown course. Often enough for the captains of these galleys, navigational science of the day was not sufficient to guarantee the intended destination. We might say that the slave ship, its crew, and its human-as-cargo stand for a wild and unclaimed richness of possibility that is not interrupted, not "counted"/"accounted," or differentiated,

until its movement gains the land thousands of miles away from the point of departure.[100]

In the context of the transatlantic slave trade, blackness was wedded to the ocean, providing the condition of possibility and the limit of reason. More precisely, the black body, like the ocean, was pornotroped, broken open, phantasmatically imagined as anything but itself.[101] Suspended in and as the disavowed oceanic of the yet to be named, black people were subjected to the wayward, fundamentally trespassive movement of colonial desire.

And while there is a potential critique of colonialism at the heart of Kant's exploratory allegory for reason, such critique is not motivated by an ethical concern for the ocean itself but rather for the "adventurous sea-farer."[102] Put another way, Kant knows that there is a real danger of being misled and making claims that are only possible when the limits of reason have been transgressed. But he also knows that in many ways this wandering (off reason's path) is required. Whether or not black people survive the recognized subject of the Enlightenment's trip is not as important as the survival of enlightened subjectivity itself. In the end, Kant's critical writings on race reveal the ways that his oceanic understanding of blackness— as at once unbound and subject to ceaseless discovery—provided the conditions for this ethical violence. I now turn to the philosophical making of that violence and the adventurous seafaring that constituted its methodological condition.

Against the Tide: Race and Kantian Contradiction

Although race is a subject in many of his writings, Kant's writings on teleology advance a presumably ethical theory of blackness. Resting on the purportedly stable shores of science and nature, Kant claims to avoid the ocean. I argue otherwise; as with Rousseau's "self-styled African," blackness becomes the occasion of an ethical breach—a wandering of the idealized Enlightenment subject onto terrain upon which the subject could not ethically stake a claim.[103] In other words, blackness and black people endure Kant's and Rousseau's roaming reason—a mode of rationality that, despite its ethical pretense otherwise, denies black people's right to philosophical subjectivity and private desire.

Still, Kant's writings on race, particularly his work on teleology, are seemingly motivated by an antiwandering ethos. Using a teleological analytic, Kant argues that before race can be understood, it must first enter the critical domain of reason and be cautiously kept away from the magnetic pull of the imagination. Imagination, for example, leads certain theorists, among them Georg Forster, to assert that racial differences, particularly those that differentiate the "Negro" from the rest of mankind, derive from multiple lines of descent (the theory of polygenesis). For Kant a theory of polygenesis requires the formation of illusory claims, including Adamic-esque postulates on the earth's differential evolutionary processes—claims that reveal a straying "from the fertile grounds of natural science into the desert of metaphysics." To speculate about the earth's originary drives—its (re)production of divergent life forms—is to make "it possible for reason to wander about in unbounded imagination."[104]

Against this impulse Kant asserts the necessity of a teleological critique of judgment. In *The Critique of Judgment* (1790), Kant identifies how a crisis in reason's method is an expression of philosophy's internal division. Philosophy is divided into two parts—a "theoretical" philosophy of nature and a "practical" philosophy of morals.[105] Because, for Kant, man is at once an observer of nature as well as a member of civil society, he must have a relationship to reason that can attend to this duality.

Moreover, reason works in the practical interest of the will while the understanding is associated with the theoretical interest in nature. Reason, unlike the understanding, is unable to intuit (namely, sensibility) the presence of objects and, as such, promiscuously makes claims beyond experience. The gulf between understanding and reason is resolved for Kant through the faculty of judgment that in turn negotiates the faculty of desire—the feelings of pleasure and displeasure—with the imperatives of causality and purposiveness as set forth by the objects in nature. Kant puts it plainly: "Judgment in general is the faculty of thinking the particular as contained under the universal."[106]

Though endowed with the task of being the middle term between understanding and reason, judgment itself is indeed also a legislative faculty. Having to arbitrate between the practical and theoretical imperatives of freedom and nature, judgment legislates a purposive relationship between subject and object. The purposive nature of a relationship between subject and object introduces teleological principles as a way to frame the ethical relationship between man and the world. A critical elaboration of teleology allows for a new way of thinking about how such exercises of will either abide by or betray the moral end of freedom. Moreover, a teleological analytic allows Kant's lifelong investment in the "unification of natural science and metaphysics" to, again, converge in an anthropomorphic interrogation (and enactment) of (un)freedom.[107] This "integration of natural necessity and practical freedom"—the critical version of the union between natural science and metaphysics—is for Kant enabled by the concept of race.[108]

Indeed, race became a crucial concept for Kant: it not only allowed for a public response to many of his critics (many of whom defended a theory of origins and polygenesis) but also helped to cement his "support [for] the use of teleology within biology, as opposed to providing merely mechanical explanations, as had become the tendency," according to Bernasconi.[109] For Kant "a science of natural history would, by contrast, concern itself with investigating the connection between certain present properties of the things of nature and their causes in an earlier time in accordance with causal laws that we do not invent but rather derive from the forces of nature as they present themselves to us, pursued back, however, only so far as permitted by analogy."[110] Following this logic, race is an inherited peculiarity that emerges as a purposive differentiation in order to ensure the preservation of the species. Moreover, Kant believes that there is an original diversity within the initial seeds of man that manifests itself when the purpose of species differentiation is required.

This set of arguments concerning originary predispositions requires that there be only one line of descent, that diversity be contained within this line, and that racial difference be understood as purposive. These arguments emerged in response to a theory of polygenesis popular at the time of Kant's writing. Among others, Forster and François Bernier criticized Kant's formulations by postulating the existence of multiple lines of descent as well as by associating race with degeneration or the "accidental imprints" of nature. Kant, in turn, questioned his opponents' claims on the basis of the observation that such philosophies on race require a "stray[ing] from the fertile grounds of natural science into the desert of metaphysics."[111]

To posit that race is an accidental effect of a chaotic shift in environment is to necessarily suggest that nature cannot serve as a category for reason. If nature does not function rationally and with purpose, then its availability to science is compromised. For Kant, nature, like moral law, necessarily operates with purpose: "[W]e are bringing forward a teleological ground where we endow a conception of an object—as if that conception were to be found in nature instead of in ourselves—with causality in respect of the object, or rather where we picture to ourselves the possibility of the object on the analogy of a causality of this kind—a causality such as we experience in ourselves—and so regard nature as possessed of a capacity of its own for acting *technically*; whereas if we did not ascribe such a mode of operation to nature its causality would have to be regarded as blind mechanism."[112]

Nature is organized as a system, as is man's relationship to his faculties of desire. If these realms were organized nonteleologically, they would run the risk of proceeding blindly—calling once again to mind all of Shonibare's headless philosophers. Inasmuch as Kant encourages his colleagues to contemplate nature's design differently, he also cautions them about the dangers of "ascribing powers to [causes], the existence of which cannot by any means be proven, and whose very possibility can, only with difficulty, be reconciled with reason."[113] To speak of race metaphysically, then, is to problematically wander, asserting an intrinsic value and meaning to content, when reason can only contend with form. Ironically, however, Kant's theoretical position weakens when it comes to the subject of the blackness of Africans. Just as "the problem of why Blacks were black, obsessed scientists throughout the eighteenth century," Kant participated in the terms of this inquiry by not only appealing to a possible biological origin—iron particles and phlogiston—but also maintaining that the "Negro . . . undoubtedly holds the lowest of all remaining levels by which we designate the different races."[114] Bernasconi theorizes how the "problem of Blackness" that obsessed the eighteenth century "kept [Kant] focused on the question of the adequacy of mechanistic explanations offered in isolation from teleology."[115] I would further ask, what anomaly did blackness present to Kant that would make him "stra[y] from the fertile grounds of natural science into the desert [or ocean] of metaphysics"?[116] In other words, what initiated the shift from a language of purposive drives to "the lowest of all remaining levels"?[117]

Mills is also interested in those moments when blackness becomes Kant's oceanic, the watery desert of, as Freud would say, his "wishful impulses."[118] For Mills, Kant's philosophy presumes that "the color of the skin is a surface indicator of the presence of deeper physico-biological causal mechanisms. If we think of the 'ontological' as covering what an entity *is*, then the physical makeup of a dog will have ontological implications (its capacity for rationality, agency, autonomy, etc.) and so similar will the makeup of these inferior humans: race does not have to be transcendental to be (in a familiar sense) metaphysical."[119]

Inasmuch as the telos of freedom and desire forged by the categorical imperative was figured as straight, upright, and principled, racialized and sexualized deviations (unprincipled movements) were its conditions of possibility. Standing with one foot in the ocean, and one foot on land, Kant giddily wandered in order to make empirical determinations of the black people in front of him. These determinations were staged at the convergence of the physical and metaphysical, where racialized and gendered bodies of color provided the brutalized ground for the crooked theorizations of truth, reason, and freedom.

In the end, for Kant and Rousseau, wandering described a movement antithetical yet indispensable for reason. In Rousseau's case, wandering provided the conditions for an embrace of private desire, a space to heal from the constraints of enlightened society. Yet wandering also provoked an ethos of restraint—a mobilization of Enlightenment racism, sexism, and homophobia—when enacted by the oppressed. Kant also worried about wandering and wanderers and in particular identified racialized and gendered bodies with a tendency toward errant movement. But it was Kant himself who wandered, who engaged in errant movement as an expression of (his) reason. In this way, wandering constituted method for both philosophers while embodying the end of the Enlightenment.

However, what the white European Enlightenment never anticipated was that those bodies who lived within that end and were consequently trampled, trespassed, and straightened out could reason, imagine, and philosophize themselves, achieving what was otherwise only murderously dreamed about. These headless philosophers, dreaming of monsters, never anticipated that those wandered upon also theorized with and against the Enlightenment, that they had objects of their own, "thing[s] [that had] no concept" and that were often "akin to freedom."[120]

T W O

Crooked Ways and Weak Pens

The Enactment of Enlightenment against Slavery

I like a straightforward course, and am always reluctant to resort to subterfuges. So far as my ways have been crooked, I charge them all upon slavery.

HARRIET JACOBS, *INCIDENTS IN THE LIFE OF A SLAVE GIRL*

Black philosophers have always theorized and embodied the Enlightenment even though its recognized authors did not cognize their engagement as such. To avoid playing "the game of the Enlightenment," to quote Louis Sala-Molins, we must recognize the centrality of these forgotten terrains of philosophical subjectivities.[1] In other words, following Sala-Molins and David Scott, the Enlightenment presumed the absence of black philosophical performance. This is a move that is replicated in the discernment of the Enlightenment as a racialized and gendered monolith that uncategorically violated as opposed to being fundamentally imagined through black life. In opposition, some theorists contend that the enactment of radical antislavery constitutes the Enlightenment's actual fulfillment. For example, with regard to the Haitian Revolution, Hillary McD. Beckles argues that "the blacks of St. Dominique . . . were first to declare the universality of liberty, to build it into the national constitution of Haiti, and commit a State to eternal opposition to chattel slavery. Enlightenment idealism was rescued and historically legitimized by enslaved people who were not expected to be its beneficiaries."[2]

Moreover, in the context of the United States, nineteenth-century black activist-philosophers moved in Haiti's spirit to design and realize a hemispherically minded black enlightenment. While such philosophical movement sometimes coalesced in antislavery writings, which asserted the natural-born rights and liberty of man (a key presumption of white Euro-American Enlightenment philosophy), the black enlightenment cannot be reduced to a set of liberatory revisions. Instead, black philosophers produced their own enlightenment project, at once independent from and in dialogue with the white Euro-American philosophical projects that otherwise figured their presence as absence. In particular, black enlightenment philosophers often expanded the terrain of reason to include insight engendered by the spiritual, enacting a mode of what Fred Moten describes as a "critique or rationalization unopposed to the deep revelation instantiated by a rupturing event of dis/appropriation, or the rapturous advent of an implicit but unprecedented freedom."[3] Put another way, by elevating the unseen's philosophical potential, these thinkers raised important questions regarding the role of a phantasmatic, rapturous movement, or wandering, in freedom's philosophical enactment while extending antislavery's aim of keeping said movement safe from the (empirical, economic, sexual, and epistemological) encroachments of others.

What is more, such innovations within the Enlightenment enacted terrain beyond the "governing configurations of the human as man," writes Alexander G. Weheliye.[4] As Sylvia Wynter argues, the last five hundred years have been marked by Western culture's "secularization of human modes of being"; from the Renaissance through the Age of Enlightenment, the human and humanism became more and more interchangeable with the white European man. The constitutive outside, or those said to lack such ontology, on the other hand, included, among others, the "New World Peoples (*indios*) and enslaved peoples (Negroes)."[5]

But even as the human-as-man apparatus remains a hegemonic configuration that we currently fight against, resistance to its governance has a long and deep history. Whereas "the anticolonial assault . . . is one fundamental moment in the dissolution of Europe's idea of itself as the embodiment of humanity's ideal," Wynter cites antislavery, more particularly, as the grounds for a reimagination of the human apart from hegemonic Enlightenment ideals.[6] She writes, "Yet that plot, that slave plot on which the slave grew his food for his/her subsistence, carried over a millennially *other* conception of the human to that of Man's."[7]

Significantly, Wynter uses the word *plot* as a way to frame antislavery resistance to the hegemonic Enlightenment. *Plot* evokes ground, landscape, a terrain delimited and hemmed in by colonial and economic logics of capitalist governance. But *plot* also refers to strategy or plan. In that way, the slave plot resonates on physical and metaphysical levels, where geography meets philosophy. Geography emerges through philosophical movement not just as material fact—as that spot in the woods or that particular Southern town—but also, following Katherine McKittrick, as an "interpretative alterable world."[8] In the context of this chapter, then, the slave plot is more than a scene (or scenes) of subjection; it is rather the phantasmatic ground for other travels through the world. Indeed, it is through a range of movement—from forward-looking and self-directed to sedentary and rambling—that the slave plot provides the terrain upon which the Enlightenment is enacted, critiqued, rephilosophized, and overcome.

Further, the nature of one's movement across the plot crucially figured, for some, in one's eligibility for black enlightenment. The project of black enlightenment, as with white European Enlightenment, sometimes presumed one's capacity for "self-management" as a key condition.[9] Self-management, for the authors Carol Lasser, Marc Arkin, and Christopher Castiglia, reflects an abolitionist and reformist sensibility that figured slavery as a (dis)abling place of unrestrained desire, violence, and unreason.[10] In this sense, for some white and black abolitionists alike, black enlightenment indicated the end of slavery, measurable in the transition of the formerly enslaved into self-regulated, restrained, rational, and upright (nondisabled) citizens of the state. A straight walk across the plot.

The black enlightenment was formed by the interanimation of two modes of performance, two modes of moving across the plot; an upright, straight-forward, composed, self-determined comportment (forward looking, planning, and, in some cases, walking) on the one hand and a wayward, inspired, divinely guided, and, for some, debilitating wandering on the other. Engaging with the philosophies of Harriet Jacobs, Martin Delany, David Walker, and Sojourner Truth, I consider the way that this performative tension innovated the political project of black enlightenment. Further, I query the role slavery played in sustaining and resolving this performative tension, and how the resolution of this tension manifested in presumptions about the proper form and terrain for enlightened comportment and movement itself.

Along these lines, I ask: How did these different black activists move across the plot and imagine their movement in relation to freedom? How did this difference in movement correspond to and enact opposing modes of philosophical comportment? How did sexual difference as well as the difference that emerges when one is born either free or enslaved presume different sets of bodily and philosophical maneuvering? In many ways, such determinations were not only shaped by particular gendered, sexualized, and classed ideas of proper black enlightenment comportment but also by the "relationship between private identities . . . and public deconstructions of those identities," in Karla FC Holloway's words.[11] On the one hand, the place of the private shaped these activist-philosophers' political and philosophical subjectivities. On the other, the private harbored slavery's memory, which in turn, sometimes bore the blame for any wayward, deregulated, and nonstraight movement said to endanger black enlightenment. In that way, the limits of a self-same, transparent black enlightenment shore up at the end of privacy, to quote Moten, in the "cut shaped in the interminable constitution and reconstitution of a kind of knowledge to which conventional philosophies of Enlightenment and opposition to Enlightenment have no access."[12]

In the case of the four philosophers I discuss in this chapter, theorizations of freedom formed in a wandering between terrains—private and public, visible and invisible. A certain kind of phantasmatic straying into the ante-articulate—a place of hurt and spirit—seemingly engendered other coordinates of freedom. Even though I don't have access to such coordinates, nor do I desire such access, I cannot presume the end of philosophical movement at the end of articulation. Importantly, David Kazanjian's theories of articulation and the Enlightenment inspire my thinking here. In his unparalleled engagement with Walker's *Appeal to the Coloured Citizens of the World* (1829), Kazanjian argues for the power of the (counter)articulation, where "articulation . . . [is] a term that is implicated in the social formations it seems simply to be describing. Articulation figures the mode of connection among discursive practices of race, nation, and equality and offers a way of understanding how relationships between discourses and bodies came to be lived in North America in the eighteenth and nineteenth centuries."[13] For Kazanjian, Walker brilliantly reveals the intense relation, for example, between Thomas Jefferson's articulation of the (white) American Enlightenment and the murderous disarticulation of black bodies and minds, a disarticulation enacted upon bodies and words: "Yet this bodily disarticulation is also discursive, since the breaking of bodies is also a breaking of information, of 'intellect,' of 'the *Word*,' so that black speech is shattered, rendered inarticulate in a discursive sense."[14]

In response to racist, disarticulating practices, according to Kazanjian, Walker offered a modality of philosophical performance that merged embodiment with articulacy, "turning an inarticulate utterance, the 'cry,' into an articulation of human nature."[15] While I agree with Kazanjian about the ways that black enlightenment philosophers, like Walker, powerfully deformed and reformed the white American Enlightenment by way of embodied philosophical subjectivity (given as the cry), I am also interested in the possibility of invisible, inaudible modes of philosophical subjectivity—those modes of reason that roam just above, before, and ahead of the articulate, in the private, untranslatable, often rapturous and unrestrained domains of its making and meaning. Routes of black enlightenment philosophical production and foreclosure that emerge in and against "a field of visibility characterized by the visible and unverifiable light of the Enlightenment."[16]

In some ways, the black enlightenment's frequent resistance to such fields disaggregated its movement from the constraints of external knowability given as *readable* comportment or kinesis. However, because the ante-articulate—the private "communion with the invisible" facilitated by such disaggregation—potentiated, for some, an (in)visible (sometimes painful) straying; it was often cast as antithetical to enlightenment.[17] Nonetheless, Jacobs's quiet encounters with the sublime, Delany's anxiety and faith, Walker's exclamatory pauses, and Truth's unfollowable prophecy extend the terrain of reason to include the wayward, unpredictable, and errant—roamings across the plot invisible to the light of enlightenment. Even as its value remained philosophically contested, such errant movement, or wandering, embraced ante-articulate moments and unseeable terrain as method, revealing the intense limitations of an empirically confirmable notion of enlightenment in realizing the end of subjection.

While the unseeable and unsayable forge slavery's plot and in some ways enact the terrain toward freedom, Jacobs's undisclosed movements proved problematic to many. Put another way, in *Incidents in the Life of a Slave Girl* (1861), the methodological value of privacy is a site of conflict. In some ways, Jacobs's strategic appeal to the supposedly enlightened sensibilities of Northern white women animated this conflict. This is to say, given the set of performative constraints among some white women reformists, Jacobs's capacity for enlightenment required a renunciation of her sexual history and private desire. At the same time, however, certain abolitionist tendencies among these same white women reformers rendered such an enlightenment precondition as impossible for black women. Still, within and against this dialectic, Jacobs created another path. By wandering along the unreadable course of her private life—in Gayl Jones's words, "the lived life, not the spoken one,"—Jacobs philosophically queried the (im)possibility of black female enlightenment against slavery.[18]

To begin, Jacobs's *Incidents in the Life of a Slave Girl* negotiates the gaze of an antislavery and women's-rights-oriented enlightened subjectivity. Aspects of this subjectivity included rational transparency, self-directedness, and passionlessness. With regard to passionlessness, many scholars, including Nancy F. Cott, posit its integral role in the presumption of a "shared womanhood"—a rhetorical principle essential to both political projects.[19] According to Cott, passionlessness transformed from a repressive figuration of (white) women into a "positive" symbol of "moral superiority."[20] The abolitionists and women's rights activists Harriet Beecher Stowe and Angelina Grimké, for example, both deployed passionlessness "as affirmation of woman's dignity in revulsion from male sexual domination."[21] Passionlessness also centrally figured in one's capacity to reform, to enlighten, and to be enlightened.

As such, to be free and capable of freedom's instruction, according to some white female antislavery activists, including Jacobs's amanuensis, Lydia Marie Childs, required a purposive desexualization. However, for black women reformers such self-determined desexualization was impossible. As Margaret Washington argues, slavery cloaked black women in "promiscuity," which in turn choked and constrained the possibilities for black female enlightened philosophical performance.[22] Nevertheless, philosophers, such as Jacobs, mobilized the choke and the cloak toward their own ends. In *Incidents in the Life of a Slave Girl*, for example, Jacobs strategically draws on the language of shared womanhood—evoking the patriarchal protections intrinsic to enlightened society and the passionlessness said to characterize (white) women's enlightenment—only to highlight its fictitious pretense: "But, O, ye happy women, whose purity has been sheltered from childhood ... do not judge the poor desolate slave girl too severely! . . . I wanted to keep myself pure; and under the most adverse circumstances, I tried hard to preserve my self-respect."[23] Further, Jacobs theorizes unenlightenment in ways that bridge the violences of the colonial, hegemonic Enlightenment with a pornotropic tendency of abolitionism to invoke, according to Lasser, "sexual spectacle to depict the evils against which it fought."[24] With regards to *Incidents in the Life of a Slave Girl*, Washington reveals that the abolitionists Amy Post and Childs both urged Jacobs to share slavery's "monstrous features" with the public.[25]

Against the pull of unenlightenment threatened by a coercively crooked engagement (and by implication, association) with slavery's "monstrous intimacies," Jacobs carves out other paths of philosophical desire.[26] Through private, unnarrated, surreptitious movement, Jacobs wanders beyond the narrow roads and scripts of others' instructions to query the possibility of black female enlightenment against (anti)slavery. In doing so, she enacts "something akin to freedom" in corners and hideaways light and dark.[27]

Harriet Jacobs

Jacobs's story commences, like many slave narratives, with the assertion, "I was born a slave." Yet it isn't until the age of seven that she learns of her status as property. Such knowledge emerges upon her parents' death and subsequent subjection in Dr. Flint's household. The brutality of Flint and his family cause Jacobs to wonder "for what wise purpose God was leading [her] through such thorny paths, and whether still darker days were in store for [her]."[28] From the beginning of *Incidents in the Life of a Slave Girl*, knowledge of slavery moves with a negotiation of the slave plot's "thorny paths," and a negotiation of being trapped on the crooked course of someone else's desire. In the face of her master's unrelenting sexual harassment and pursuit, Harriet laments: "My master met me at every turn, reminding me that I belonged to him, and swearing by heaven and earth that he would compel me to submit to him. If I went out for a breath of fresh air, after a day of unwearied toil, his footsteps dogged me. If I knelt by my mother's grave, his dark shadow fell on me even there. The light heart which nature had given me became heavy with sad forebodings."[29]

Jacobs's minimal freedom to be alone in nature, at her parent's grave and at other places of solitude and reason, is continually undermined by the master's endless pursuit. Meeting her "at every turn," Flint enacts a bodily surveillance that escalates into fantasies of incarceration. His attempts to regulate and contain Jacobs's movement are the conditions of possibility for his own private desire. For example, believing that Jacobs's resistance to his sexual harassment involved her discomfort with his wife's presence, Flint offers to relocate Jacobs outside the plantation, "in a secluded place, four miles away from the town."[30]

While Jacobs refuses to move and be moved into that prison, the consequences of such resistance paradoxically coalesce as another tight space—

shame. At this point in the narrative, Jacobs admits to a "relationship" with a white senator from town, Dr. Sands; this is a relationship that results in pregnancy. When pressed by Flint about moving into the secluded cottage, Jacobs publicly admits to her pregnancy. By such admission, Jacobs loses a foothold in her own private path. With the public expression of private, illegal desire, private illegal wandering, Jacobs now moves under the weight of other people's impending (mis)readings.

Upon learning of the unwed pregnancy, Jacobs's grandmother kicks her out of her home. Shut out, Jacobs's only remaining move is to walk "on recklessly, not caring where [she] went, or what would become of [her]."[31] Tragically, Jacobs is restrained by the suffocating bounds of other people's reason—the slave owner Flint on the one hand and her grandmother on the other. What is more, Jacobs's negotiation with these kinetic constraints was arguably compounded by the abolitionist and women's rights enlightenment imperatives requiring her to sustain her reader's empathy (through appeals to passionlessness) while displaying "the relentless forces of [slavery's] sexual undoing."[32] Having to disentangle while delicately sharing the condition of the enslaved female's sexual being occasions, in *Incidents in the Life of a Slave Girl*, moments of articulatory tightness (along with bodily) with "words stuck in [her] throat."[33]

Powerfully, through reckless walking, Jacobs responds to being choked by the crooked forces of slavery and antislavery. While the critic Saidiya Hartman argues that it is the recklessness of her relationship with Sands that threatens to "sever identification" with her readership, I would add that her reckless walking is just as troublesome for these enlightenment projects' voyeuristic tendencies.[34] After being kicked out of her grandmother's home, for example, Jacobs's reckless movement moves her past the reader's prurient gaze. Fleeing to the middle of the woods, she "sat there alone. . . . [Her] mind was full of horrid thoughts."[35] These horrid thoughts are not made available to others' reasoning and, in that way, the thoughts divert an abolitionist imperative that equated an "impassioned speech" (one that was straightforward about [sexual] crookedness) with an opening of "consciousness to reason."[36]

Jacobs's reckless walking and ruminations (in place of telling) work as obstacles to such incursions, and they philosophically enact a new path. Her wanderings at once express an unrestrained philosophical desire and resist the voyeuristic crookedness at work in some abolitionists' requests for straightforward truth telling. Put another way, by closing off the portal of the reader's gaze, Jacobs prohibits any further white wanderings that interfere with her own. This is important because it is precisely Jacobs's resistance to others' tight spaces that inform her unnarrated trips.

For example, determined to save her unborn child as well as her other children from continued subjection, Jacobs plots her escape. Shortly before making her plans known, she continues her (reckless) private philosophizing by speaking with God:

> I knew the doom that awaited my fair baby in slavery, and I determined to save her from it, or perish in the attempt. I went to make this vow at the graves of my poor parents, in the burying-ground of the slaves. "There the wicked cease from troubling, and there the weary be at rest. There the prisoners rest together; they hear not the voice of the oppressor; the servant is free from his master." I knelt by the graves of my parents, and thanked God, as I had often done before, that they had not lived to witness my trials, or to mourn over my sins. I had received my mother's blessing when she died; and in many hours of tribulation I had seemed to hear her voice sometimes chiding me, sometimes whispering loving words into my wounded heart. . . . The graveyard was in the woods, and twilight was coming on. Nothing broke the death-like stillness except the occasional twitter of the bird. My spirit was overawed by the solemnity of the scene. For more than ten years I had frequented this spot, but never had it seemed to me so sacred as now. A black stump, at the head of my mother's grave, was all that remained of a tree my father had planted. His grave was marked by a small wooden board, bearing his name, the letters of which were nearly obliterated. I knelt down and kissed them, and poured forth a prayer to God for guidance and support in the perilous step I was about to take. As I passed the wreck of the old meeting house, where, before Nat Turner's time, the slaves had been allowed to meet for worship, I seemed to hear my father's voice come from it, bidding me not to tarry till I reached freedom or the grave. I rushed on with renovated hopes. My trust in God had been strengthened by that prayer among the graves.[37]

Jacobs's place of reason is the slaves' graveyard, where "the weary be at rest." On the Sabbath she travels to this place in nature for instruction on her next "perilous" step. The scene itself is sacred. "Nothing broke the death-like stillness" and the overall "solemnity" of it all. It is at this moment, the mo-

ment before the perilous step toward freedom, when Jacobs's consciousness wanders with the sacred insight of the weary, the private instruction
of the no longer violated. Kneeling to kiss her mother's grave, Jacobs recalls
hearing "her mother's voice, sometimes chiding [her], sometimes whis-
pering loving words," inspiring rhythms of deregulated movement into a
"wounded heart."[38]

In the slaves' graveyard, reason courses along the errant, sublime, and
rapturous grooves of private desire. As observed with Immanuel Kant,
the sublime, what Jacobs philosophizes as awe, is a feeling of magnitude,
incapable of being fully expressed by reason. Awe produces either extraordinary pain or pleasure. In short, awe moves. According to the *Oxford
English Dictionary Online* awe is simultaneously "(2) . . . the attitude of
a mind subdued to profound reverence in the presence of supreme authority, moral greatness or sublimity, or mysterious sacredness. . . . (3) the
feeling of solemn and reverential wonder, tinged with latent fear, inspired
by what is terribly sublime and majestic in nature. . . . (7) something that
inspires fear; a cause of dread; a restraint."[39]

Like Kant's sublime, Jacobs's awe at once responds to the indescribable
presence of greatness and, by itself, inspires a (self-)restraint. Gayatri Spivak writes, "It is not too excessive to say that we are programmed, or better,
tuned to feel the inadequacy of the imagination (thus *tripping the circuit*
to the superiority of reason) through the pain incited by the Sublime. The
language is persistently one of inescapable obligation, although the concept in question is that of freedom."[40]

While Kant didn't believe that black people were capable of accessing
this "feeling of solemn and reverential wonder" (the ambulations of private
desire and pain), it was nonetheless central to the production of, resistance
to, and innovation within black enlightenment philosophies. In Jacobs's
case, these ante-articulate occasions become a place of philosophy precisely because they open up rather than being closed off by reason. Moreover, unlike Kant, Jacobs isn't moved into reason's superiority, "the poverty
that derives from the attempt to seal ourselves off," according to Scott, but
rather reason's private reconfiguration.[41] This is why Jacobs writes, "Nothing broke the death-like stillness except the occasional twitter of the bird.
My spirit was overawed."[42] On the rapturous edges of this overawe, her
father's spirit wanders as her philosophy of anticaptivity, reminding her
"not to tarry till [she crossed the plot] reach[ing] freedom or the grave."[43]
She escapes the following day.

At midnight Jacobs escapes from the Flint plantation. "The night was so intensely dark that [she] could see nothing" while groping her way to her first hiding place.[44] Here I want to signal again how Jacobs's path toward freedom often becomes itself through invisibility and, as such, not as *straightforwardly* available as her abolitionist readers might have liked. Because slaves were prohibited from leaving the tight space of the plantation—with its "penal protocols" of containment—a common complication of nighttime escape was slaves' inability to see where they were going.[45] Jacobs writes, "I dropped on my knees, and breathed a short prayer to God for guidance and protection. I groped my way to the road, and rushed toward the town with almost lightning speed."[46] Physically blinded by the night, she is guided by the private light of will and the grace of God. What is in excess of the visible field allows her to arrive unharmed.

It is upon her arrival that Jacobs goes into hiding. Leaving her initial hiding place for fear of implicating the acquaintance who harbored her, Jacobs moves into a friend's attic. It is here that she spends her initial days, "feeling . . . the most fortunate slave in town."[47] As cramped as the space itself is, Jacobs feels "a gleam of satisfaction" knowing that she could watch the movements of her former slaveholders without being seen. Reflecting on this pleasure, she asks the reader, "Who can blame slaves for being cunning? They are constantly compelled to resort to it. It is the only weapon of the weak and oppressed against the strength of their tyrants."[48]

As Hartman argues, "the exercise of cunning," in conjunction with "the chapter's language of guilty prostration lures the reader by manipulating her [crooked] investments and desires."[49] In other words, cunning performs several labors. First, by "deposing the reader as judge"—"who can blame slaves for being so cunning?"—Jacobs anticipates the abolitionist reader's own culturally specific moral and ethical ideas of enlightened (straightforward) comportment.[50] Further, by "manipulating [their] investments and desires" Jacobs sustains their crookedly influenced empathy under the pretense of straightforwardness while wandering to keep her retreat safe.[51]

Returning to the narrative, after the first hiding space is no longer safe, Jacobs moves to a small garret behind her grandmother's shed: "The garret was only nine feet long and seven wide. . . . There was no admission for either light or air."[52] Jacobs lies there cramped, unable to stand or turn without hitting the makeshift roof. After boring three rows of holes, she is able to see her children without being seen. Thus she creates another loophole for her privately choreographed philosophical desire. In this way, the chapter's title, "Loophole of Retreat," abounds in signification. Donald Gibson writes, "A loophole is . . . a small opening in a *fortress* wall through which arms may be fired, a place allowing defensive action, and also, because it conceals observer from observed, unobserved offensive action."[53]

Similar to her previous hiding place where only she could fit, the garret also holds just enough space for one person—a kind of barrack from which only she can mount an offensive. Despite being in a cramped position, Jacobs again persists as an "unseen mover."[54] Not only can she see her children without being seen but also she has time to think: her thoughts "wandered through the dark past, and over the uncertain future."[55] Importantly, in this space Jacobs's mind moves however it wants and for an unrestricted duration. One critic of *Incidents in the Life of a Slave Girl* describes this moment in the text as Jacobs's "garret sojourn."[56] An occasion where, once again, wandering names those modes of travel within captivity, a kind of philosophical movement taking place in the boundless space of other grounds.

Powerfully, through hiding and holding silence, wandering into the invisible terrain of spirit and memory, Jacobs errantly moves across the "slave plot." McKittrick argues, "Once the racial-sexual body is territorialized, it is marked as decipherable and knowable."[57] By traveling along unseen and unbound coordinates, along the rapturous edges of what remains undisclosed, Jacobs resists the enlightenment's various and differently motivated (sometimes crooked) territorializations undergirding expectations of black female straightforwardness. In so doing she asserts a project of black female enlightenment where moral integrity and rational self-determination become themselves in private.

Indeed, for Jacobs the place of the private is the place of philosophy. That is, key to her enactment of black female enlightenment against slavery was keeping certain things to herself. This assertion of privacy alongside unnarrated trips, walks, and ruminations offered a "different sense of place that allows her to explore the possibilities in the existing landscape."[58] In other words, the private describes another kind of ground as well as a way of moving through it. It is the unbound space that swirls around the literal slave plot and that pulls against the territorializing constraints at work in some abolitionists' need for transparency. Furthermore, it is where Jacobs can wander against the forces that otherwise try to straighten out (reform, render transparent, and police) her movement.

This chapter's epigraph is Jacobs's assertion, "I like a straightforward course, and am always reluctant to resort to subterfuges. So far as my ways have been crooked, I charge them all upon slavery."[59] What is powerful about this claim is the way in which it gets at the complexity of her project of black female enlightenment. On the one hand, Jacobs's investment in straightforwardness is tied to her investment in the principles of moral propriety at the heart of hegemonic feminist enlightenment. At the same time, however, her resistance to the essentially trespassive character of enlightenment's calls for transparency takes crooked form. But this notion of crookedness doesn't index ethical corruption; rather, in order to sustain a relationship to private desire, she wanders away from a transparent relationship to word and geography. Jacobs finds freedom in the "complicated geographies" enacted by what remains unseen and unsaid.[60] In the places where the road bends and the traveler disappears from view.

Moreover, one might say that Jacobs enacts plenitude not only in the bend in the road but in spaces of confinement. In the face of her grandmother's disappointment at her unwed pregnancy, Jacobs matches directionlessness—"where could I go?"—with a kind of boundless walking.[61] Similarly, from the vantage points of her tight-lipped refusal to share details of her private life and the garret, Jacobs uses the tight space to enact other kinds of free terrain. Other ways of moving across the slave plot.

This can all be contrasted with the freedom movement of Delany. For Delany, tight spaces were not the grounds for freedom's innovation and enactment. Rather, they were spaces to be rejected for their association with seemingly perverse, sometimes sacred, ante-articulatory, and often feminized movements. Such movements, in the case of Delany's text *Blake; Or, the Huts of America* (1859–1861), often suffered pathologization by the main character for bearing what historian Peter Hinks describes as a "trace of connection to the culture of slavery."[62] Indeed, *Blake* was one of Delany's major contributions to the late nineteenth-century conversation on the politics, performance, and philosophy of antislavery and emancipation. Appearing in chapter form in the weekly serial *The Anglo-African Magazine*, Delany's novel is a fictionalized account of a formerly enslaved West Indian man's quest to liberate his wife and other people from tight spaces and, more particularly, their illegal possession by American and Cuban slaveholders. Through the liberatory quest of his main character, Henry Holland (Blake), Delany advances his straight and upright philosophy of freedom and black enlightenment. Key principles of this philosophy include "the necessity for black communities to develop their own sense of pride and community awareness, . . . a sense of moral rectitude . . . and ethical grace," and a possible resettlement of black peoples in the African country of Liberia.[63]

Instructively, unlike Jacobs's *Incidents in the Life of a Slave Girl*, this philosophy of freedom almost entirely depends on a visibly kinetic, straightforward, and planful mode of performance. More specifically, throughout *Blake*, reason and unreason, along with black enlightenment and unenlightenment, are codified through gesture and speech and as straight, transparent movement and divinely guided stasis, respectively. In fact, the author himself believed that enslaved and recently freed people of African descent whose notions of uplift did not include formal literacy, self-initiated black industry, and secularized, middle-class definitions of moral and ethical propriety were unequivocally oppressed and inactive. In *Blake*, this inactivity particularly characterizes black people who supposedly remain attached to slavery—its tight spaces, relations of power, and locale (the South). Further, early on in the novel Delany figures those who believe in divine, not secular, salvation as intellectually and morally uncultivated and, in that way, wretched obstacles to a "manly course."[64] In contrast to the self-mobilizing philosopher, these black people oscillate between stillness and an externally imposed mobility (affectability), hindering the full elaboration of the black body's revolutionary telos.

With regard to this telos's history, Baker argues that an anxiety concerning tight spaces for the newly emancipated black body produced an ideology of modernism that cast the unstill, cosmopolitan black body as its representative sign: "During the ships' passage, shackled black bodies were subject to perhaps the *ur*-definition of 'tight places'"—a mode of real and phantasmatic spatial relations that produced the performative conditions for black immobility.[65] Against the telos of the black body imposed by the slave ship itself—where racialized captivity and confinement brutally figured as the ends of blackness—Delany's self-authored revolutionary telos moved beyond the regulative logic of "tight spaces."[66] Within *Blake*, tight spaces and the bodies that occupy them are left behind.

An exemplary tight space, for Delany, was the state of slavery. In that state, black people (enslaved or free) worked for whites, believed in salvation by Christ, were juridically and symbolically immobile (standing still, as it were), and, according to Baker, "sp[oke] 'Negro'" (the inverse of formal literacy and the sign of ignorance).[67] The performative conditions of a black modernity, then, depended on a *straight*forward, transparent, and readable moral and intellectual movement beyond the pull of enslavement's telos. In the novel Henry's task is to enact that end.

Martin Delany

Henry is the novel's enlightened main character—a figure whose free comportment becomes as essential for the political project of antislavery as armed resistance. In many ways, through Henry's interactions with his yet-to-be enlightened enslaved community, Delany establishes his position on the performative conditions for black freedom. For example, upon learning of the sale of Henry's wife to Cuban slaveholders, he admonishes his unfree-acting mother-in-law, Mammy Judy: "Don't tell me about religion! What's religion to me? My wife is sold away from me by a man who is one of the leading members of the very church to which both she and I belong! Put my trust in the Lord? I have done so all my life nearly, and of what use is it to me? My wife is sold from me just the same as if I didn't. I'll . . ." His mother-in-law responds: "Come, come, Henry, yeh mus'n talk so; we is po'weak an'bline cretehs, an' cah see de way uh da Laud. He move' in a mystus way, his wunduhs to puhfaum." They continue their discussion:

> "So he may, and what is all that to me? I don't gain anything by it, and . . ."
>
> "Stop, Henry, stop! Ain' de Laud bless yo' soul? Ain' he take yeh foot out de miah an' clay, an' gib yeh hope da uddah side dis vale uh teahs?"
>
> "I'm tired looking the other side; I want a hope this side of the vale of tears. I want something on this earth as well as a promise of things in another world. I and my wife have been both robbed of our liberty, and you want me to be satisfied with a hope of heaven. I won't do any such thing; I have waited long enough on heavenly promises; I'll wait no longer. I . . ."
>
> "Henry, wat de mauttah wid yeh? I neveh heah yeh talk so fo'-yeh sin in de sight ub God; yeh gone clean back, I reckon. De good Book tell us, a tousan' yeahs wid man, am but a day wide de Laud. Boy, yeh got wait de Laud own pinted time."
>
> "Well, mammy, it is useless for me to stand here and have the same gospel preached into my ears by you, that I have all my life time heard

from my enslavers. My mind is made up, my course is laid out, and
if life last, I'll carry it out. I'll go out to the place today, and let them
know that I have returned."

"Sho boy! What yeh gwine do, bun house down? Bettah put yeh
trus' in de Laud!"

"You have too much religion, mammy, for me to tell you what I
intend doing."

Then the narration explains:

After taking up his little son, impressing on his lips and cheeks kisses
for himself and tears for his mother, the intelligent slave left the abode
of the careworn old woman, for that of his master at the cotton place.

Henry was a black—a pure Negro—handsome, manly and intelligent, in size comparing well with his master, but neither so fleshy nor
heavy built in person. A man of good literary attainments . . . he [went]
immediately to the place [and] presented himself before his master.[68]

Henry's response to his mother-in-law's faith in the Lord's timing (which
he equates with a white time or white people's timing) imaginatively sets
into motion Delany's theory of effective oppositional movement. For
Henry, blind faith in the Lord's promise of salvation constitutes an im-
passe and defers a relatively straighter, self-directed, and "manlier" course
for freedom. It sustains what the author refers to as the tightly spaced
"darkened regions" of a so-called slave intellect.[69] In contrast, Delany's (and
his representative character Henry's) performative program for black enlightenment asserts the secular light of necessity, the pursuit of moral and
ethical freedom, the course of the outer-reaching man, and the straightforward movement of going "immediately" *out* of the slave quarters and
out on *his* own.

Further, Delany's invention of a difference in speech helps delineate
a noncourse from a course that is "laid out." For example, the voice of
Henry's mother-in-law, in their interaction with the "intelligent" slave,
is marred by the "incomprehensible," inarticulate, and presumably unenlightened tones of a slave vernacular, or as Baker would put it, a speaking "Negro."[70] Moreover, Henry's mother-in-law remains locked into the
performative, teleological conditions of the plantation. Her caricatured,
melodramatic gestures and speech figure as unrelentingly oppressive and
immobile.

Further, Henry suggests the fundamental unenlightenment of his mother-in-law's decision to wait for justice. Interestingly, in *Blake* waiting is an embrace of contingency and unpredictability otherwise figured as antithetical to the planfulness of a secular black enlightenment. In *Incidents in the Life of a Slave Girl*, Jacobs makes, even as she creatively subverts, a similar distinction between slavery and crookedness on the one hand and freedom and an enlightened straightforwardness and planfulness on the other. The difference with Jacobs, however, lies in her openness to the different temporalities and geographies engendered by divine guidance. Even as she asserts a relation between moral degradation and the unplanned and nonstraightforward, she enacts philosophical desire precisely at those places. In that way, those places engender an innovation and subversion of a relation between morality, enlightenment, and transparency.

In *Blake*, however, divine guidance is initially opposed to the plan; the plan, given as "reflective forethought, a studied deliberation, and a carefully measured calculation," is the sign of "enlightened self-consciousness," writes Scott.[71] Indeed, in the novel, the plan is an enlightened movement up and out of the tight space, far past the putative premodernity below the Mason-Dixon Line. For Henry, the exercise of a plan begins with the self-assured assertion: "From this time hence, I become a runaway."[72] After this enlightened revelation, Henry escapes from the slave plantation, striding directly toward the unfree worlds beyond the Mason-Dixon Line. It is, ironically, there where "a hundred thousand bondsmen . . . [seem anxious] to *await* him."[73]

While his "bondsmen" await, he walks directly across the plot. This purposive performative distinction, for the author, corresponds to a deeply philosophical difference. For example, whereas striding and walking connote a sense of direction and plan, waiting implies a yet-to-be enlightened and unregulated mode of bodily comportment. In a conversation with one of his Southern bondsmen (who asks, "how many step man got take fo'e kin walk?"), Henry replies predictably: "Intelligence among yourself on everything pertaining to your designs and project. You must know what, how, and when to do. Have all the instrumentalities necessary for an effective effort before making the attempt. Without this you will fail, utterly fail!"[74]

However, as the novel progresses, Henry's journey is less planned as it becomes guided by chance, contingency, and divine intervention. While

in New Orleans, an "alone and friendless" Henry reflects on the difficulties
of enlightening and mobilizing his bondsmen out of their tightly spaced
"darkened region[s]."[75] It is during this meditation on his brethren's resistance to black enlightenment that Henry's manly course shifts from an
anchored, self-directedness to a "floating on the cold surface of chance."[76]
His straightforward course is compromised by the private, unbound drifts
engendered by political despair.

Yet, as Henry begins to wander, his "anti-mystical racial rationalism"
kicks in to remind him of the plan.[77] Delany writes, "With renewed determination, Henry declares that nothing short of an unforeseen Provi-
dence should impede his progress in the spread of a secret organization
among the slaves."[78] Here a renewed self-determination cites "a gospel and
dynamics of uplift," in Baker's words; an imaginative proximity to unenlightenment causes Henry to trip the circuits up and out of his tight space
below the Mason-Dixon Line and into the straightened out "superiority
of reason."[79]

Further, just as New Orleans suffocates, the United States begins to
feel similarly claustrophobic; a scene of unenlightened activity, once again,
directly precedes this tight sensation. The occasion is the reunion between
Henry and the families left behind on the Franks' plantation. On seeing
the dejected look of Mammy Judy at the news that Henry has yet to free
her daughter, he becomes "choked with [private] grief which found an
audible [public] response from the heart of every child of sorrow present."[80] While the children are made to bear his unenlightened (private)
comportment, Henry publically asserts his revolutionary desire. He leaves
for Cuba the following day.

Once in Cuba, Henry reclaims his preslavery name, Carolus Hen-
rico Blacus, and reunites with his revolutionary-minded cousin, the poet
Placido. Together, in the interest of a transatlantic insurrection, they organize the slaves of Cuba against the slaveholding empires of Spain and
the United States. Interestingly, Cuba is where Carolus reestablishes a
relationship with God, the figure previously criticized for enabling a set
of movements that were neither straight nor self-directed.[81] Once the revolution is set into motion, he prays:

> O God of clemency, in humble petition we again prostrate ourselves
> before Thee, to acknowledge our feebleness and unworthiness to come
> before Thee. We are more and more sensible that without thy divine

aid, we can do nothing. O, guide and direct us in this the greatest of undertakings: be a leader in our wilderness traveling; director in our wilderness wanderings; chief in our wilderness warfare; benefactor in our wilderness sojourning; and light in the midst of the darkness in which we are now enveloped. O, fit and prepare us for the work that is before us—a mighty undertaking: go with us to the battlefield—be our buckler and shield, sword and spear, and strengthen us for the conflict; and be with such of us who fall in the struggle, though the dark valley and shadow of death. Be our great Captain, I pray thee; for it is written in thy holy word, "the Lord is a man of war, for the Lord is his name." If thou art for us, Lord, none need be against us. These things and thy name shall be ever praised, and have all the glory![82]

The closer that Carolus gets to the revolution, the more important heavenly guidance becomes. As he humbly acknowledges, this pursuit of freedom is a mighty undertaking. In fact, it is its status as the "greatest of undertakings" that seems to require the most profound and wildest of wanderings. On the eve of revolution, Carolus admits that God sees all, in the nooks and corners, in the bends and turns, in the places you get to by not being empirically confident that they exist at all.

How do we think about Carolus's renewed faith? In some ways, it indexes Delany's own paradoxical relationship with Christianity, a system of faith at once oppressive to black people (and used to justify racial slavery) and crucial to his plan of black immigration to Africa. Robert Levine explains, "Increasingly convinced that there was an intimate connection between 'the Moral, Social, and Political Elevation of Ourselves, and the Regeneration of Africa,' Delany solicited Henry Ward Beecher for funds on 17 June 1858, two months before he wrote [J. H.] Kagi, so that he could travel to Africa and 'negociate with the natives for Territory or land' and thus help to establish an 'Enlightened and Christian nationality in the midst of these tractable and docile people.'"[83]

Delany's insistence on Christianity as a black enlightenment tool becomes possible once he is outside the United States and amid landscapes said to require regeneration. As in Carolus's prayer, God as guide emerges to decenter a man-as-guide model when the idealized enlightened subject discovers himself in "the wilderness."[84] At once, in the context of the prayer, the wilderness figures as a metaphoric state of unenlightenment, degeneration, "sojourning," and "wandering."[85] Arguably, with regard to

Delany's black enlightenment interest in *settling* Africa, God reemerges in an exemplary wilderness (the imperialist construction of Africa) to guide the guideless while choreographing the legitimate wandering of those presumed to be already free.

This idea that there exists an unmappable terrain, a wilderness, just on the other side of reason's narrowly paved, straight roads, and that such terrain moves in the place just before liberation, holds rich possibility. However, Delany's insistence on a straight progress narrative that begins (even if by wandering) in the imaginative wildernesses of Africa and slavery and ends in the flattened-out terrain of a secular black American enlightenment forecloses that possibility. In fact, the condition of possibility for Delany's black American enlightenment depends on a radical dephilosophization of the wilderness itself and the wandering it engenders. Even though wandering itself enables such dephilosophization, the regenerative logic of Delany's black enlightenment presumes a neat distinction between the lands of the crooked and straight. For Delany and for Walker, Africa and slavery exemplarily figure as crooked terrain, wildernesses that threaten to throw them off course in their straight pursuit of freedom.

In many ways Delany disavows those (sometimes tight) places where the plan falls apart and the road bends—those moments when the course ceases its progressive movement and shifts to the side or, even worse, backward. Indeed, Delany's main character's forward-looking gaze sharply contrasts with Jacobs's roaming with her parents' spirits and other specters from the past. For Jacobs, wandering describes an indiscriminate movement—one that took her "through the dark past, and over the uncertain future."[86] Perhaps this is what makes wandering threatening for those, like Delany, who were wedded to planful, straightforward movement; in wandering, one cannot anticipate where and when one travels and the state of the terrain upon arrival.

This is perhaps also why Delany appeals to God in the midst of his wilderness sojourns. God figures as a guide, as a salve for the unpredictable spatio-temporal character of wandering. Similarly, Walker, a fellow philosopher and the author of *Appeal to the Coloured Citizens of the World* (1829), appeals to God for salvation from a certain kind of movement: a wayward movement that unpredictably leads him to places of hurt and pain. In Walker's work, as in Delany's, an antiwandering ethos is mobilized against places that bear what Hinks calls a "trace of connection to the culture of slavery."[87]

David Walker

In some ways, the U.S. South is one of those places that harbored this "trace" and, as such, threatened to move Walker off course. According to one of Walker's contemporaries, Henry Highland Garnet, the South, particularly the Lower Cape Fear region of North Carolina, bore this trace and "harrow[ed] up his [Walker's] soul. Said he, 'If I remain in this bloody land, I will not live long. As true as God reigns, I will be avenged for the sorrow which my people have suffered. This is not the place for me—no, no. I must leave this part of the country.'"[88]

By way of complication, Hinks argues that Walker's relationship with the South was more complex than Garnet allows. According to Hinks, Walker was born free in Wilmington, North Carolina, but lived side by side with slaves. Because of this cohabitation, Hinks speculates that Walker likely felt restrained because he was "grouped with the unfree."[89] Still, even as slavery's presence imposed kinetic constraints, the revolutionary, anti-slavery spirit of the black South (including everywhere from Charleston to Haiti) moved the young philosopher. In thinking Garnet's and Hinks's claims together, I query the black South's role in the enactment of Walker's philosophical desire and, beyond that, the way that the methodological inhabitation of slavery's trace—its presumed locale and mode of comportment—shapes his performance of black enlightenment. In other words, how and in what way did slavery—its places and traces—shape Walker's movement across the plot? How did slavery disrupt his preference for straight and transparent travel?

Indeed, Walker's *Appeal to the Coloured Citizens of the World* tells the story of this travel, from moving forward and shrinking back to wandering somewhere else. He reflects, "Having travelled over a considerable portion of these United States, and having, in the course of my travels taken the most accurate observation of things as they exist—the result of my observations has warranted the full and unshaken conviction that we, (colored people of these United States) are the most degraded, wretched, and abject set of beings that ever lived since the world began, and I pray God, that none like us ever may live again until time shall be no more."[90]

Traveling, for Walker, produces philosophical insight into the supposed wretchedness of the current and former enslaved as well as reveals the strange relationship between slavery and enlightenment. As we saw in *Blake*, implicit in the *Appeal to the Coloured Citizens of the World* is an argument connecting the degradation of (Southern) slavery to unenlightenment as well as the suggestion that formal education, manhood, and middle-class values forge the straight path toward freedom. Seemingly, the document reconciles the causes of racialized, gendered wretchedness, embodied in some ways by the *place* from which Walker fled, the Lower Cape Fear, and considers how this condition is produced as well as remedied by a fundamentally reimagined, forward-looking American Enlightenment.

An exemplary expression of American Enlightenment, for example, takes the form of Thomas Jefferson's *Notes on the State of Virginia* (1785). In this document Jefferson famously argues that a black person's "imagination is wild and extravagant, escapes incessantly from every restraint of reason and taste, and, in the course of its vagaries, leaves a tract of thought as incoherent and eccentric as is the course of a meteor through the sky."[91] He further maintains that the "eccentric" absence of reason is attributable to "nature" and not to condition.[92] In many ways Jefferson's claim that black people privilege sentiment over reason resonates with the European Enlightenment's claims about white women. For Kant, (white) women are more inclined to sense than reason, "love pleasant[ries] and . . . [can] be entertained by trivialities."[93] Implicit in Jefferson's formulation is an understanding of black men (the default gender under attack) as feminized, unrestrained, and irrational.[94] The language of comportment (how one holds oneself, behaves, performs) was, for Jefferson and other recognized Enlightenment thinkers, always already racialized, gendered, and classed.

Walker's *Appeal to the Coloured Citizens of the World* is a formalized response to Jefferson, and the white Euro-American Enlightenment project more broadly, as well as a call for a black enlightenment—an uplift project that dissociated enlightened comportment from racial difference while idealizing a formally educated man as its forward-looking, straight-moving subject. Nonetheless, the text's contradictory and complicated relationship with the racist Enlightenment constitutes a (dis)abling tension. For example, the *Appeal*'s preamble begins with an indictment of Euro-American waywardness, the vicious movements of recognized racial enlightenment projects. Walker starts here because it is the source "from which most of our miseries are derived."[95] It is this misery, a misery with a history that extends from the violently colonized nations of antiquity to the nineteenth-century United States, that has had God's ears ringing "with the cries, tears and groans of his oppressed people."[96] For Walker, this sound produces a troublesome dissonance in this *"Republican Land of Liberty!!!!!"*[97]

The use of exclamation points above indicates a deliberate and heart-felt emphasis on the racialized, performative contradictions at the heart of America's self-understanding. Emotion erupts into the text to make the affective impact of this violence clear. Further, the exclamation point con-stitutes an internal dissonance within the *Appeal to the Coloured Citizens of the World* that breaks up the even (enlightened) tone that Walker sustains via language and ideology. On the one hand, Kazanjian argues that this dissonance is the sound of a new enlightenment's inauguration, the excla-mation point "an embodied articulation, a 'cry' that makes 'human nature' a sign of a future justice, a freedom to come."[98] While I agree with Kazan-jian that emotional movement enacts new liberatory subjectivities, I am just as interested in the ways that a change in affect eludes the constraints of political and philosophical codification and, beyond that, empirically knowable enlightened comportment. Moreover, what is at stake when par-ticular scenes of subjection, the vicious enactment of racial enlightenment, engender a bending, a movement astray, of Walker's sound and phrase? To what extent does such bending indicate the emergence of a different terrain and a different kind of philosophical movement, or wandering? Such bends (dis)articulate "a freedom to come," and they do so in ways that disaggregate black enlightenment from the constraints of a visible, transparent, straightforward, and planful movement. Still, because such bends threaten to endanger the forward-looking philosopher, they are sub-sequently straightened out through rhetorics and ideologies of rational self-management.

Like Delany and, in a different way, Jacobs, Walker's resistance to racist violence took the form of a black enlightenment project, with improve-ment of the self becoming interchangeable with antislavery. Undoubt-edly, the assumption that racism could be most effectively dismantled once black people *acted free* reveals a larger anxiety around the impact of slavery on black performance. Recall Jacobs's admission: "I like a straight-forward course, and am always reluctant to resort to subterfuges. So far as my ways have been crooked, I charge them all upon slavery."[99] The differ-ence between Jacobs and Walker, however, consists of their relationship with crookedness. While both philosophers associated slavery with crook-edness, Jacobs often embraced the crook in the path or the tight space en-gendered by slavery—cunning, silences, and garrets—as the condition of possibility of freedom. For Walker, on the other hand, crookedness or the degradation wrought by enslavement was a gendered and fundamentally unenlightened mode of comportment, counterposed to an uplifted (transparent, straightened-out, and self-determined) manhood, "the prized figure of the discourse of racial uplift," according to Hartman.[100]

Acting free presumed an uncorrupted and incorruptible manhood, and it should be considered within a "rising new spirit" of black reform—a movement that, as Hinks writes, "promoted racial solidarity and moral elevation."[101] Just as this early nineteenth-century movement negotiated antislavery resistance and black solidarity, it moved by way of an ideology of emancipation that aspired to "a fuller participation in the dominant white middle-class culture of the North."[102] It is just this painful paradox that engenders what Hartman calls "the burdened individuality" of freedom—an ideological double bind that is marked by "the onerous responsibilities of freedom with the enjoyment of few of its entitlements, the collusion of the [Enlightenment's] disembodied equality of liberal individuality with the *dominated, regulated, and disciplined embodiment of blackness*, the entanglements of sovereignty and subjection, and the transformation of involuntary servitude effected under the aegis of free labor."[103]

Acting free, then, involves the disciplining of blackness and black performance. In Walker's case, it is as much a self-discipline as it is a disciplining of the unenlightened. The straightening out works both ways: "And when my curious observer comes to take notice of those who are said to be free (*which assertion I deny*) and who are making some *frivolous pretensions to common sense*, he will see that branch of ignorance among the slaves assuming a more cunning and deceitful course of procedure. He may see some of my brethren in league with tyrants, selling their own brethren into *hell upon earth*, not dissimilar to the exhibitions in Africa but in a more secret, servile and abject manner. Oh Heaven! I am full!!! I can hardly move my pen!!!"[104]

Taking a "standpoint outside himself"—to be the "curious observer," as it were—sustains a straight and disinterested course of argumentation and allows Walker to discipline himself as a black man of reason.[105] The straightness of his course, however, is compromised by the irruption of crooked, "deceitful course[s] of procedure," introducing dark, dangerous roads and "African" detours into his path.[106] In particular, Walker evokes Africa, and the equally elusive concept of *what happens there* as a way to criticize the absence of enlightenment among the enslaved. Further, "Africa" is an undifferentiated, southernized scene of unenlightenment that also threatens to throw Walker off course—a mental roaming that again leads him into that crooked trace, the ante-articulatory domain of emotion's philosophical unpredictability. Here pens stop moving and wander off the page.

Nevertheless, by preceding as well as serving as emotion's condition of possibility, Africa figures as a performative imaginary of unreason, becoming tied to a whole set of terms that Walker's European counterparts had already invented. Africa's metonymic relationships with Wilmington, the Lower Cape Fear, femininity, irrationality, and antienlightenment—the kinetically (im)mobilizing traces of black enlightenment—are embodied and repressed through Walker's urgent call for his brethren to be "MEN."[107] Against the wayward pull of the trace, then, Walker calls upon black men "of sense" to do the work of straightening out their more wretched brethren—moving them forward across the plot.[108]

Indeed, the wretched and the crooked are the reasons for the *Appeal to the Coloured Citizens of the World*. What is more, they always already index a corrupted male subject. Women (both enslaved and free) are nowhere to be found. Their absence speaks to a larger anxiety surrounding women, reason, and the black enlightenment's idealized subject. Further, we know that Walker's mother was born free and his father enslaved. Can we assume, even still, that she remained among the wretched given that Walker's subjects of enlightenment are "men of colour, who are also of sense?"[109] The irony stands, however, that despite her absence, a "mother's blessings" were the *Appeal*'s performative conditions.[110]

According to Garnet, before Walker "turned his back upon North Carolina," he first turned toward his mother.[111] This is the story told by the preface and forgotten by the *Appeal* itself. Despite her absence, the blessing moves the text. When Walker's pen threatens to stop moving, for instance, it might just be the specters of Walker's mother and a feminized Lower Cape Fear (as well as other unspeakable locations) that stop the writing, endangering the straight and upright course that the *Appeal to the Coloured Citizens of the World* otherwise engenders. Perhaps, the feminine, the "trace of connection to the culture of slavery," in Hinks's words, privately changes the shape of Walker's movement, from "solemnly" taking "a stand" to "shrink[ing] back into nothingness."[112]

Shrinking back before God attends to Walker's realization that black men have the potential to be enlightened. In some ways, the act of shrinking back and roaming into a feminized nothingness is revealed as philosophically productive even as the invocation of visible, enlightened comportment forecloses that possibility. This also reveals the *Appeal to the Coloured Citizens of the World*'s simultaneous enactment of secular and sacred desire. In fact, the frequent appeal to God, even if it is the occasion for some unpredictable movement into the holy domain of the ante-articulatory, speaks to Walker's larger belief in divinely sanctioned "natural rights."[113]

For Walker, even as God endowed all men with enlightened potentiality, the secular stylization of a particular social and ethical comportment made black enlightenment possible. In the face of God, Walker shrinks back into a constitutive, though disposable, terrain of black enlightenment, one forged by the wayward ante-articulate wanderings of a feminized nothingness. This nothingness, what must go unmentioned even though its tear-streaming ambulations move the *Appeal*, might be the place where his mother resides. "*Handled* by her in ways that he cannot escape," in Hortense Spillers's words, Walker's *Appeal to the Coloured Citizens of the World* dramatizes his mother's absent presence in the forces (places, traces) that threaten to lead him astray.[114]

Walker's pen and the abundance of exclamation marks demonstrate the irrepressibility of emotion, those things feminine and private, those things unseemly to this man "of sense," while at the same time making illegitimate this force as philosophically productive. In some ways this illegitimacy manifests in his mother's unspoken vulnerability to violation as well as her exclusion from black enlightenment subjectivity. On the one hand, against Spillers's injunctive, Walker says no—albeit emphatically and with a decidedly unmasculine pitch—to the "female" within.[115] On the other, in the appeal to God, Walker wanders southward, past nothingness and toward a *something* to which he could not possibly make a direct appeal.

Tragically, black women who were associated with the vestiges of slavery—residing in the South, lacking formal literacy and middle-class respectability, or who were born enslaved—were the someones to whom Walker could not appeal directly. Not only were poor, often illiterate black women marginalized in discourses on black enlightenment but, as we saw with Jacobs, they were further silenced by concurrent projects of racial and sexual freedom. The critic Louise Newman discusses their exclusion from white women's abolitionism and suffragist discourse:

The exclusion of enslaved black women from the categories of both "slaves" and "woman" was a common feature of white abolitionist-suffragist discourse, although white women sometimes invoked claims to a universal sisterhood that contained assumptions about a universal womanly character. At the same time, the tropes of sisterhood and uplift began to foster and reflect a new self-understanding among white women that they, as white women, had a moral responsibility to reform an evil social and political system. As historian Jean Fagan Yellin has pointed out, these tropes were readily apparent in iconography that white female abolitionists used on their stationery and transformed into folk art through their needlework. The imagery depicted a kneeling slave-supplicant asking the question "Am I Not A Woman and a Sister?" a phrase that white suffragist Frances Gage put in the mouth of Sojourner Truth when she retold Truth's 1851 address ("Ar'n't I a Woman?) in the article Gage published in 1863.[116]

As observed with Jacobs, white abolitionist-suffragist discourse cast enslaved black women as fallen. Put another way, because of the level of amoral sexual brutality experienced while in captivity, black women figured as aimless in their relation to white feminist humanism—a figuration juxtaposed to the already uplifted and self-directed white woman.

Moreover, black women who bore that trace—against which Walker and Delany planned a straightforward movement—were fixed outside a path toward enlightenment. In the case of Sojourner Truth, for example, the trace of slavery figured in other people's marginalizing representations of her, shoring up as a kind of bent or broken (formally illiterate) speech, a bent or broken mode of comportment. Indeed, in some ways, because she lacked the ability to formally record her own word, to literally write her own lines of freedom, she was subjected to the crooked tracings of others. This is to say that Truth's marginalization was exacerbated through her coercive theatricalizations by literate others—theatricalizations that manifested themselves at the level of externally imposed gestures, accents, and deeds.[117]

Arguably, there is an intense relationship between the trespassive figurations of Truth as boundless "plot space" (a body that rehearses, performs and becomes legible according to the needs of others) and a deeper anxiety over her putatively "unreadable," privately inspired philosophical performances.[118] In many ways, Truth's itinerancy, illiteracy, unreadability, and unwavering commitment to the invisible bends of divine guidance presented a crisis for a patriarchal, uplift-oriented politics that otherwise required her to stay posed, transparent, and translatable, as well as in place. Even as others attempted to script her (or straighten her out) within a certain path, Truth's sojourns, or wanderings, enacted an often divinely guided freedom on its own terms and terrain.

Sojourner Truth

Born in Hurley, Ulster County, New York, in the late 1790s, Truth (known then as Isabella) grew up enslaved and spent most of her childhood in a "cold, dark, and damp cellar . . . on the eastern side of Roundout Creek," Nell Painter writes.[119] Isabella lived there with her parents, James and Betsey, and her brother, Peter. Upon the slave owner Charles Hardinbergh's death, Isabella's family broke up, sending Isabella to work for two more owners, John Neely and John Dumont. Enduring great cruelties at the hands of Neely and Dumont, Isabella survived through prayer, learning from her mother that if "she spoke out loud to God and asked Him for direction, He would always come to her rescue."[120]

According to the *Narrative of Sojourner Truth* (1881), Isabella's "dialogic relationship with God" was such that when the time came to leave the Dumont plantation, she sought God's assistance in revealing the "deeper pattern" for her escape.[121] Because slaves in New York were to be emancipated in 1827, Isabella promptly informed Dumont of the date of her departure. While Dumont initially agreed to emancipate Isabella at this time, he subsequently changed his mind upon a reassessment of Isabella's changes in labor value (she suffered a bodily injury). Though she consented to stay longer to compensate for her decline in value, Isabella eventually left: "In 1826, Isabella heard the voice of her God instructing her when to set out as a free woman. Just before dawn in the late fall, she left the Dumonts' carrying only her baby, Sophia, and a supply of food so meager that it fit in a cotton handkerchief."[122]

God directed her steps "to the safe asylum" of the Van Wagenen residence, a distant acquaintance.[123] She stayed with the Van Wagenens for a few months though foresaw an eventual return to her former master, John Dumont. Despite the atrocities committed by Dumont, including the illegal sale of her son, Peter, to a Southern slaveholder, Isabella was divinely informed that she should still return to him. It was on the occasion of her return that Jesus Christ illuminated the eternal presence of his friendship with Isabella.

This phantasmatic encounter occurred as she mounted herself and her child onto Dumont's carriage for the passage back to the farm. It was then that she felt the omnipotence of God. He was everywhere, guiding her every step and maneuver. But it was also at this moment that she experienced God's omnipotence to be as miraculous as it was frightening: "With the breath of his mouth, [a] lamp [is blown out] so that no spark remains."[124] Contemplating the possibly annihilating potential of a deep proximity to God, Isabella was soon soothed by the intervention of "a friend who appeared to stand between herself and an insulted Deity."[125] This friend, she observed, was Jesus. As her amanuenses Olive Gilbert and Frances Titus recount, at this private philosophical moment, Isabella became symbolically baptized by the Holy Spirit.

From that philosophically formative moment, Christ continued to be a consistent mediating force between Isabella and the overwhelming luminescence of God; he worked with her to enact a private path of reason in the undisclosed domain of God's light. A divinely shaped movement across the plot. For example, while in bondage on the Dumont plantation, Isabella philosophized on the property's edge. As with the slave's graveyard in *Incidents in the Life of a Slave Girl*, "the place she selected . . . was a lonely spot, and chosen by her for its beauty, its retirement, and because she thought that there, in the noise of those waters, she could speak louder to God, without being overheard by any who might pass that way."[126]

During her private philosophical sojourns, outside the visible reach of the plantation, Isabella had to be cautious so as to not be "overheard." What is further interesting about Gilbert and Titus's account (within which this anecdote is featured) is the way that Isabella's communion with reason is untrespassed by her amanuenses. Gilbert and Titus, who otherwise attempt to "commodif[y] [their] subject's interior life" in the *Narrative of Sojourner Truth*, leave Isabella's conversations with God alone.[127] Not only did Isabella recount the Lord's Prayer in the private tones of the Dutch language, but she also spoke with an invisible interlocutor.[128] The fact that the methodological conditions of her philosophy are indecipherable at once reveals their successful subversion of colonial surveillance while foreshadowing how Isabella's purported eccentricity suffered diagnosis precisely because of these kinds of resistances to other people's reason, reading, and understanding. Isabella's path toward freedom, as with Jacobs's, became itself in a kind of wandering against translation, a resistance to others' needs for transparency. We will return to examine the performative effects of this resistance, but for now it is important to understand the steadfast role God played in Isabella's enlightenment.

Importantly, the conversations with God that began at that "small island" intensified with time, inspiring her religious conversion to Methodism. Methodism, in particular, enabled Isabella to discover what Painter describes as "a new means of power, what Pentecostals call the power of the Spirit, that redressed the balance between someone poor and black and female and her rich white masters."[129] Having been racially excluded from New York City's prominent John Street Church, she joined the Zion African Church. It was during this time that she met and began to work for James Latourette. Latourette, "having left the regular Methodist church, because of its falling away from the ideals of John Wesley," began to organize small meetings for the dissatisfied faithful, among them Isabella.[130] Known as the Holy Club, this particular sect promoted principles such as self-righteousness, moral propriety, and asceticism. The small group eventually became tied to a burgeoning movement called New York perfectionism, which "sought to eradicate the corruption of this world, just as John Wesley's Methodism was meant to purify the Anglican Church."[131] What is more, for Isabella, these ethical and religious commitments were buttressed by the belief that one's experience with racial and sexual subjection had no bearing on moral rectitude and one's capacity for enlightenment (unlike black reformism). Washington writes, "Thirty years of enslavement and sleeping on pallets in Dutch kitchens shaped Isabella's understanding that neither unfortunate circumstances nor proximity to 'evil' was synonymous with moral degradation."[132]

Arguably, this refusal to associate slavery with degradation or wretchedness is partly responsible for Truth's marginalization in historical narratives of antislavery activism. Though she is remembered as an iconic (albeit stagnant and excessive in that iconography) protoblack feminist, her black radicalism is often overshadowed by the critiques of prominent black statesmen during that era, including Frederick Douglass and Delany. Delany, for example, heavily criticized black people's association with white people, particularly associations that contained though were not necessarily defined by an economic relationship (Isabella worked for the Grears, the Piersons, and the prophet Matthias during her membership in their Seventh-day Adventist groups). Painter writes, "For the most part, unseen holy women like [Catherine] Ferguson and Isabella, who performed household labor and were known more for piety than for wealth or agitation, served as targets of criticism. The educated black abolitionist, Martin Delany, for instance, berated blacks satisfied to live as servants."[133]

Because the ethical and metaphysical, more than the juridical and economic, shaped, in Painter's words, Isabella's "politics of race," many figured her "ways out of humiliation" as backward.[134] Black and white itinerant female preachers, though attuned to the sinfulness of racism and sexism as instantiated practices, prioritized being true to themselves and God as paramount goals. This feature, in conjunction with the oft-observed fact of female preachers' tendency toward being "unconstrained and outspoken," rendered their contributions to black history relatively neglected.[135]

On the one hand, speaking outside, being outspoken, indicates a potential phantasmatic movement beyond the bounds of secular reason. In fact, Isabella changed her name to Sojourner Truth after making such sacred outspeaking and out moving her life's mission. However, Truth's unbound outspokenness, along with the private, indecipherable wandering with God that moved before and after the word, upset the imperative of transparency at the heart of prominent black reformers' and abolitionists' straight paths.[136] Like Delany, Douglass admits to being *thrown off* by Truth's movement. Painter writes,

> Frederick Douglass's first meeting with Truth occurred at Northampton [a utopian society in Massachusetts], as Douglass was charting a course into freedom divergent from hers. Like many other fugitive slaves, Douglass associated illiteracy with enslavement, and strove to complete his emancipation through the acquisition of fluency—elegance, in his case—in reading and writing. He saw himself as a statesman-in-the-making and modeled his comportment on the well-educated antislavery leaders with whom he worked.
>
> Though some twenty years younger than Truth, Douglass patronized her industry and amiability, calling her one of the community's most useful members "in its day of small things." What most galled Douglass was Truth's lack of sympathy with his own means of personal rebirth. While Douglass was schooling himself to "speak and act like a person of cultivation and refinement," Truth, he said, "*seemed to feel it her duty to trip me up* in my speeches and to ridicule my efforts." Doug-

lass saw Truth as "a genuine specimen of the uncultured [N]egro," who cared very little for elegance of speech or refinement of manners.[137]

There are several interesting points to remember from this observation. As demonstrated earlier, the association of illiteracy with enslavement, or the trace of slavery, was a key feature of black reform literature emerging during this period. More precisely, philosophers such as Walker and Delany posited an underlying connection between so-called backward speech and behavior, speaking out or being outspoken in Truth's case, and an alleged complicity with an enslaved (as opposed to reformed, enlightened, and forward-looking) posture.

Furthermore, in Douglass's case, something about the way Truth moved and spoke tripped him up. I'm reminded here of the allegedly African scenes in Walker's *Appeal to the Coloured Citizens of the World*, how recalling images of subjection made his pen wander, bend, and stop. Indeed, as with Jacobs's trips to the graveyard, these scenes resonate with Spivak's arguments on the sublime.[138] The feeling of the sublime is a feeling of magnitude, incapable of being fully expressed by reason. It produces either extraordinary pain or pleasure. It moves. In the case of Truth, her very presence moved Douglass enough for his feet to begin tripping the circuits into reason's superiority, making claims that Truth herself was a "genuine specimen of the uncultured [N]egro," who "cared very little for elegance of speech or refinement of manners."[139]

It is precisely this patronizing refusal of Truth's profundity that affected the representation of her in subsequent years. For Douglass and others, Truth became tantamount to "otherness through the use of what they [historians, critics, reformers, and others] thought was *Negro* dialect and they dwelled at length on descriptions of her body," writes Painter.[140] Because she refused to be straightened out by prevailing logics of appropriate enlightened and secular comportment and because her path toward reason resisted transparency, Truth endured others' trespasses. Those who tripped the circuits into reason theatricalized Truth as "quaint," and according to Donna Haraway, a "special human, not one that could bind up the whole people through her unremitting figuring of critical difference— that is, not an unruly agent preaching her own unique gospel of displacement as the ground of connection."[141]

Because she was consistently determined to be unreadable (not transparent) and, with that, not easily assimilable into counterhegemonic projects of racial and gender sense making, Truth remained vulnerable to the peripatetic whims of the literate public's imagination—that is, those who recorded, codified and made readable, and ultimately nonconsensually theatricalized her countless philosophical performances. Tragically, the descriptions of these philosophical performances, most notably Truth's famous (and invented) speech act "Ar'n't I a Woman?," push the limits of accuracy with accent, gesture, and imagery. Many (mis)heard Truth in a number of ways, but I have chosen two, the first by Marius Robinson, the editor of the *Anti-Slavery Bugle*, and the second by the (white) women's rights advocate and abolitionist Frances Dana Gage, to illustrate the radically divergent impressions that Truth's movement made. Marius Robinson says,

> One of the most unique and interesting speeches of the convention was made by Sojourner Truth, an emancipated slave. It is impossible to transfer it to paper, or convey an adequate idea of the effect it produced upon the audience. . . .
>
> [Robinson begins to recap Truth's speech.] May I say a few words? Receiving an affirmative answer, she proceeded; I want to say a few words about this matter. I am a woman's rights. I have as much muscle as any man, and can do as much work as any man. I have plowed and reaped and husked and chopped and mowed, and can any man do more than that? I have heard much about the sexes being equal; I can carry as much as any man, and can eat as much too, if I can get it. I am strong as any man that is now. As for intellect, all I can say is, if a woman have a pint and man a quart—why cant she have her little pint full? You need not be afraid to give us our rights for fear we will take too much,—for we can't take more than our pint'll hold.[142]

Frances Dana Gage also provides a reenactment:

> Slowly from her seat rose Sojourner Truth, who, till now, had hardly lifted her head. "Don't let her speak," gasped a half-dozen in my ear. . . . There was a hissing sound of disapprobation above and below. I rose and announced "Sojourner Truth," and begged the audience to keep silence for a few moments. The tumult subsided at once, and every eye was fixed on this almost Amazon form, which stood nearly six feet high, head erect, and eye piercing the upper air like one in a dream. . . .
>
> "Well, chillen, whar dar's so much racket dar must be som'ting out o' kilter. I tink dat, 'twixt the niggers of de South and de women at

de Norf, all a-talking 'bout rights, de white men will be in a fix pretty soon. But what's all this here talking 'bout? Dat man over dar say dat woman needs to be helped into carriages, and lifted over ditches, and to have de best place eberywhar. Nobody eber helps me into carriages, or ober mud-puddles, or gives me any best place"; and, raising herself to her full height, and her voice to a pitch like rolling thunder, she asked, "And ar'n't I a woman? Look at me. Look at my arm," and she bared her right arm to the shoulder, showing its tremendous muscular power. "I have plowed and planted and gathered into barns, and no man could head me—and ar'n't I a woman? I could work as much and eat as much as a man, (when I could get it,) and bear de lash as well—and ar'n't I a woman? I have borne thirteen chillen, and seen 'em mos' all sold off into slavery, and when I cried out a mother's grief, none but Jesus heard—and ar'n't I a woman? When dey talks 'bout dis ting in de head. What dis dey call it?" "Intellect," whispered some one near. "Dat's it, honey. What's dat got to do with woman's rights or niggers' rights? If my cup won't hold but a pint and you holds a quart, wouldn't ye be mean not to let me have my little half-measure full?"[143]

The differences between Robinson's and Gage's versions are nothing less than striking. While Robinson ("who was familiar with Truth's diction") performed her speech in so-called standard English, Gage represented Truth with an "inconsistent dialect," "modeling Truth's idiom on a conception of Southern Black plantation speech to which readers of Uncle Tom's Cabin had been accustomed."[144] The association between Southern black plantation speech and Truth at once "fails to account for Black speech patterns in the Ulster County area [upstate New York, where Truth was enslaved]" and implicitly renders the idiom of black plantation speech the sign par excellence of ignorance.[145] Interestingly, for example, Gage's rendition finds Truth unable to "locate" the word "ignorance." Here, most explicitly, the conflation of a plantation speech with ignorance becomes the occasion for one's movement off course, being lost as it were in the murky waters of the trace, or what Walker might call the "mist" (of ignorance).[146]

Gage's Truth is quaintly unaware, her speech powerful though muddled in such ignorance that it succeeds in losing Gage's attention: "Turning again to another objector, she took up the defense of Mother Eve. I cannot follow her through it all. It was pointed and witty and solemn; eliciting at almost every sentence deafening applause."[147] This comes at the end of

Truth's speech, at the end and beginning of Truth's philosophy. This is precisely where Gage admits to having lost Truth. Gage cannot follow her through it all.

Deep below the superficial assumptions concerning the supposed incomprehensibility of Truth's diction, there exists the inescapable fact that something in the way Truth philosophized and performed threw Gage off. They were no longer on the same path—in this case (white) women's advocacy. Truth stood fixed somewhere else, enmeshed in an antebellum imaginary that Gage created and that black reformists determined as unenlightened and unfree—a terrain with limits that Truth maneuvered and exceeded. Haraway argues, "Perhaps, we need to see her [Truth] as the Afro Dutch-English New World itinerant preacher whose disruptive and risk-taking practice led her to 'leave the house of bondage,' to leave the subject-making (and humanist) dynamics of master and slave, and seek new names in a dangerous world. This sojourner's truth offers an inherently unfinished but potent reply to Pilate's skeptical inquiry, 'What is truth?'"[148]

Isabella's new name revealed that the truth was in the unreachable terrain of her sojourn. Her path toward freedom stayed its own, independent though sometimes concurrent with the courses that moved beside it. Sojourner's Truth, truth's sojourn, sometimes tripped people up, and contained private bends and turns that prevented others from following it. At the place before and ahead of articulation, what Walker might have called a "nothingness," Truth theorized justice.[149] Moreover, by ceding control to God, Truth, like Jacobs, and in more vexed ways, like Walker and Delany, philosophized in the bends of divine guidance; in that way, all four philosophers restored the domain destroyed by the European Enlightenment—the mythic, the spiritual—in their expressions of black enlightenment. But it was Sojourner Truth who unwaveringly and primarily expressed a philosophical openness to wandering with the invisible. What is more, along the bends and turns of the unseen, she enacted a philosophy of freedom, picking from the harvest of the ante-articulate, or in Scott's words, "the ungovernable grove of [her] alternative values."[150]

In the end, it is this philosophically performative spirit of ungovernability that brings these black activists together. Even though the philosophical movements presumed to lack rational self-determination suffered frequent pathologization, it was often through an unrestrained wandering that freedom itself was realized. While I don't know nor am I interested in finding out what these philosophers communicated to the invisible, I cannot discount the possibility that freedom moved in that engagement. That philosophy was made in an undisclosed wandering across the plot, in the silence of private rumination and in the trembling, "rapturous" exhortation of appeals to the divine.[151]

This realization is shaped by a political and ethical commitment to freedom; life's movement exceeds the visible, aural, tactile, and the material. Even if the hegemonic Enlightenment logic of truth presumed that everything lived could be seen and captured, histories of antislavery resistance and philosophy theorize otherwise. For those subjected to the most vicious of state constraints, truth is often found, according to Hartman, outside the "dominative imposition of transparency and the degrading hypervisibility of the enslaved."[152] In the crook and the garret, at the moment when speech and comportment wander against all efforts to straighten out and render transparent, freedom's path is (un)written. In this way, if we really listen to Sojourner Truth, then we must acknowledge other landscapes of philosophical desire. What is more, if we really believe in Truth's philosophical intervention, then maybe it's best to leave the "deeper pattern"[153] of her philosophical desire alone.

THREE

Writing under a Spell

Adrienne Kennedy's Theater

— *FOR TRAYVON MARTIN* —

Writing about the twentieth-century playwright Adrienne Kennedy's one-act plays, the *Village Voice* critic Alisa Solomon provocatively titled her critique "Sojourner's Truths." For Solomon, "Adrienne Kennedy's plays are like towering rock formations. Frightening and beautiful, their craggy terrains drop off suddenly and provide only the most tentative of footholds. Images threaten to avalanche, careening plots almost knock us off a cliff, but Kennedy's precise backtracking language prevents these disasters."[1]

Significantly, Solomon renders Kennedy's theater a kind of treacherous, untravelable landscape and further frames that (un)travelability as "Sojourner's Truths." While Solomon doesn't theorize the bridge between these two philosophers, it is important to situate such narratives of untravelability and unfollowability within the context of post-Enlightenment. For example, many figured Truth as unfollowable, attributing her unfollowability to a purported backwardness and her supposed anthropological and ideological undecidability. Such a move expresses enlightenment's promiscuous epistemological desire and also confines Truth's movement to the empirical, the surface topography of her philosophical performances. But given her relationship with God (her private interlocutor), Truth's philosophy moved on various plateaus at once, the visible and invisible, the divine and the lay. In this way, her philosophical performances always already resisted other people's desires to pursue and travel through.

Similarly, Kennedy's theater unpredictably wanders between various terrains, times, spaces, states, the visible, and the invisible. And, like Truth,

Kennedy's glides between and among worlds suffer policing by post-Enlightenment logics of realism.[2] Arguably, such logics emerge out of a racialized, gendered differentiation between what Denise Ferreira da Silva describes as inner and outer determination: "In the *stage of exteriority* it [reason] operates as the exterior ruler of affectable things, and in the *stage of interiority* it is the force that guides the production of human knowledge and culture."[3] In the Enlightenment and post-Enlightenment eras, according to da Silva, black people continue to figure as affectable, lacking the moralizing, internal presence of reason as guide. As such, they become subject to a range of surveilling and disciplining scripts, and their visible wanderings (of body, speech, tone) are policed as such.

A crisis emerges, however, when minoritized people refuse their scripts or endeavor to write them outside of reason's regulatory schemes. Tragically, punishments—death or incarceration in prison or mental institutions—become enlightened society's answer to such resistance. In the case of Kennedy, her scripts are hard to follow and, in some ways, partially hidden. As such, her characters and scripts receive a psychiatric diagnosis. Historically speaking, psychiatry emerged as a regulative, straightening-out device for such occasions, according to Françoise Vergès, where "the anarchist, the communard, the vagabond, . . . [and] the colonized" were presumed to lack or, more nearly, refused to disclose their private maps.[4]

Indeed, there is a long history of medicalizing minoritarian wandering, or presumed maplessness. In the nineteenth century, according to Ian Hacking, "disorders" such as drapetomania (the psychosis purportedly at fault for slaves' desire to run away from subjection) and dromomania (the aimless wandering of the typically white working poor) emerged to police the inconvenient, *unproductive* movement of the oppressed. What is more, while the worldly wanderings of the elite leisure classes, "the grand tours of British aristocrats, county landowners," and so on were the conditions of possibility of capitalist imperialist subjectivity, poor people's "mad" flight from social, civic, and economic "responsibility" (the mappings of others' desires) figured as disease.[5] As Vergès observes, during the late nineteenth and early twentieth centuries, "the colonizing soldier lent his place to the psychologist, militarist rhetoric to humanitarian rhetoric. The land has been conquered, the soul of the native was the new territory to map out and describe."[6]

This chapter, therefore, is not interested in charting or mapping, or offering a diagnostic frame for the *reading* of Kennedy's wandering scripts and characters. While this chapter is about two of Kennedy's most famous plays, *Funnyhouse of a Negro* (1964) and *The Owl Answers* (1965), in many ways, it refuses to be. Making arguments about Kennedy's plays is complicated, precisely because of the sometimes stifling, diagnostic nature of argumentation and interpretation. As the performance critic and philosopher Fred Moten argues, "interpretation [is often the] deferral of freedom or of justice, a deferral enacted in singularized and differentiated readings and legitimated by the law which structures the production of readings."[7]

I hope to attend to the radicalisms at the heart of Kennedy's wandering theater while acknowledging the partiality and limits of such a maneuver. While an ethical and political interest in racial and gender justice inspires my engagement with Kennedy's art, I take care not to undermine such ethics in my engagement. So perhaps paradoxically I am interested in the ways in which *Funnyhouse of a Negro* and *The Owl Answers* resist the teleological constraints of reading and understanding through the wandering speech, movements, and minds of Kennedy's characters. Along these lines, I am also deeply concerned with those occasions when wandering, in its resistance to analysis and other technologies of reason, becomes wedded to pathos for some law-abiding readers.

Arguably, the persistence of Enlightenment definitions of madness— or movement "away from the proper path of reason," according to Michel Foucault—continues to animate anxieties around Kennedy's theater.[8] Because her plays refuse to provide "footholds" and safe passage for others to follow, her wandering characters and plots get locked up, condemned, and foreclosed.[9] However, at the same time, Kennedy seemingly anticipates such a maneuver in her plays. She does so by dreaming into being black female wanderers who, through speech, movement, and reverie, undo the very scripts they're dreamed into.

The Elusive Play

Kennedy messes with the transparency of the script itself—the presumption that an assemblage of words is enough to locate a character's identity and desire. In many ways, scripts by Kennedy aren't straight lines but serpentine paths where characters wander and hide.

What's more, Kennedy's wanderers move along private scripts, inhabiting scenes described as "dramatiz[ations of] . . . something that is done as a result of the story."[10] This story before the story, the sublime before the reason, the travel before the place, is often a story about being black and female where blackness and femaleness become bloodied, (im)possible, holy, and bludgeoned sites of salvation. This story before the story might also be the stuff of Kennedy's dreams, the frightening and frightened imagery on the pages of her travelogues-cum-diaries. The *ur*-story may be shaped by those unreadable (sojourner's) truths, forging a relation between her surrealism, black radicalism, and nonlinear lyricism on the one hand and the writing that comes out of solitude on the other, when, for Kennedy, days of writing are always already "days of images, fiercely pounding in [her] head."[11] Days of walking and wandering. Days of being confined to the bed because of pregnancy-related complications. Days where the only noise is the eerily reliable sound of owls. Days where plays are written though the playwright claims that it is impossible to say that *she* wrote them: "Somehow under this spell they become written."[12]

While Kennedy describes these beginnings in the preface to her *Adrienne Kennedy: In One Act* collection (1988), they remain (somewhat) elusively offstage. As such, this uneasy relation between the semiprivate preface and the semipublic stage raises the following questions: What are the stories that she misses when she writes? What are the stories missed by audiences when they watch? What are the stories that come through despite the fact that the audience might not see them? How is the inability to pin down these (origin) stories, the desire at the heart of her art, a result of the anticaptivity quality of wandering? How might these stories before the story, what is hidden from view, move within the ante-articulate?

Indeed, Kennedy's plays wander as much as they elude the wanderings of others (just as Truth's sojourns and Harriet Jacobs's recklessness succeeded in losing their abolitionist audience). That is part of what happens when plays are written under a spell. When one produces art along lines of flight occasioned by magic, dreams, holy guidance, and faith, something happens in the space between the creator and the object created. The philosopher José Gil argues,

> Magical-symbolic thought and practice not only resolve the antinomies of power but also—and it is definitely the same thing—the antinomies of the power of discourse. Is this not to say that this way of thinking provides a solution to the problems posed by the transcendental dialectic of Kant? What was at stake there—in the question, what is it possible to know?—was the power of scientific discourse

itself. For magical-symbolic thought there is no obstacle getting to the noumena, and it is the same for the hypothetical Kantian figure of the *intellectus archetypus*, which knows the unconditioned: magical words are action, thought coincides with being, time and space do not impede the grasping of the thing in itself—because on the contrary, they are organized in such a manner that they can be transformed by appropriate techniques (such as those at work in the therapeutic ritual) and at the same time remain linked to their normal perception—in order to create from it the conditions of possibility and the formal framework for knowledge of the absolute.[13]

While the art and philosophy made "under the spell" troubles post-Enlightenment imperatives of transparency, knowability, and self-directedness, the spell remains post-Enlightenment's very condition. The "knowledge of the absolute," occasioned by the descent into the spell, animates the transgression of a limit articulated by Kantian reason as its necessary condition and absolute threat. As we saw in chapter 1, the deluded use of the imagination by recognized Enlightenment philosophers rationalized racial and sexual subjection. Yet, because reason needed to deny such methodological straying, the European Enlightenment's racial and gendered Others became the unwitting embodiments of a delusional imagination.

Powerfully, however, the remobilization of the imagination by the purportedly affectable opened up other pathways for the enactment of reason and freedom. For Kennedy in particular, surrealism, the twentieth-century artistic movement, provided the space for such phantasmatic innovations along with a critical disturbance of post-Enlightenment distinctions. Because these distinctions, real and unreal, reason and unreason, truth and shadows, spells and philosophy, are relied on to justify neoimperial impositions of external guidance and rule, such subversions have profound implications. By creating other lifeworlds for the enactment of philosophical desire, surrealists not only critique and refigure the logic of such guidance but also advance its existence in an unreachable realm. According to the critics Franklin Rosemont and Robin D. G. Kelly, "surrealism—an *open* realism—signifies *more* reality, and an expanded *awareness* of reality, including aspects and elements of the real that are ordinarily overlooked, dismissed, excluded, hidden, shunned, suppressed, ignored, forgotten or otherwise neglected."[14]

For the director and critic Robert Scanlan, Kennedy's use of surrealism works at the level of strategy, "for a 'grip' on something intractable in the black experience."[15] Provocatively, this grip on "something intractable"— what remains uncanny, ungovernable, essential, absolute, and elusive at the heart of black experience—suggests a regulatory device. However, at the same time, it is the fundamentally deregulated form of surrealism itself, and its expanded terrain of elusive movement, that figures as a possible, albeit paradoxical, anchor. Maybe then for Kennedy the errant opening of reality provides a grip onto another lifeworld, one that makes new relations to neglected life possible, relations that subvert the differentiation of unlivable terrain—medicalized and derealized, disavowed and diagnosed—by restoring the untravelable and unfollowable as freedom's very conditions.

Sadly, though, Kennedy's reimagining of terrain suffers from the imposition of outside maps. More precisely, while her plays *Funnyhouse of a Negro* and *The Owl Answers* resist the tyrannies of stillness operative within the diagnostic laws of reason, reading, and interpretation, the language of psychosis moves in to effect another kind of containment. Famously, Billie Allen, the actress who played *Funnyhouse of a Negro*'s main character, the Negro Sarah, described her as "psychotic."[16] Years later, the critic Philip Kolin also employed a lexicon of mental illness in his diagnosis of the same character. This diagnosis emerges in Kolin's book *Understanding Adrienne Kennedy* (2005), which promises, in its title, to provide an "understanding" of the elusive artist. In many ways this understanding heavily relies on a language of psychiatric assessment; for example, Kolin reads *Funnyhouse of a Negro* as a "schizophrenic play," featuring "alters in a dissociative world."[17] He also claims that "the shocking world of the *Funnyhouse* . . . symbolizes her mad fantasies and the impossibility of escape. As psychotherapist Gaetano Benedetti contends, 'hallucinations of mad people are dreams from which they cannot awake.'"[18]

This language of psychiatric pathology constitutes a form of lockdown that, by itself, sustains the very same "impossibility of escape" otherwise critiqued. Moreover, the use of Benedetti's argument about "mad people" (who are technically schizophrenic—"mad" is a different designation) further works to dismiss Kennedy as not only crazy but pathologically otherworldly. What gets missed in these designations, according to the anthropologist João Biehl, are the ways in which psychosis, as both sign and difficult experience, "lies not in the psychotic's speech but in the actual struggles of the person to find her place in a changing reality vis-à-vis people who no longer care to make her words and actions meaningful."[19]

In his important work on a Brazilian asylum, *Vita*, Biehl thinks about the social and economic processes that conspire to create such "a category of unsound and unproductive individuals who are allowed to die."[20] In *Vita* (2005), the title of his book and the asylum itself, Biehl engages with zones of social abandonment, places where the "mentally ill and homeless, AIDS patients, the unproductive young, and old bodies" are left behind.[21] In many instances, according to Biehl, these populations are disposed of at the asylum precisely because their existence figures as unproductive and to be corrected by the state's own maps and scripts. This is precisely why I bring his work in here. What happens to Kennedy's theater happens regularly at the hands of state institutions. In fact, for Biehl, psychosis and other diagnoses are effects of post-Enlightenment logics that ascribe value to purportedly composed (able) bodies and (sane) minds. For bodies and minds who wander against such regulative scripts, pathology and abandonment are a matter of *course*—zones of abandonment, zones of unlivable terrain where those who fall out of line are left behind.

Returning to the main character of *Funnyhouse of a Negro*, the critical reduction of Sarah's speech and behavior as psychotic reveals an anxiety around black women who wander outside post-Enlightenment scripts. Even though we live in a postbellum era, anxieties around black (female) wandering—a straying from externally imposed names and scripts— endure. As Hortense Spillers argues, the "ruling episteme that releases the dynamics of naming and valuation remains grounded in the originating metaphors of captivity and mutilation so that it is as if neither time nor history, nor historiography and its topics, shows movement, as the human subject is 'murdered' over and over again by the passions of a bloodless and anonymous archaism, showing itself in endless disguise."[22] Against such murder, Kennedy's main characters drift away from the pull of name and identity at the heart of imperial, empirical, and epistemological desire. Contrary to Kolin's wish, they refuse understanding and, consequently, suffer punishment.

Indeed, many black and white theatergoers reviled *Funnyhouse of a Negro* for its inability to be understood, followed, and codified. As the playwright remarked in a lecture given at Brown University in 1989, critiques of *Funnyhouse of a Negro* included its presumably negative representations of black people and the fact that the main character, Sarah, *ap-*

peared psychotic. Moreover, according to Joni L. Jones, the play's straying from a "generally accepted understanding of black theatre which tends toward linear realism" resulted in its ambivalent relation to black radical aesthetic movements of the time, most notably the black arts movement.[23] The play's inability to be followed and understood resulted in a set of aesthetic and political dismissals, and it also potentially inspired Kennedy's own musing that "the person who wrote them [one-act plays] is quite crazy."[24]

Given Kennedy's relationship with surrealism and the spell that engendered her plays, however, craziness doesn't easily imply a pathological designation of cognitive illness. Instead, "the person who wrote them" indexes the other dimensions of being, living, moving, and knowing offered by what is unseen. With regard to *Funnyhouse of a Negro*, the play itself formed in dreams. During the lecture at Brown University, she recalled that "every morning, she [her mother] would tell me her dreams[,] . . . speak[ing] in images. Her dreams were always very tragic. The monologues of my plays are exactly like them, especially *Funnyhouse*." The fact that Kennedy's monologues "are exactly like" her mother's dreams not only suggests a philosophical bridge between worlds but further undermines any desire to follow her. More specifically, something about the dramatization of dreamwork upsets the logic of pursuit at the heart of a "hermeneutic drive"; perhaps in that way, speaking in dreams constitutes a mode of reason that can be heard but not fully followed.[25]

While, for Sigmund Freud, an interpreter of dreams must "follow the main road that leads to the interpretation of dreams" and avoid the detours on the other side of what is manifest, Kennedy's art disturbs that process.[26] In other words, Freudian dream interpretation presumes the transparent availability of thought, the availability of philosophy underneath the wayward images in dreams. He writes:

> Their [latent dream-thoughts] most powerful image is the repressed instinctual impulse, which has created in them an expression for itself on the basis of the presence of chance stimuli and by transference on to the day's residues—though an expression that is toned down and disguised. Like every instinctual impulse, it too presses for satisfaction by action; but its path to motility is blocked by the physiological regulations implied in the state of sleep; it is compelled to take the *backwards course* in the direction of perception and to be content with

a hallucinated satisfaction. The latent dream-thoughts are thus transformed into a collection of sensory images and visual scenes. It is as
they travel on this course that what seems to us so novel and so strange
occurs to them. All the linguistic instruments by which we express the
subtler relations of thought—the conjunctions and prepositions, the
changes in declension and conjugation are dropped, because there are
no means of representing them; just as in a primitive language without
any grammar, only the raw material of thought is expressed and abstract terms are taken back to the concrete ones that are at their basis.
What is left over after this may well appear disconnected.[27]

Against the readability of dreams, Kennedy's art wanders. More precisely,
if Kennedy's monologues begin at images and if such images withhold
their philosophical impetus, they already move at the detour of what is
manifest. In this way, for Freud, they make reading hard, and, for that reason, "backwards." But even here in Freud's formulation of the movement
of dreamwork, forward and backward are seemingly impossible as the only
directional coordinates. Perhaps, for the analyst, forward and backward
become necessary for the successful (efficient) traveling along a course,
otherwise so "novel and strange." But it is the fullness of the course that remains important—one that roams in all different ways, past the watchful
eye of a post-Enlightenment-minded interpreter and into an undisclosed
domain of powerfully inefficient wakeful wandering.

Significantly, Kennedy's plays dramatize this wandering as well as its
endless regulation. In 1964, *Funnyhouse of a Negro* debuted at the East
End Theater in New York City, raising with it a set of questions that concern the aesthetic, psychic, political, performative, and philosophical implications of being pursued. In the opening scene, Sarah asks the various
personas that (de)form her identity (otherwise referred to in the play as
"herselves")—Jesus, Patrice Lumumba, Queen Victoria, and the Duchess
of Hapsburg—why her father, the "blackest one of them all," keeps returning: "He is arriving again for the night. (*The Duchess makes no reply.*) He
comes through the jungle to find me. He never tires of the journey."[28]

Being pursued by blackness constitutes, for the psychoanalytic critic
Frantz Fanon, an existential dilemma for the unassimilable (perhaps so-
cially psychotic) black person—someone who at once yearns for solitude
and the ability to escape from his or her own skin: "I slip into corners, I
remain silent, I strive for anonymity, for invisibility. Look I will accept the

lot, as long as no one notices me!"[29] In this sense the resistance to racial definition coincides with a resistance to, or avoidance of, visuality. At the same time, however, being pursued by blackness indicates another kind of movement. More precisely, interactions prompted by corporeal difference are often just as shaped by mythological musings, phantasmatic "tom toms, cannibalism, intellectual deficiency, fetishism [and] slave ships."[30] In that way, the movement of blackness is both phantasmatic and physical.

Moreover, in the context of *Funnyhouse of a Negro*, this doubledness of blackness at once arrests and liberates Sarah's own philosophical comportment. The main character's resistance to blackness's simultaneously physical and phantasmatic pursuit, embodied in some ways by her father, suggests (as it does in Fanon's philosophy) a resistance to external discovery and definition. As two of herselves, Queen Victoria and the Duchess of Hapsburg, discuss:

> VICTORIA: (*Listening to the knocking.*) It is my father. He is again arriving for the night. (*The* DUCHESS *makes no reply.*) He comes through the jungle to find me. He never tires of his journey.
>
> DUCHESS: How dare he enter the castle, he who is the darkest of them all, the darkest one? My mother looked like a white woman, hair as straight as any white woman's. And at least I am yellow, but he is black, the blackest one of them all. I hoped he was dead. Yet he still comes through the jungle to find me.[31]

However, even while this resistance to discovery and definition figures, for some critics, as an expression of internalized racism, there is an openness in Kennedy's art that agitates against a single story. Perhaps the avoidance of her father's arrival indicates the presence of her own kinetic desire, raising questions such as: if it's the case that blackness moves on both a physical and mythological level and, in that way, describes a movement that always already hovers above and outside the body down below, then why can't the nature of that movement be remobilized in Sarah's interest?

Indeed, just as Sarah laments her father's arrival, she also yearns for similarly ungraspable movement—a yearning that takes place as wandering and often from behind closed doors. For Kennedy it is crucial that Sarah be left alone "in her room with her belongings" while the "rest of the play happen[s] around her." In her room, where she says that all of "myselves [can] exist," Sarah dreams into being impossible selves, worlds, and movements while eluding the (de)forming threat of others' pursuit,

other's knocks on the door.[32] This tension in *Funnyhouse of a Negro* between unfettered movement on the one hand and the material experience
of trespass on the other also evokes the contradictions within travel itself. Just as travel, according to Frances Bartkowski, "calls up the capacity
for movement, a lack of fixity," it also means "border crossings and identity checks."[33] This is a liberatory and precarious experience of "shifting
grounds."[34]

In many ways, Sarah mobilizes such shifting ground toward her own
ends. Not only does she exist as multiple selves but she also confesses to
know nothing of place. This might be why she suffers private pursuit and
public critique but not captivity. If the ground endlessly shifts and Sarah
embraces a composite of disparate, mistaken identities, then perhaps the
"blackest of them all" might never find her. "[Her] station is so radically
marked by [her] costuming of the self," Bartkowski writes, that place itself becomes continually reinvented, draped over, and nullified.[35] Consequently, the radical "costuming of self" and place subverts capture and
containment.

Alternatively, Kennedy's evasion of "identity checks" along with a resistance to pursuit often translated into "not presenting a positive image
of Blackness," according to Michael Kahn.[36] For example, for some critics,
"Sarah/Negro's nihilistic renunciation of the African heritage results in
the death of her father, thereby implying self-destruction."[37] According to
this logic, such identitarian and topographical renunciations—her rejection of a singular ground, heritage, or place in the world—purportedly kill
off blackness. Further, for some critics, the rejection of unmovable grounds
and places results in problematic yearnings. In particular, Sarah's longing
to be "pallid like Negroes on the covers of American Negro magazines"
purportedly evidences a fixed movement of self-hatred rather than an errant drive toward self-transgression.[38]

Again, while Sarah's self-hatred remains an important question, I
think that self-denial also suggests liberatory potential. Contrary to Kimberly Benston's reading, if nobody is there to answer the door, if there are
no "tracks and signs for the ardent pursuer of this evasive subject to follow," then Kennedy's characters and their (her) stories cannot be located.[39]
Their (her) constant moving around and against the enclosures of self,
ground, and place destroys the maps and, with it, the attempts at their
(her) capture. In so doing, wandering enacts a philosophy of living where
and "when one is no longer marked by the dynamics of recognition or by

temporality."[40] Put another way, in a monologue in the first scene of the play, Sarah reveals that *who she is* has everything and nothing to do with where she can and can't be found:

> Part of the time I live with Raymond, part of the time with God, Maxmillian and Albert Saxe Coburg. I live in my room. It is a small room on the top floor of a brownstone in the West Nineties in New York, a room filled with my dark old volumes, a narrow bed and on the wall old photographs of castles and monarchs of England. It is also Victoria's chamber. Queen Victoria Regina's. . . . When I am the Duchess of Hapsburg I sit opposite Victoria in my headpiece and we talk. The other time I wear the dress of a student, dark clothes and dark stockings. Victoria always wants me to tell her of whiteness. She wants me to tell her of a royal world where everything and everyone is white and there are no unfortunate Black ones. For as we of royal blood know, black is evil and has been from the beginning. . . . As for myself I long to become even a more pallid Negro than I am now; pallid like Negroes on the covers of American Negro magazines; soulless, educated, and irreligious. I want to possess no moral value, particularly value as to my being. I want not to be.[41]

Kennedy's Sarah and the rest of herselves "endlessly and restlessly move along a continuum of time, matter, and space," explains Paul K. Bryant-Jackson.[42] From her white boyfriend Raymond's apartment to conversations with God to a bedroom cluttered with revolutionary icons and the royal voices of statues that speak, Sarah traverses real and imagined terrain. This traversal across time, space, and matter is endless, restless, and not circumscribed by the limits of place or destination. Moreover, the refusal of external localizations—presumptions about where she lives and what doors she will open—works in tandem with the refusal of externally imposed identifications.

Sarah's affirmation of her desire "not to be," then, does not necessarily indicate a white-identified narrative of blackness as unlivable, immobile, and inhuman. To insist that these are the playwright's politics is, in more ways than one, *misguided*. While many of Kennedy's critics read such scenes as "not supportive of the Black movement," philosophers such as Frantz Fanon might argue otherwise.[43] For Fanon, such ontological refusals have less to do with internalized racism than with a resistance to being externally "overdetermined."[44] In the essay "The Fact of Blackness," for example, Fanon's desire to ride the train in silence, anonymity, and invisibility, is over and over again interrupted by the trespassive stares of his fellow passengers.[45]

Returning to Sarah, the idealization (and racialization) of anonymity could suggest a longing for unfettered travel, where ontological refusals rely on topographical withholdings. Recall that this formulation concludes Sarah's meditation on her desire to "become an even more pallid Negro than [she is] now; pallid like Negroes on the covers of American Negro magazines; soulless, educated, and irreligious. I want to possess no moral value, particularly value as to my being."[46] Sarah, profoundly performative, wants to be able to be nowhere, to exist in elsewheres outside the radars of those who desire to fix her somewhere. In this way, "I want not to be" expresses anticaptivity while potentially indicating a grip onto another world—a world where one can wander while refusing being.[47]

Moreover, such purposive refusal of name along with the adoption of many names indicts and agitates against the historical violences at the heart of (post-)slavery's own errant naming procedures. Turning again to Spillers, she argues that during the antebellum era, such (mis)naming expressed both racial violence and (un)lawful property rights: "The captivating party does not only 'earn' the right to dispose of the captive body as it sees fit, but gains, consequently, the right to name and 'name' it."[48] Indeed, in the postbellum era, such black female (mis)naming endures as slavery's legacy, where a promiscuous nominalism animates various architectures of containment. But in *Funnyhouse of a Negro* Sarah's adoption of various names constitutes a wandering that resists such regulation. By simultaneously renouncing and claiming multiple mistaken identities and becomings, Sarah advances an inherent mobility in her identificatory choices.

At the same time, however, such identitarian errancy suffers from endless policing. As Gilles Deleuze and Félix Guattari put it, if "the *self is only a threshold, a door, a becoming between* . . . multiplicities," then Sarah at once lives outside the range of other people's visions and is pulled between terrains of (un)fettered movement.[49] Interestingly, *Funnyhouse of a Negro*'s monologues feature different characters standing in corridors, knocking on doors, and repeatedly entering and exiting. And all of it often happens at the same time; as the characters in the play traverse multiple thresholds and "careening plots," in Solomon's words, the incessant door knocking of others equally haunts the characters.[50]

These are the "terribly beautiful" contradictions that Kennedy welcomes: the self as threshold, hallway, and knock on the door; becoming and captivity; unfixedness and fixity; wandering and circumscribed movement; pleasure and fear; and the real and unreal.[51] Interestingly, Kennedy partially attributes these contradictions to the ocean, as she wrote portions of *Funnyhouse of a Negro* on a ship bound for Ghana: "Being on the ocean in these charming writing rooms (perhaps being on water) seemed to join the real and the unreal in my writing in a way that I had never before envisioned."[52] Kennedy continues, "Away from my old books, but now besieged and surrounded by a myriad of real, astounding new imagery (ocean, staterooms, the decks, standing at the rail), my unconscious and conscious seemed to join the real and unreal in a new way."[53]

For Kennedy, the ocean facilitates profound creativity. Along with other philosophers, Kennedy believes that there is something about being suspended on water that joins "the real and unreal," making the ocean the literal and figurative site for the imagination. Indeed, the ocean and oceanic became the unwitting stage for imperial wandering, the reckless (un) making of the Enlightenment. The stepping outside and the walking-on-water exercises of the emissaries of imperialism coalesced as a murderous choreography—a violent, unpredictable movement resulting in what Spillers describes as the pornotropic deterritorialization of African humanity.[54]

In this way, reason violently formed and deformed on the ocean. In fact, Foucault argues that "water and madness have long been linked in the [forgotten] dreams of European man."[55] During the Renaissance, for example, the mad went from being "allowed to wander in the open countryside" to being incarcerated aboard so-called ships of fools.[56] Water, "the sea with its thousand roads," became a fitting home for the supposed uncertain and irrational; bodies figured as unpredictable as the sea itself.[57] What is more, as scene of black subjection, the ocean moved along imperialism's own psychotic foundations.

Regarding Kennedy, the unpredictable, simultaneously dangerous and beautiful, character of the ocean arguably facilitated her (un)writing the enduring and elusive complexity of black female subjectivity in the modern world. Crucially, Kennedy's theater begins on the water, in the nowhere between shores. By reinvesting the unreal with aesthetic, ethical, intellectual, and radical potential, Kennedy not only resignifies upon "nowhere," making it a utopia for black female identity, but also complicates a reading of Sarah's desire for "anonymity" as unsound and politically backward.[58] Further, the main character's simultaneous desire for and mistrust of white friends might have something to do with their oceanic death wishes.[59] Here death suggests an existentialist yearning for transcendence, where their loss of self oceanically requires the occupation of Sarah's body. This is precisely the process that Sarah mistrusts and counters with her own anonymity and polynominalism. If she mistakes herself as opposed to being mistaken, then her status as a "wild and unclaimed richness of possibility" (or ocean) moves from being necessarily static to peripatetic.[60] Further, by identifying as multiple selves where "renaming also marks a propensity to wander or migrate or stray," Sarah wanders toward a recharged, unlocalizable "nowhere," a black oceanic if you will, outside the range of her white friends' encroachment.[61]

Still, to her neighbors and landlady, Sarah remains pathologically immobile, not radically nowhere, in her hiding place. In the next scene, her landlady gossips that Sarah refuses to *leave* her apartment because she is traumatized by her father's suicide: "Ever since her father hung himself in a Harlem hotel when Patrice Lumumba was murdered she hides herself in her room."[62] While Lumumba, the late anticolonial fighter and the first prime minister of the Republic of Congo, appears as one of Sarah's four selves, his assassination figures as cause for her father's suicide. In both scenarios, Lumumba remains a profound choice of character. On the one hand, Lumumba not only critiqued Belgian colonization of Africa but poetically framed such violence as wandering. His poem "Dawn in the Heart of Africa" muses:

> For a thousand years, you, African, suffered like beast,
> Your ashes strewn to the wind that roams the desert.
> Your tyrants built the lustrous, magic temples
> To preserve your soul, reserve your suffering.
> Barbaric right of fist and the white right to a whip,
> You had the right to die, you also could weep.
> On your totem they carved endless hunger, endless bonds,
> And even in the cover of the woods a ghastly cruel death
> Was watching, snaky, crawling to you
> Like branches from the holes and heads of trees
> Embraced your body and your ailing soul.
> Then they put a treacherous big viper on your chest.[63]

Against Belgium's endless and restless crawling, Lumumba mounted a massive philosophical and ideological program for Congolese independence. On June 30, 1960, the people of Congo's struggle culminated in their emancipation. Lumumba, however, was subsequently assassinated.

Lumumba's murder moved Kennedy in such a way that "he became a character in [her] play[,] . . . a man with a shattered head."[64] Interestingly, the landlady later describes a conversation with her reclusive tenant, recounting how Sarah changes her story: "He did not hang himself, that is only the way they understand it[,] . . . but the truth is that I bludgeoned his head with an ebony skull that he carries about with him. Wherever he goes, he carries black masks and skulls."[65] Moreover, as Sarah identifies her father with Lumumba, she simultaneously admits to *their* assassinations. While I initially read this confessional moment as Sarah's identification with colonial power (those responsible for Lumumba's interrupted arrival and murder), the play's inherent multiplicity resists such political straightforwardness. Once again, there may be more profound and complicated reasons inspiring her decision to murderously interrupt and avoid his nocturnal arrival.

Returning to the play, Sarah's father, unlike Lumumba, was a Christian missionary "who went to Africa years ago" and "erect[ed] Christian mission[s] in the middle of the jungle in one of those newly freed countries."[66] Suggestively, it is immediately after the description of her father's imperial crusade that the duchess (as Sarah) makes a plea to Raymond, the funnyman master of the funnyhouse, to hide her. In the end, Sarah does not want to be found, and in her twisted, supposedly psychotic storytelling, she creates the undisclosed location of her own funnyhouse. Unfortunately, however, the knocking continues. In the next scene the stage directions read: "somewhere near the center of the stage a FIGURE appears in the darkness, a large dark faceless MAN carrying a mask in his hand."[67]

At this moment, Sarah's father seems to have trespassed upon her "nowhere," slowly becoming her. The scene starts with the man (who is her father, Lumumba, Jesus, the Duchess of Hapsburg, Queen Victoria, and now Sarah, all at the same time) describing the beginning (which is Genesis; the story of her, and their, birth; the opening scene of the play; and so on). As her father hallucinates the reasons for his daughter's rejection, it is rumored that "he put out his hand to her, tried to take her in his arms, crying out—forgiveness, Sarah, is it that you never will forgive me for being black? Sarah, I know you are a child of torment. But forgiveness. That was before his break down."[68]

Forgiveness, in this scene, is a loaded proposition. Forgiveness for being black may and may not refer to Sarah's supposed internalized racism. The ironic and hopelessly twisted articulation of revolutionary blackness moves alongside Sarah's memory of her father in Africa—his desire to be Jesus and his drunken rape of her mother. It is unclear which aberration or narrative of trespassing requires forgiveness. Perhaps, following Moten, blackness in Kennedy "is only in that it exceeds itself; it bears the groundedness of an uncontainable outside."[69] Indeed, blackness might be this uncontainable outside—whether it takes the form of psychosis, haunting, revolution, a radical nowhereness, peripatetic alterity, liberation, or the trespassing knocks on the door. Further, the ironic and incessant black becomings of the characters in this play—where Sarah roams as Lumumba as her father as Jesus and peripatetically back again—accelerate to confound and complicate each individual and their collective unity's political subjectivity. This makes it hard to say that this play is about a specific kind of blackness, black performance, or politics. But what it does is suggest a deep connection between black identity and wandering that agitates against the peripatetically possessive encroachments of others.

And even on the play's last page, these encroachments continue. In fact, in the last scene, the already-blurred lines between individual characters almost completely dissolve. This occurs as the jungle begins to cover the entire stage: "SCENE: . . . In time this is the longest scene in the play and is played the slowest, as the slow, almost standstill stages of a dream. By lighting the desired effect would be—*suddenly the jungle has overgrown the chambers and all the other places with a violence and a dark brightness, a grim yellowness.*"[70] The thresholds and corridors that separate the duchess's chamber, the Harlem hotel room, and Sarah's Upper West Side bedroom begin to crumble and the jungle swarms the stage. The characters become all, "wandering about and speaking at once."[71] Perhaps, they all become one because of their wanderings, curvy ramblings, and crooked movements, because, Deleuze and Guattari explain, "the One is said with a single meaning of all the multiple. Being expresses in a single meaning all that differs. What we are talking about is not the unity of substance but the infinity of the modifications that are part of one another on this unique plane of life."[72]

It is in this last scene, on this "unique plane," that everything and everyone blurs: "A dark brightness, a grim yellowness."[73] This might be the beginning of the end of civilization, where the limits of reading and understanding shore up. There are no clear lines between selves and people, between paths and escape routes. Blackness becomes whiteness becomes yellowness and back again. The jungle is Europe is a lonely apartment on the Upper West Side. This is a polyphonic, perambulatory, and highly trafficked moment where the characters "all appear in various parts of the jungle. Patrice Lumumba, the Duchess, Victoria, wandering about speaking at once."[74]

This is precisely what is great about Kennedy—too much happens, moves about. Arguments about what happened to Sarah and her father, and how race figured, form and deform in a wandering script. Identities are trespasses. *Funnyhouse of a Negro* is and isn't about a young black woman who runs from blackness toward a deadening, transcendent whiteness. It also may have been a story about a young black woman who runs toward and finds revelation in blackness. Yet the play's very wandering, the endless shape-shifting of characters and story, resists such narrative, spatio-temporal, and political enclosures.

The play's ending only potentiates other beginnings. According to the play's stage directions, "the Negro Sarah is standing perfectly still, we hear the KNOCKING, the LIGHTS come on quickly, her FATHER's black figure with bludgeoned hands rushes upon her, the LIGHT GOES BLACK and we see her hanging in the room."[75] This can mean anything. It could be any persona hanging there. I haven't seen the play on stage and I'm not sure I want to. Something about the text, its writing and unwriting of itself, messing up and with the questions of what happened, to whom, and why, offers a generativity (on and off the page) that I fear the staged production might try to diagnose, reduce, read, and represent. It is this generativity, the wandering that emerges between what and who is (un)written and how it's imagined, that agitates against the lockdown of reading and representation toward the unmarked hideout of freedom.

The Owl Answers

Something happens in that bend, in the place where the script wanders off the page. There is a plenitude, an expansive terrain engendered by such ambiguities in meaning, character, speech, and movement. Indeed, it seems that at those places where the script turns away from transparency and understanding, where the lines between selves and places dissolve, that Kennedy's characters enact philosophical desire. Moreover, what's crucial is not just these hidden terrains but the travel that engenders them. The turning away, hiding, and wandering of Kennedy's characters and with that, the rejection of identitarian and topographical fixity, constitutes their philosophical method.

In 1965, one year after *Funnyhouse of a Negro*'s debut, Kennedy released another play shaped by phantasmatic, philosophical travel—a play where the script wanders off just as much as its characters. *The Owl Answers* begins in transit as the main character, Clara Passmore, rides the subway in search of answers. Wondering about who and where she is and whether anyone at all will love her, her musings move along with the train. At the same time, as in *Funnyhouse of a Negro*, her wandering endures restraint at the hands of another set of shape-shifting characters. The list of characters reads:

> SHE who is CLARA PASSMORE who is the VIRGIN MARY who is the BASTARD who is the OWL.
> BASTARD'S BLACK MOTHER who is the REVEREND'S WIFE who is ANNE BOLEYN.
> GODDAM FATHER who is the RICHEST WHITE MAN IN THE TOWN who is the DEAD WHITE FATHER who is REVEREND PASSMORE.
> THE WHITE BIRD who is REVEREND PASSMORE'S CANARY who is GOD'S DOVE.
> THE NEGRO MAN.
> SHAKESPEARE, CHAUCER, WILLIAM THE CONQUEROR.[76]

Like the characters themselves, the plot of this play comes cloaked in other disguises. The plot moves and hides by way of the main characters' roaming questions, including, "[Who Am I]—the reader becoming in some sense a version of the heroine, asking at every turn, 'Where am I?'—and grasping at every moment for some preliminary outline or map."[77] As with *Funnyhouse of a Negro*, reading *The Owl Answers* is difficult if what is sought is the play's story, the bottom line or punch line, the unmoving ground that helps one make sense of or to follow the play. Nevertheless, this experience of difficulty might occasion some political and ethical reflexivity, raising queries regarding the trespassive potential of (a longing for) textual understanding and the complicity between such longing and post-Enlightenment constraint.

This is crucial as this play's main character already suffers endless trespass. As the lights go up on the first scene, it soon becomes clear that the main character moves on a subway. Seated on a rough box, Clara Passmore's body jerks back and forth and up and down by the phantasmatic movements of a subway train.[78] This play's soundtrack consist of a subway's screeching noise, and it also features disembodied voices calling for guards to keep the main character locked on the train while others harassingly remind her that "one drop of black blood makes her black." As these sounds and voices play, lights go on Clara Passmore as she furiously and defiantly writes on a train that won't stay still. Though her papers ripple and fall chaotically, the main character nevertheless writes for the first ten minutes of the play.

As Clara Passmore writes and gets pushed, other characters walk through the (her) scene: the Tower of London's guards, Shakespeare, William the Conqueror, Chaucer, and Anne Boleyn—collectively known as "They" (we are told their names because their costumes are not necessarily indicative of their identities). Other people also walk, wander, perform balletic movement, and haphazardly spin across the stage. The play moves slowly from the private wanderings and frenetic writing of a lone black woman to a highly exposed and trespassed main character. Moreover, just as her private movement suffers criminalization from within the play, such kinetic constraint also swirls in from the outside. As with *Funnyhouse of a Negro*, for example, Kolin jumps on Clara's train to diagnose her behavior as dissociative identity disorder.[79]

Among other things, what such reckless movement does is derealize injury. Through the prison house of psychiatric diagnoses, the wandering of the already wounded traveler also endures additional constraint. In the interest of another way, then, I ask, following Claudia Barnett: if the subway in Kennedy's work serves as a metaphor for the unconscious, then what might be at stake for this black woman traveler that an ever-increasing set of people not only intrude upon her (and her private writings) but continually break down her subway car's walls?[80] Tragically, in fact, the more they wander, the less the subway remains hers to ride and write on. The more they wander, walk, stride, spin, diagnose, dance, trample, the less she can rest in her own ramblings. The more they wander, the greater the risk that they (he) will lock her up in the prisons and mental institutions of their choosing.

Further, for Barnett, the subway is a scene of trespass as well as philosophy. In the context of European Enlightenment philosophy, she argues, the trope of the abyss or the thing underground tends to figure as the highly theatricalized, unenlightened, racialized, insane, and feminized space of unreason.[81] In *The Owl Answers*, this is also the stage for Clara

Passmore's visible movement. Tragically, then, as with the abyss of Western philosophy, Clara Passmore's subway becomes an equally overpopulated and trespassed space where private musings endure public restraint, or in the case of Plato's cave, being "dragged" out into the sunlight.[82]

In this underground, unreason struggles to live autonomously while enlightenment vampirically denies such life. Further, such vampirism depends on its own transgressive wandering, a promiscuous movement between realms of light and dark. In fact, Plato writes that it is the role of philosopher-lawgivers to "act as leaders and king-bees in a hive." He instructs the philosophers, "Descend in turn and live with your fellows in the cave and get used to seeing in the dark: once you get used to it you will see a thousand times better than they [the prisoners] do and will distinguish the various shadows, and know what they are shadows of, because you have seen truth about things admirable and just and good."[83] Because the man of reason is necessarily of the en*light*ened world and yet fully capable of periodic wanderings into the nocturnal realm of his half-blind, frightened brothers, his sight is (for Plato) most philosophically sound. As lawgiver, it is his duty to not only cultivate his sight but to be able to "drag" the fearful prisoners who choose to reside in the cave, which is the prison, which is the womb, which is the tomb, which is the abyss, which is the subway, "up the steep and rugged ascent and not let go till they had been [painfully] dragged" into the sunlight.[84] Those who resist being dragged and turned wait in the dark, consigned to an irrational life of blind roaming. Or, worse still, psychiatric diagnosis.

For Plato, such darkness, or the underground, (dis)ables sight, creating the illusion that the shadows are the whole truth. This is also where Clara Passmore (un)writes herself into being, in the lightless, subterranean vessel of a New York City subway train. Barnett writes, "The prisoners of the cave [or riders on the subway] see illusionistic images which reflect no truth; they see shadows without subjects and hear voices without speakers."[85] But in *The Owl Answers*, the images reflect the truth of Clara Passmore's ride, a ride that is busy and overpopulated by too many voices, images, and speakers. Again, this is the truth of her ride. Whether or not these images are real is irrelevant to a subject who is pushed too hard and far enough to be bothered. What is more, the irony stands that despite the fact that, according to Kolin, "space in Kennedy's plays is not physical," Clara Passmore's revelation of her private musings endlessly contends with physical restraint.[86]

For example, They want to lock her up: "They start at a distance, eventually crowding her. Their lines are spoken coldly. SHE WHO IS is only a prisoner to them."[87] As she struggles to keep writing and expressing her ideas, they crowd her physically while incarcerating her psychically, calling her a "bastard" and instructing the guards to "keep her locked there."[88] Denying her claims to her "richest white father" (whose funeral she was prevented from attending, and whose love is perhaps, in some ways, one of the things she's searching for), they further *penal*ize her desire to search at all: "Shakespeare crosses to gate and raises hands. There is a SLAM as if great door is being closed."[89] Indeed, throughout the play, They furiously and urgently agitate for her arrest, seemingly anxious around Clara Passmore's continued attempts at travel. Plainly stated, the more she wanders, the more they call for her lockdown.

But where is she to be locked up, and what form does that prison take? A dark underground, a New York City subway (which is St. Peter's, which is the Tower of London, which is a Harlem hotel room), which also might be Plato's cave. As the scene morphs from subway car into the Tower of London into a Harlem hotel room into her womb into St. Peter's into bastard, it shuttles between a promiscuous openness and what critic Houston Baker calls "tight spaces," or the "psycho-social figurations of the sexually forbidden."[90] In that way, regardless of its promiscuous form, the prison haunts her wanderings with the incarceral tones of others' trespassing sounding upon her ancestral musings.

Consequently, the process by which Clara Passmore secures her rights of locomotion forms somewhere in between wandering and trespass, as well as between truth and murderously guided shadows. Amid "their" confining speech to "keep her locked there," however, Clara Passmore struggles to free herself of the tight space. Her resistance involves ancestral musings, where she describes her leisurely walk with her father, her "goddam father," who is the "richest white man in the town," who is the "dead white father," who is "Reverend Passmore." Her reveries move her to England, "the place of [her] ancestors": "We rose in darkness, took a taxi past Hyde Park through the Marble Arch to Buckingham Palace, we had our morning tea at Lyons then came out to the Tower. We were wandering about the gardens, my father leaning on my arm, speaking of you, William the Conqueror."[91]

Unfortunately, however, They ceaselessly disrupt her dream. For them, Clara Passmore's unbound travel spells danger for the stories these icons tell about themselves. Put another way, "keep her locked there" responds to Clara Passmore's illegitimate wandering while sanctioning white wanderers' unlawful roaming. For example, as the Richest White Man in the Town stepped outside the racial and sexual scripts regulating his own movement, "someone that cooked for him" provided the unnamed ground for his travels.[92] Further, as he moves, haunts, and denies his paternity, Clara Passmore suffers incarceration and the equally miserable condition of riding the train with his corpse at her feet. Not only must she ride with the corpse who, along with the icons, continually denies her ancestry, but she must "drag" him to "a dark, curved high-back chair."[93] Even after death, it remains her labor to move him.

Against this labor, she flees toward Anne Boleyn, a character who functions as "an image of imprisonment" and of love.[94] Clara Passmore's turn toward Anne enacts the performative contradictions at the heart of her (Clara Passmore's) ancestral musings, as love's hysterical beginnings emerge from the walls of a prison. With "so many subtle, uncertain, shiftings," in Deleuze and Guattari's words, love figures in *The Owl Answers* as both "revolutionary potential and reactionary danger."[95] As such, ancestral yearning is both embraced and denied—a violent and ecstatic doubledness that resonates with prior imperial forgettings. These are occasions where explorers murderously forgot the very beings that secured their ecstatic transcendence.

Returning to the play, as Clara Passmore appeals to Anne Boleyn for insight into her (Clara Passmore's) crisis in love, the figure of empowerment herself metamorphoses into another prisoner, the Bastard's Black Mother. Kneeling in prayer, the Bastard's Black Mother explains to her child that the reason for her "owldom" lies in the violence of her conception: "Clara, you were conceived by your Goddam Father who was The Richest White Man in the Town and somebody that cooked for him. That's why you're an owl. (*Laughs.*) That's why when I see you, Mary, I cry. I cry when I see Marys, cry for their deaths."[96]

Animality, for Clara Passmore's mother, results from the union between the Richest White Man in the Town and "somebody that cooked for him." While there may be specific interpretative possibilities bound up with Kennedy's choice of owls as the main character's (anti)ontological expression, the larger narrative of animality abounds in signification. If Clara Passmore is half human and half animal, she occupies the "phantom world [animality] that has haunted, throughout its long history, the domain of human subjectivity."[97] Akira Lippitt queries this proximity between human and animal worlds, lending insight into why an interracial union might result in the birth of an owl. He writes, "Despite the distance of animal being from the human world, the uncanny proximity of animals to human beings necessarily involves them in any attempt to define a human essence. The effort to define the human being has usually required a preliminary gesture of exclusion: a rhetorical animal sacrifice. The presence of the animal must first be extinguished for the human being to reappear."[98] Historically, the racialized and sexual wandering of an otherwise "pure" white power structure depended on the animalistic figure of the mulatta. Animality here refers to her purported rapacious sexuality, a racialized sexuality that by its very definition fulfills the political and philosophical protocols of an inhuman being, the animal. As Lippitt continues, animals a priori figure as outside the categories that produce subjects: consciousness, language, reason, and spatio-temporal connection (animals do not have the capacity to register the significance of being in the world and, therefore, are without one).

For the mulatta, whose name itself is an extension of the Spanish word for *mule*, animality indexes racist and sexist assumptions about her supposedly necessary and expendable wild (life) sexuality, as well as confirms her illegitimate claims to personhood. As the critic Jeanie Forte argues, "She [the mulatta] must be available as the site of sexual plenitude for the dominant male, but disappear as the evidence of his transgression. She is there to confirm his virility and to support racist classism against the subjugated community, but does not exist within the whole of culture, which indeed would deny her existence."[99]

Kennedy's development of a mixed-race character who becomes an animal, then, not only powerfully speaks to these political and philosophical discourses of black female sexuality but also isolates how hypersexualized narratives of mulatta identity facilitate and result from an unlawful wandering. Because she exists at the limits of the so-called pure lines separating white from black, the human and its end, her body provides the imaginative ground for trespassive meditations on identity and desire. As Forte continues, the mulattas within Kennedy's plays "are objects of desire for both black and white men, not by virtue of some individual attraction, but because of the sexuality imputed to their skin color."[100] In the context of *The Owl Answers*, Kennedy's mixed-race character endures endless (sexual) trespass while she is stranded at an overly trespassed station on someone else's train.

This may be why the Bastard's Black Mother prays for new names for her daughter. As Mary, Clara Passmore would inhabit an untrespassed and untrespassable sexuality, a sexuality that neither wanders nor is wandered upon. Yet, while the Bastard's Black Mother might momentarily pray her daughter's sexuality into a place outside the coordinates of her captors, Marys inevitably die: "You're an owl. (*Laughs*.) That's why when I see you, Mary, I cry. I cry when I see Marys, cry for their deaths."[101] The Bastard's Black Mother dreams of her daughter as Mary and, at the same time, mourns the impossibility of that dream. As Clara Passmore and her mother dream, Shakespeare, William the Conqueror, Chaucer, and an infinite amount of others enter and exit. These trespassers disrupt their musings and criminalize their right to see at all. Their antiwandering ethos further manifests in threats of incarceration and endless inquiries about Clara's travels:

> If you are his ancestor, what are you doing on the subway at night looking for men? What are you doing looking for men to take to a hotel room in Harlem?
>
> Negro men?
>
> Negro men, Clara Passmore?[102]

Powerfully, Clara Passmore responds nonstraightforwardly; the search for her father's love becomes obscurely linked to the pursuit of men to take her to a Harlem hotel room, "to love, dress them as [her] father, beg to take [her]."[103]

Toward the end of the play, Clara Passmore describes the story of her ancestry to an anonymous "Negro Man" on a New York City subway. Afterward they smile, join hands, and go to a Harlem hotel room. Once there, seated together on the bed, she asks him to call her Mary. The anonymous "Negro Man," confused by this request, asks her about it. She turns to explain only to have her words and desire shouted over by They, who are at once in England, in the subway train, in her mind, and in the Harlem hotel room. After fleeing and then returning to the same room, the Bastard's Black Mother enters the scene and joins Clara Passmore. The hotel room becomes increasingly crowded as real and phantasmatic presences wander in and out. Doubled over in pain, as the icons' screaming and trampling increases in ferocity, she begins to lose her footing and becomes an owl. As They wander, "she tries to get out of the room, but he will not let her go."[104] The chase ends climactically as the transformation of Clara Passmore into an animal is complete.

At last, They reach the limits of her being and she becomes an animal. Her search ends and does not end in her animalistic imprisonment. Rather, she "stares into space and speaks: Ow oww."[105] Staring, drifting, and wandering into the partially unseen space of her desire, Clara Passmore might now be able to fly out and away. In the end, owldom is not an occasion for sacrifice so that the human can fully emerge. Rather, the figure of the owl takes on new meaning as it instead responds to the crisis of the icons' trespasses by offering other possibilities for black female being in the world. What is more, the indecipherable speech of the owl works as a "broken injunction *against* telling . . . those lives and hereditary relationships (inherited and otherwise passed on, taken up) that are insistently buried, repressed, disavowed."[106] And the speech agitates against this telling by speaking in ways immune to trespass, in ante-articulate tones that wander against the call for incarceration into other undisclosed domains of freedom. Beyond the script and off its page.

Conclusion

Even though Kennedy's plays are not staged in *real* places but on sets that replicate her mind, her characters' bodies still suffer exterior policing. In *The Owl Answers*, for example, Clara Passmore can't dream and write without other voices and movements interrupting her reveries. Still, some readings of Kennedy's theater deploy the language of psychosis and, in doing so, derealize an experience of trespass and constraint; according to these readings, Kennedy's characters deteriorate (only) as a result of their minds' unruly wanderings. This logic presumes that the self is embattled from within and not by the trespassive forces that make the episteme of psychosis possible in the first place. In other words, the language of psychosis itself constitutes a trespassive movement, regulating that which appears as nonsensical, troublesome, disruptive, and dangerous. Modes of social (dis)engagement are imagined as at once "pleasant [but also] probably not useful or valuable," to quote psychologist Jonathan Schooler.[107] Dangerous dancing.

So while drapetomania and dromomania are no longer in the *Diag-*

nostic and Statistical Manual of Mental Disorders (DSM), dissociative fugue remains. In fact, daydreaming itself borders on the diagnostic terrain of the dissociative when observed to disrupt productivity. For the cognitive psychotherapist Michael Kane, "whether or not mind wandering causes distress often depends on context. . . . We argue that it's not inherently good or bad; it all depends on what the goals of the person are at the time."[108] In this context, the discourse of goals reveals a productivist investment. Put another way, if mind wandering doesn't easily serve capital, it may be in need of cure or constraint. Once again, the logics of transparent self-determination, rationality, and productivity at the heart of post-Enlightenment subjectivity reveal their complicity with the state's antiwandering ethos. In other words, drifts away from the pulls of life, labor, and identity become subject to a range of disciplinary maneuvers. Constraints manifest in everything from a teacher's admonishment of a student who stares out the window too long to the psychiatric diagnosis of a person who wanders away from his or her identity and presumed social responsibility. The latter appears in the *DSM-IV* as dissociative fugue, a "disorder" characterized by "sudden, unexpected travel away from home or one's customary place of work, accompanied by an inability to remember one's past and confusion about personal identity or the assumption of a new identity."[109] While I am not interested in classifying Kennedy's plays as complex fugue states, I query the social conditions that render her characters' wandering psychiatric—the social conditions that make the rejection of identity, labor, and one's name the sign of psychiatric deficiency.

This is important because just as dissociative fugue remains a diagnostic code, racialized and gendered bodies are disproportionately targeted for pedestrian "stop-and-frisk practices" and black kids are arbitrarily gunned down while walking down the street.[110] So even though Kennedy's plays happen in the mind, they're not always private. Just like a city street, the mind sometimes figures as surveillable terrain, subject to trespass and constraint. This isn't to say that there aren't places and movement that remain invisible to surveillance. Rather, as with Clara Passmore, physical roaming often expresses philosophical desire, a searching. When that physical movement suffers policing, sometimes the phantasmatic travel suffers as well. When visible wanderings of body, speech, and tone figure as unproductive or inefficient, the terrains of the mind often endure similar pathologizings. These are places where public interest collides with private desire and black wandering is written up as a violation.

"I Am an African American Novel"

Wandering as Noncompliance in Gayl Jones's *Mosquito*

What is at stake in being a reclusive artist who makes reclusive work? Art and life that wander on the other side of the known world, on the border between private desire and public interest. According to the critic Sally Eckhoff, the African American writer Gayl Jones is famously private, her life barely known.[1] The extent of Jones's publicity stays confined to the (un)known worlds of her novels. In fact, by Jones's own admission, she is a novel, a "complex blending of every story element and non-story."[2]

Jones's assertion is part of a larger performance undertaken by the artist in 1994. In "From *The Quest for Wholeness*: Re-imagining the African American Novel: An Essay on Third World Aesthetics," Jones-as-novel theorizes the relation between the self as an aesthetic form and the ongoing, unfinished process of decolonization. Decolonization, in this context, becomes possible through formal innovations—imagining new ways and patterns to tell stories—and the new philosophical subjectivities such innovations engender. For Jones-as-novel these subjectivities emerge from the tenuous "correspondence between what a novel is and who/what a novelist is."[3] Moreover, the uneasy alignment between author and novel in conjunction with the performative assertions of self as novelistic opens up other pathways for freedom: "Aesthetic revolutions . . . are wars of independence."[4] In other words, claims of being a novel sustain what Eckhoff calls a "portable fortress" and paradoxically keep the author herself from being read.[5]

Powerfully, Jones-as-novel writes herself and resists being written.

This is part of the performance, of what it means to be decolonized. To be written is to be colonized. Jones argues, "a novel is colonized, for example, when patterns of stories and patterns of ideas in stories and how stories are made from one storytelling tradition are imposed upon another storytelling tradition; that is, when the storyteller from the dominant culture says that you must tell stories the way I tell them, or when one storytelling tradition is seen as the mere subgenre of another."[6] In the context of post-Enlightenment, such dominant ways of storytelling often privilege what Srikanth Reddy describes as "abecedarian progression."[7] *Abecedarian progression* refers to a mode of storytelling characterized by progressive linear movement and the presence of a discrete beginning, middle, and end. Further, abecedarianism and abecedarian storytelling, as Reddy convincingly argues after Diderot, expresses the post-Enlightenment imperatives of linear progress and, with it, rationality, self-possession, and composure.

As a decolonized novel, then, Jones refuses the kinetic constraints of a singular story as well as a singular, dominant way of telling it. To be more precise, even though Jones is "one novel, [she is] novels within novels, and novels plenty. Perhaps [she is] even simultaneous novels, for novels-within-novels generally set up or imply a hierarchy."[8] As such, the polyphonic and polytemporal theater engendered by Jones's novelistic performances potentiate other kinds of errant terrain, new literary-scapes and lifeworlds where black women write themselves (sometimes outside the lines and scripts) and refuse the writings of others. What is more, the enactment of self as a decolonizing, Afrocentric, and inherently multiple novel resists a modality of post-Enlightenment subjectivity discernible as self-sameness. Historically, and in the context of post-Enlightenment, self-same subjects must reject their inherent multiplicity in order to sustain the illusion of transparent self-determination. Put another way, self-same identity requires that the inner wanderings of word, desire, and spirit be quelled. Hent de Vries writes, "Enlightenment clarifies everything in terms of repetition and returns everything to the same, to an (abstract) identity. It contents itself with a subject that cannot lose itself in identification with the other [or otherness, *mit anderem*]. Therefore it must also disavow in advance what's qualitatively new—the singular or an unanticipated and unpredictable event—and sanction anew what myth once termed 'fate': Whatever might be different [or other, *anders*] is made the same."[9]

Against the determinisms of fate and its antiwandering conceit, the decolonizing, performing Afrocentric novel embraces its multiplicity and the ongoing process of becoming free. Perhaps becoming a novel provides the conditions of possibility for freedom from post-Enlightenment constraint. More precisely, if it is the case that Jones's identity is, first and foremost, performatively novelistic, then it is as highly mobile as the act of composition itself. Being able to compose and decompose herself, wandering in between, around, and through words, times, and spaces, Jones-as-novel disrupts the cartographic impulse of being someone else's story. This is not the same as the novel being her story, a terrain where Jones the author and artist can be fixed and read. Rather, by inhabiting a form that "assures the deterritorialization of the world," in Gilles Deleuze and Félix Guattari's words, Jones-as-novel can experiment with modes of being and becoming otherwise rendered (im)possible.[10] This is to say, being a form that is assuredly a different kind of world enables a range of philosophical performances otherwise criminalized by this one. By being a novel, and more specifically a decolonizing one, the self is unfinished, endlessly wandering past its own limits, even as "the world effects a reterritorialization of the book."[11]

Such reterritorializations, indeed, often result in the collapsing of word with world, even though the "book is not an image of the world," according to Deleuze and Guattari.[12] These conflations not only violate the author's own privacy but also presume a set of worldly conditions to which the book itself must replicate. Such worldly conditions, for example, constrain the speech and movement that wander into other realms, inhabiting various times, spaces, and states of mind. Put another way, such worldly conditions presume that the life of the novel must abide by its own (the world's) post-Enlightenment preferences—linear spatio-temporal progress, coherence in speech and action, rationality, and self-determination. But, as Jones-as-novel philosophizes, just as the novel is not its author, it is also not bound by the constraints of its author's world.

Imagining a different lifeworld for the novel calls for other modes of engagement. On the level of content, Jones-as-novel cautions her readers and listeners to not "mistake [her] for politics, or economics, or sociology, or history."[13] This is important because, historically speaking, being mistaken or miswritten as "politics, or economics, or sociology, or history" often accompanies an experience of subjection. Perhaps this is what Hortense Spillers means when she describes black people, and black women in particular, as "so loaded with mythical prepossession that there is no easy way for the agents buried beneath to come clean."[14] In other words, even in the postbellum era, black women continue to be written against their will; becoming the unwitting central characters in somebody else's story. Stories of crisis, trespassive criminal sexualities, and nonproductive desire. Stories about post-Enlightenment rationality, self-possession, and their Other.

Significantly, Denise Ferreira da Silva, Karla FC Holloway, and Candace Jenkins theorize such governance through a language of performance. For these critics, black women are written between two competing "scenes of regulation"—one structured by a racist, sexist narrative of black female degeneracy and the other formed through a black "self-imposed sexual and familial propriety."[15] In both cases, black women figure as novels with the same beginning (antebellum slavery) and the same end (private loss). Against such narrative and performative closures, according to Jenkins, novels such as Jones's *Eva's Man* (1976) enact other storytelling possibilities. In Jones's art, counterstories move within black privacy—previously (un)read stories of sexuality, sexual vulnerability, and constraint, and stories about lives that move in excess of others' wayward desires.

While I agree with Jenkins, I think that there's a way that the private in Jones's novels might be where stories are written but not necessarily read. This doesn't necessarily imply their absence but rather their roaming fullness beyond the word and world. More precisely, in Jones's novels this abundance in movement often comes from what's unwritten, the ante-articulate and undisclosed ambulations before and ahead of the word. Or, to put it another way, the story is more than what's written, the movement more than its visible composition. Whereas in *Eva's Man* (1976) and *Corregidora* (1975) a certain scarcity of words engenders phantasmatic ambulations, in *Mosquito* (1999) the excess of words facilitates surreptitious movement. Beginning with *Eva's Man*, Eva's strategic indirection and sparse prose subvert the patriarchal constraints of her dominating lover, Davis:

> "I punched my belly, swollen with too much eating in, and being constipated. I'd get nervous with him there, and nothing would come out.
> "What are you doing?" I asked.
> "Traveling."
> He asked me what I was doing.
> "Traveling."[16]

Eva's nervousness around Davis makes her constipated, uncomfortable, her body becoming a tight space of its own. As she sits on the toilet, nervous with him in the other room, she admits only to "traveling" when asked about her doings.

"Traveling" is not elaborated in the text; it doesn't describe or preface a readable scene, a discrete or isolatable moment in a story. Instead, traveling evokes a movement that takes place in the swelling around words, when their own limits make them hard to get out. In *Corregidora* and *Eva's Man*, daydreams, unnarrated toilet-bound travels, and stares at the ceiling join other occasions of unreadable, unbounded movements. Jones writes, "You ask where's the story: I'm the story, me/you, myself/ourselves. I am a complex blending of every story element and non-story, and like I said multicultural through Afrocentric. (And Afro-eccentric)."[17]

Jones-as-novel's assertion of self as a moving composite of story and nonstory philosophically performs "wars of independence," a liberation from the telos of other people's reading and writing practices.[18] Still, because this resistance evokes movement on other ground, at once unseen, private, and impossible—given post-Enlightenment's investments in readable transparency—the war of independence remains unfinished. What is more, this inherently processual, multiple, and nonteleological movement of decolonization courses alongside the performative novel's own errant kinesis; in both performative domains, characters hold onto their stories as much as their nonstories while freedom hangs in the form's future to come.

In the future to come enacted by the novel, stories are written, though it's impossible to say that the author wrote them. As with Eva's response to Davis, stories endlessly (de)compose from within protective fortresses and according to private scripts and patterns. Claudia C. Tate says of the character Eva "She would tell her story, a story that she had previously refused to tell anyone. But still in her act of telling, she refused to divulge something that would give coherence to her story."[19] Given the futuristic ambulations of novelistic selves, coherence figures as both impossible and unwanted.

Nevertheless, post-Enlightenment-minded readers (readers stuck within the constraints of this world) tend to punish such subversions. For example, such readers include those who critiqued Jones's first two novels for having "strayed from the straight and narrow path of African American literary uplift," Trudier Harris writes.[20] This straying in *Corregidora* and *Eva's Man* might refer to their depictions of black erotic life's "ugliness" and pain—a representation that, according to Jenkins, renders the "salvific" (uplift) impulse ineffective.[21] At the same time, the antistraying critique might have something to do with Jones-as-novel's formal (aesthetic) drifts away from the post-Enlightenment world. In the end, being outside the path results in the dismissal of Jones's innovations; not only is Jones's art underengaged but her work endures the most vicious kinds of misreadings. As with Adrienne Kennedy, these misreadings have everything to do with the inability to know, recognize, and codify the kind of art that Jones produces and, beyond that, to know, recognize, and codify Jones. Moreover, as I've argued, this empirical and epistemological anxiety dangerously flirts with a long history of writing black women's stories without their consent. Spillers situates this writing within the ongoing context of state violence: "These undecipherable markings on the captive body render a kind of hieroglyphics of the flesh whose severe disjunctures come to be hidden to the cultural seeing by skin color. We might well ask if this phenomenon of marking and branding actually 'transfers' from one generation to another, finding its various *symbolic substitutions* in an efficacy of meanings that repeats the initiating moments? . . . This body whose flesh carries the female and the male to the frontiers of survival bears in person the marks of a cultural text whose inside has been turned outside."[22]

By being a novel, Jones effectively removes her own private story from view. In the lifeworlds engendered by her novels, black female subjects also wander, introverted or extroverted, on and off the page. Their stories are withheld and, by definition, unfinished. Moreover, within *Mosquito*, Jones-as-novel makes fortresses out of words while instantiating a new modality of black female philosophical performance—one that both formally and conceptually resists the various "technologies of hypervisibility," in Avery Gordon's words, at the heart of the Enlightenment's legacy.[23] As the prose wanders, the story splits into multiple spaces, places, and times. Beginnings, middles, and ends roam away from a linear structure and characters' lives thrive in that wandering movement; this is a movement that might begin publically—somewhere on the page—but drift off and away from the reader's gaze. While these novelistic innovations powerfully enact untouchable subjectivities and terrains, the critical response reveals the anxiety surrounding such wandering and other strategies of independence.

We *know* from the blurb on the *Mosquito* book jacket that the main character Mosquito's "journey begins when she discovers Maria, a stowaway who nearly gives birth in the back of the truck."[24] But because this beginning is one of many, *Mosquito* gets criticized for offering an unsettling sprawl in place of a map. The following are excerpts from critics' reviews of *Mosquito*. Henry Louis Gates, for the *New York Times*, writes: "Would that an editor like [Toni] Morrison had helped Jones locate where she wanted her narrator to be, and to bridle in this sprawling, formless, maddening tale."[25] Tamala Edwards, from *Time* magazine, maintains: "Mosquito is a carnival of digression and free association, though, with the plot hijacked for paragraphs, if not pages, by muddled tangents."[26] And Tom LeClair, writing for *Salon*, argues: "At first Jones' main character has the appeal of Huck Finn, fresh talk from a naive, good-hearted outsider. But after 50 pages and with little narrative momentum, her 'confabulatory' charm wears off and 'Mosquito' reads like 2,000 pages of Gertrude Stein's 'Melanctha,' aggressively digressive, frequently vapid and stupefyingly repetitive."[27] While Gates imagines a bridle as cure for a wandering narrator, Edwards and LeClair, respectively, figure Jones-as-novel's digressions as terroristic and aggressive. This anxiety around hijacked, aggressive plots along with unbridled black women narrators bespeaks of a larger nervousness around their worldly noncompliance. In other words, the epistemological and empirical interests at the heart of these critiques are troubling for several reasons. To begin, a particular kind of antidigression in these reviews becomes oddly complicit with the state's apparatus of capture of, in this case, black women.

This is to say, just as black transwomen, like Cece McDonald, get punished for refusing the disciplinary maneuvers of racist homophobes, authors such as Jones must also negotiate harassment by post-Enlightenment cultural logics (even as those logics might otherwise critique the state).[28] In light of this correlation, Robert McRuer argues that "the composition of a coherent and disciplined self has, in fact, often been linked to the composition of orderly written texts."[29] The clarity and efficiency of one's writing measures one's post-Enlightenment compliance. Further, for McRuer, the valorization of product over process, the final version over the draft, expresses an investment in "straight composition."[30] Here straightness again indexes "compulsory ablebodiedness and heterosexuality," suggesting that such pedagogical maneuvers and the disavowals they require align with the state's own pathologization (and criminalization) of desire and unpredictable embodiment.[31]

Against this straightening out, McRuer argues for the deromanticization of composure and the new formations of queer and disabled identities that de- or ante-compose enables. I would add here that an aesthetics of ante-composure is as important for racial freedom as it is for sexual and physical liberation. Considering Jones-as-novel, then, not only raises important questions about her aesthetic relation to ante-composure but also queries whether her perceived resistance to composure and coherence energizes the disciplinary maneuvers of post-Enlightenment-minded readers.

Against the Lockdown

Interestingly, Jones-as-novel's resistance to composure is often aligned with the author's own resistance to state management. Jones published *Mosquito* relatively soon after her release from psychiatric detention. Joining her late husband in his resistance to arrest (the Kentucky police had a fourteen-year-old warrant out on him for an assault charge), the couple barricaded themselves in their home. At which time they attempted suicide together; only she survived. Afterward she was sent to Eastern State Hospital. *The Healing* (1998) and *Mosquito* appeared after her release and twenty-year hiatus from writing. In light of this, Greg Tate, a prominent critic and musician, ethically responds to the penal protocols of the plot-obsessed critic:

> When white boys write books as cunning and convoluted as this one we call them postmodern, experimental, exemplars of the literature of exhaustion; when B-boys drop prose this polemical we call them conscious rappers; when musicians of African descent take this much space to tangentially riff, we declare them avant-garde. There is a possibility that Jones is satirizing that story of prolix, polyglot, white-boy book as well as paying homage to such freestyle masters as Chuck D, KRS-One, Cecil Taylor, and the Art Ensemble of Chicago. *It is also worth considering as one attempts to plow through this wordy book that at this stage in world history, if you are a Black woman writer who the state put on lockdown mere seconds after you'd broken a 20-year silence, your next move had best be a long, unbroken howl, full of glossolalia and fury. . . . Mosquito is Gayl Jones unbound, but certainly not untethered nor without her still prodigious storehouses of language, craft, and storytelling prowess. All those who believe in keeping the faith ought to say a little prayer for Gayl.*[32]

While I agree with the ethical spirit of Tate's engagement here, I question tautological claims that connect novel to novelist. *Mosquito* isn't Jones nor is Jones *Mosquito*. The presumption of such tautologies actually violates the intensity of the move Tate prays Jones will make. Yes, after Jones leaves the institution she publishes *Mosquito*. But who returned to the world after the lockdown was Jones-as-novel, not Jones herself. Where the author went is nobody's business.

Keeping the author out of view is perhaps the task of this particular novel. Jones-as-novel is hard to read and at once self-cites as part of a larger decolonizing tradition (that includes but is not limited to the nontransparent ex-slave narrative) and sustains a "portable fortress."[33] Further, Jones-as-novel achieves this protection of desire through aesthetic innovation, particularly improvisation. With regards to improvisation broadly and Cecil Taylor's performance, *Chinampas* (1987), particularly, Fred Moten advances improvisation's capacity to object and enact a space beyond reading. For Moten, improvisation declares not only reading's impossibility but also its limits, "what is transmitted on frequencies outside and beneath the range of reading."[34]

As Jones herself also theorizes, a prominent feature and strength of African American aesthetic traditions is wandering, an improvisatory movement underneath, around, and through the word. Along these lines, *Mosquito* might be what Jones calls a "jazz text," characterized by an "interplay of voices improvising on the basic themes or motifs of the text, in key words and phrases. Often seemingly nonlogical and associational, the jazz text is generally more complex and sophisticated than blues text in its harmonies, rhythms, and surface structure (its deep structure can be as complex, but there its intricacies are noticeable). Jazz text is stronger in its accents; its vocabulary and syntax are often more convoluted and ambiguous than blues. It is often more difficult to read than a blues text, tending to abstractions over concreteness of detail."[35]

In some ways, Jones's (maybe) jazz text, with its unpredictable and nonteleological composition, (un)writes freedom. More profoundly, the text (un)tells that story through *Mosquito*'s multiple moving lines. Lines that some try to hold down in the interests of a plot. But ultimately these lines always move, flee, and defy the threat of capture. In the end, which is always the middle and the beginning, *Mosquito* remains a journey with multiple entryways as well as multiple hiding places. Perhaps it is an example of what the philosopher Maurice Blanchot identifies as literature's end, a "workfulness" where "what it creates is always recessed in relation to what *is*, while this receding only renders what *is* more slippery, less sure

of being what it is, and because of this as though attracted to another measure: that of its unreality where in the play of infinite difference what *is* affirms itself, though all the while stealing away under the cover of the no."[36]
The workfulness explicit in the "fugitive spirit" of *Mosquito*'s prose steps
ahead of the external pressures of narrativity and meaning.[37] You do not
get to know where the story begins and ends because it endlessly ambles
outside the word.

Further, as what *is*—*Mosquito*'s multiple bottom lines of freedom as
told and untold in the peripatetic prose of Gayl Jones's main character—
affirms itself, critics scamper amid the "carnival of digression" for their
answer to what they think *is* is. What *is* moves under the cover of the no
or in the zigzagging freeways of a refusal to disclose and comply, and because of this Jones's *Mosquito* fundamentally refuses such wayward epistemological demands. In that way, the novel extends a tradition of black
radical noncompliance inaugurated by the slave narrative's refusal "to tell
y'all the whole story."[38]

Tragically, however, the refusal to comply incurs various forms of state-
sanctioned punishment, including institutionalizations in Eastern State
Hospital and pejorative dismissals of one's art. More than a decade earlier,
Jones-as-story philosophizes this phenomenon by asking about the fate
of those whose private withholdings disrupt public expectation. Those
who want to write their own stories instead of being written. Those who
want to keep this world from harming them while daydreaming others
into being.

> "So what did the doctors say you had?" he had asked.
>
> "Schizophrenia," she had answered. "I don't believe them, though.
> I think that's what they always say when they have no answers."
>
> "You're no escapee from a mental institution?" he asked, half
> joking.
>
> "No," she promised. "I didn't do any bad things. I didn't harm peo-
> ple. I was just too withdrawn. I built my own world."[39]

When critics and other agents of the post-Enlightenment don't have answers for who Jones is and the kind of work she produces, they resort to a
rhetoric of aesthetic and psychiatric pathology. Author and book collapse
upon one another. That is to say, by aligning Jones with her work, critics
attempt to cohere or psychologize (straighten out) her work, rendering
Jones's text the text of Jones. But Jones isn't Mosquito. She and her char-

acters are novels within novels, stories within stories. Words and the gaps between them engender lifeworlds where black women wander as novels, endlessly composing, decomposing, and writing themselves.

So my ethical interest lies not in offering a totalizing reading. Because totalizing readings often require slowing down the composition, just as slowing down a song helps you hear its lyrics, I resist such a performative maneuver here. As I've been arguing, disturbing the composition often harasses the composing body. Slowing down the story, in other words, might exist on a continuum alongside state-sanctioned stop-and-frisk practices. Both modalities of incarceration interrupt the wandering of the writer, the writing of the wanderer. Instead of presuming the static form of an already composed text, *Mosquito*, I presume its infinite composability. As a jazz text, infinite composability is its performative and philosophical condition. In a conversation with the reader-collaborator and performer, Mosquito muses:

> I know I read it somewhere about that jazz music, 'cause if I heard it I be remembering all of it, so I musta read it somewhere. Be saying every jazz musician is a composer 'cause that what jazz is. Them classical musicians they's got to interpret the music, they has got to interpret the music the way them classical composers have wrote that music for them to interpret it. But them jazz musicians they composes it as they plays it. They might all be playing "Chitlins con Carne" but they gets to compose it for theyselves. I be wondering if it be possible to tell a true jazz story, where the peoples that listens can just enter the story and start telling it and adding things wherever they wants. The story would provide the jazz foundation, the subject, but they be improvising around that subject or them subjects and be composing they own jazz story. If it be a book, they be reading it and start telling it theyselves whiles they's reading.[40]

For this novel's main character, infinite composability potentiates a collaboration between storyteller and listener. In this way, if *Mosquito* provides the "jazz foundation," this is what I heard.

Mosquito begins, "I was on one of them little border roads in South Texas, you know them little narrow roads that runs along the border between South Texas and northern Mexico."[41] Mosquito and her truck drive into the middle of the road, on one of many narrow and twisty lines that make the geopolitical distinction between the United States and Mexico.

She begins on the border, describing every detail of its multiple lines, the plants and trees that grow there, and how they remind her of the "new-fangled" inventions at the trade fair.[42] As she studies the natural history of this highly charged geopolitical line, she professes her love, not for the line but for the land: its distinctiveness and its elusive power. The land and the act of driving through it produces this love, where love means, among other things, knowing "where you is."[43]

Driving a truck through this beloved land, Mosquito ruminates on knowing the trees despite the fact that their names escape her. As she journeys past the alligator juniper, spruce, and fir trees that dot the landscape, Mosquito turns toward thinking about the Southwest's own rhizomatic racial history. Spending time with "the wisdom of the plants" suggests a conceptual and formal insight—that is, the "wisdom of the plants" surreptitiously (de)forms the story's telling. Deleuze and Guattari write, "Even when they have roots, there is always an outside where they form a rhizome with something else—with the wind, an animal, [and] human beings."[44]

Somewhere on this outside, somewhere in the middle, *Mosquito* endlessly begins. Beginning at the middle is, in the context of post-Enlightenment logics of efficient storytelling, both nonproductive and noncompliant. In other words, by messing with a conventional storytelling structure, the novel cultivates a new world that agitates against a productivist investment in "sequence and consequence . . . , playfully dismantling Enlightenment narratologies of rational order and linear progression in the process," argues Reddy.[45] Further, against causality and the teleological constraints of post-Enlightenment storytelling, Mosquito's swerving tire and mind tracks (along with the plants' private wisdom) help the novel (un)write this story's life (and these stories' lives).

Interestingly, according to the summary on the book jacket, "Mosquito's journey begins when she discovers Maria, a stowaway who nearly gives birth in the back of the truck." But if that's the beginning, it certainly refuses the constraints of being the only one. As Reddy argues, following Edward Said, a singular beginning would be transitive, "problem- or project-directed," surplus labor for the middle and end that is said to follow.[46] However, in this novel's case, beginnings are multiple, free-floating, highly mobile, and, because they are nonteleological, intransitive. As such, the story becomes itself through its wandering—beginnings untethered to the ground of other people's imaginations and others' need for coherence and order. Indeed, understanding this feature of the story is important in that if readers hear what they think is a beginning, it more likely belongs to them than the novel that is in their hands.

For example, against the transitive narrative of beginnings posited by *Mosquito*'s press, I hear different beginnings and other stories. Such sounds include the narrator's comparison of the commotion with the noise of a prairie fox—a sound that renders the "primary" scuffling a distant background noise.[47] Moving again with what I hear, prairie animals become aphrodisiacs become African gods and goddesses become perfectibility baptism becomes the confabulatory brochure about citizen rights becomes the philosophical distinction between humanity and animality.

In my mind and in my ear, the story (de)composes and (re)composes on the page as the main character meditates on the beautiful and disastrous dimensions of other peoples' wandering in the Southwest: "Here there's even McDonald's that shaped like them adobe's architecture, and not the McDonald's architecture that in the East or Middle America or them south-central and southeastern states."[48] And before she returns to the commotion, she broaches the subject of her own religion. She mentions her affiliation with the perfectibility Baptists, though "[she] prefers not to talk to [the reader] about Perfectibility baptism."[49] This refusal to discuss perfectibility baptism begins a six-hundred-page-long series of information withholdings. Beginning her strategy of keeping certain things to herself with the subject of perfectibility baptism seems significant in multiple ways. For example, perfectibility baptism figures centrally in Mosquito's philosophical enactments. While perfectionism's relationship to the highly anticipated commotion in the back of the truck becomes one of distraction, its status as the not quite center protects (as opposed to diminishes) its importance. In an interview with Charles H. Rowell, Jones queries "how does the (anybody's) 'trivial event' enter fiction, what place does it have along with the (anybody's) 'significant event'; how do you make the reader re-see the trivial moment as significant events when that's the question. This is digression, but I think it might be something to be considered in a discussion of the 'events' and their selection in a Southern black literary tradition and in the works of specific writers within that tradition."[50]

For Jones, the trivial is also the place of the story. The cactus-shaped mug picked up by Mosquito at a trade show, for example, is as important as religion. It is the reader's failure to listen that results in pejorative dismissals of Jones's "carnivals of digression."[51] Moreover, what sadly gets missed are the ways in which these tangential, trivial events are meaning-ful; the beauty in a carnival of digression is its ability to "preven[t] the introduction of the enemy, the Signifier and those attempts to interpret a work that is actually only open to experimentation," according to Deleuze and Guattari.[52]

Indeed, I wonder whether preventing the incursion of the enemy (whether it's the post-Enlightenment-minded reader or border watcher) might be the undisclosed mission of this book's (non)story. The main character always seems to be two steps ahead of the reader: "[I know] that there is no doubt spies and informants amongst y'all that will go around to the truckstops anyway or asks some of the peoples in the union whether they knows me and has they seen my truck. How big is it, how many axles it got, how many tons is it, what color is it? It got to tell y'all that the roof of my truck ain't the same color as the rest of my truck. So those of y'all that thinks y'all knows my truck to be one color don't know the fullness of my truck."[53]

In line with the philosophical investment in the sidetrack and in being sidetracked, Mosquito's fugitive perception shuttles again from that "scuf-fle" to the question of her truck's color to the color's capacity to attract birds. Here birds make me think about abolitionism, because conductors on the Underground Railroad, as Renny Golden and Michael McConnell explain, used "an elaborate system of passwords, special calls, or birdcalls . . . to elude capture."[54] Also, maybe birds are the archangel of this story's safety; their ante-articulate sounds and calls foreground the imperative of listening essential for Mosquito's philosophy of freedom. Mosquito listens to them as she returns to that scuffling sound, a sound that prompts her to pick up a flashlight and stun gun. With gun in hand, she switches topics to the dexterity of circus jugglers and yoga practitioners and, in so doing, guards that scuffling sound.

As the scuffler enjoys freedom, Mosquito continues her musings on her Chicana bartender, intellectual, and activist friend Delgadina's abil-ities in physical and philosophical contortion along with other "colored peoples [stun-gunning, science-fiction-style salvation of] the Universe."[55] From somewhere Mosquito ruminates on the racial politics of gun control, why Oprah might want to get herself a stun gun, and the racialized history of the outlaw. Outlaws become the question of that scuffling becomes a wondering (or wandering) whether the sound in the back of the truck is a prairie fox becomes trickster animals in the Southwest that use camouflage to protect themselves become that time she and Delgadina went to Marine World in Arizona becomes whether that marine tour guide meant Indians from India or Native Americans when talking about the Rajiformes fish becomes the fetishistic commodification of Native American reservations in the Southwest.

Mosquito wonders about those Native American trading posts that cater to the white tourist-consumer-wanderer as she phantasmatically descends into the histories of those whose roads she rides. She remembers

> hearing a poem where someone talked about the road like that, and took them roads back to they beginnings and what and who traveled on them before the modern peoples traveled on them roads. I thinks about this whole land when it were just the lands of the Kiowa, Cheyenne, Arapaho, Comanche, Apache, and what Delgadina call the Clovis Culture before them. . . . I daydreams of myself sometimes riding the prairies on a wild, Spanish mustang. I ain't know the full history of this land, but sometimes I hears pieces of the story. The fabled cities of gold, explorer-mapmakers, the California Gold Rush, Chief Peta Nocona, Comanche, Quaker Indian agents, New Mexico cattle rustlers who would masquerade as native Peoples, native rebels like Quanah. I ain't like to hear the white man's version, 'cause everybody knows that. I likes to hear the other people's eclectic stories of the Southwest.[56]

A daydream facilitates this particular philosophical travel. Mosquito daydreams often. In the worlds enacted by the novel, daydreaming keeps the story composable while enabling the main character to critically roam "among other cultures."[57] This critical roaming, to be sure, is different from the enactments of "New Mexico cattle rustlers who masquerade as native Peoples"; instead Mosquito wanders to unearth the other history of the Southwest.[58] Shape-shifting into different bodies, spaces, and times at once, according to Deleuze and Guattari, "causes flows to move that are capable of breaking apart both the segregations of their Oedipal applications—flows capable of hallucinating history, of reanimating the races in delirium, of setting continents ablaze."[59] By substituting herself for a member of a Native American tribe, suspending herself in a beginning without end, Mosquito theorizes the deep historical connection between the ancient histories of Native American movement (lockdown) and her own. This philosophical understanding composes a private music, perhaps accompanying her dreams "of [herself] sometimes, riding the prairies on a wild, Spanish mustang."[60] At least, that is what I thought I heard.

Seemingly inside and outside the dream, Mosquito cruises the real and phantasmatic landscape of Native American subjugation while formally and conceptually referencing her own (ancient) strategies of anti-captivity. Her digressive tale in combination with the sporadic, not-so-straightforward allusions to abolition makes her phantasmatic descent into the space/time of Native American roaming a potential foundation for another story. At the same time, such shape-shiftings—or wanderings past the ontological and spatiotemporal constraints of this world—expand the terrain for the main character's own movement. Imagining herself in other spaces, times, and bodies not only indexes the novel's coalitional ethos but also elucidates how wandering, in this case, mental roaming, unsettles identitarian and topographical fixity.

What is more, the palimpsest created by Mosquito's mind and tire tracks at once broadens the possibilities for identity and community and protects the wanderers within. In the middle of the half-told stories, amid these other openings, beginnings, and escape routes, Mosquito returns to that scuffle. With her stun gun and flashlight still in tow, Mosquito discovers a young, pregnant Mexican woman hiding behind a tub of detergent. She discloses the first word spoken by the young woman only after a brilliant digression on the politics of multiracialism, the overabundance of border patrols at the U.S.-Mexico border, and why it would be "good if them Mexicans would build up that Mexico and then use that wall to keep the Americans out. Or the Norteamericanos. 'Cause we's all Americans. We's the Americas, so we's all Americans. Or we could call usselves Turtle Islanders, like them Native American name."[61]

The post-NAFTA racial politics of border patrol link up with the brutality of Manifest Destiny and, in so doing, distract the reader from finding out what that woman in the back of the truck said. Unceremoniously, Mosquito minimizes the young woman's utterance when she recalls that she "whisper[ed] what must be the only word of English she know, Sanctuary."[62] While *sanctuary* resonates in its immediate definition and in its relationship to a political movement identified as the "new underground railroad," Mosquito stalls for Maria Barriga (the young woman's *given* name) by presenting it as a whispered and probably inconsequential utterance.

Sitting with Maria, Mosquito tells her about the people she's picked up along her route, "that Navajo and the Oklahoma African, and the roustabout," and about being mistaken for African when she was in Canada and "them old slaves refugitives and them new African refugees."[63] These reveries turn as Mosquito, reflecting on Maria "looking at that stun gun I got," recalls the Mexican and black women who were (sometimes gun-toting) generals in history.[64] The work of art formed out of the encounter between Mosquito and Maria endlessly composes, improvises, and produces multiple entryways for the specters of Harriet Tubman, Sojourner Truth, and countless revolutionary Mexican and black women to enter. As the sentinels of radical history move and, in some ways, guard this work of art, Mosquito discloses her full name: "I'm Sojourner, I says. Sojourner Jane Nadine Johnson."[65]

Mosquito, Sojourner, Jane, and Nadine are added to the main character's long list of names, "like them people got aliases and shit, different people be knowing them by different names. . . . And them is all my real names."[66] Because Mosquito probably "know[s] so well that naming is power and that power both confers and limits identity, shape, and place," Mosquito's introduction as Sojourner to that humanized back-of-the-truck commotion is profoundly significant.[67] The name Sojourner indexes an important black radical, though one who is far too often overlooked, and it also foregrounds a set of nineteenth-century movements against captivity. Further, Jones's deliberate naming of Mosquito as also Sojourner begins other stories, other improvisational possibilities. As a listener, for example, I wonder what the relationship might be between a twenty-first-century black female truck driver and a nineteenth-century itinerant, antislavery, and perfectionist preacher. In many ways these new stories remain unwritten—for example, it is often not Truth but Tubman who tends to be associated with a profugitive movement, namely the Underground Railroad.

Although the Underground Railroad figures as one of the many entryways into this work of art, and although Tubman is a historical figure whom Mosquito wants to teleport into the present, it is Sojourner Truth for whom she is named. It is also Truth who responds to the call for "sanctuary" uttered by Maria in the back of the truck. This is an important, errant move on the part of the novel insofar as it is Truth who "remains outside the canon of ex-slave narratives," according to Nell Painter.[68] The reasons for this exclusion most likely include Truth's lack of formal education, that is, "formal" literacy, purportedly manifest in a so-called backward speech as well as her hard-to-read road map for liberation, which "blended millennialism, black abolitionism, and women's rights into a voice that transcended any one of these struggles."[69] Importantly, in *Mosquito* the anticaptive force of Truth's itinerant religiosity along with her elusive philosophical performances prove to be essential for our thinking of contemporary anticaptivity as Tubman's work on the original railroad. But because Truth, like the main character, still figures as hard to read and hear, bound by the performative constraints of this world, the profundity of her radicalism is often missed. Donna Haraway observes:

> Perhaps what most needs cleaning up here is an ability to hear Sojourner Truth's language, to face her specificity, to acknowledge her, but *not* as the voice of seven apocalyptic thunders. Instead, perhaps we need to see her as the Afro-Dutch-English New World itinerant preacher whose disruptive and risk taking practices led her "to leave the house of bondage," to leave the subject-making (and humanist) dynamics of master and slave, and seek new names in a dangerous world. This sojouner's truth offers an inherently unfinished but potent reply to Pilate's skeptical query—"What is truth?" She is one of Gloria Anzaldúa's *mestizas*, speaking the unrecognized hyphenated languages, living in the borderlands of history and consciousness where crossings are never safe and names never original.[70]

Truth's and Mosquito's "critical roaming" composes a nonteleological movement, "inherently unfinished," always rearranging and beginning again, always improvising upon others' failures to hear. For Truth, "in her Jesus like travels [she] seemed always to be seeking the deeper pattern that connects us all together."[71] Similarly, in *Mosquito* the main character's digressive reveries and encounters enact, realize, and protect her burgeoning philosophy of interconnectedness and coalition. Hijacked plots make way for barely noticed words and positions, the chain of associations becoming long and deep enough for Mosquito and Maria to be able to *walk* together from the back of her truck, past the border patrol, and to the sanctuary of "this mission school run by this Carmelite nun."[72]

Further, this collaborative movement extends an international political project identified as the new Underground Railroad. The sanctuary movement involves a range of philosophical acts designed, in the name of God, to protect the fugitive from danger. For some of its conductors, this movement is as old as the Bible itself, with "Moses . . . set[ting] aside cities and places of refuge in Canaan, the Promised Land, where the persecuted could seek asylum from 'blood avengers.'"[73] Further, the nineteenth-century antislavery Underground Railroad critically enacted this antirefugitive spirit and inspired the twentieth-century formation of this often overlooked political movement.[74]

More precisely, the sanctuary movement began in the 1980s in response to an anticommunist U.S. foreign policy in Latin America that resulted in countrywide state repression and massive civilian casualties. The refugees, fleeing the U.S.-sponsored violence in their homelands, migrated to the shores of the United States only to be locked out by the Refugee Act of 1980. To sustain the fiction that violence in Latin America was a particular and individualized phenomenon, the Refugee Act stringently enforced the entry of only those presumed to be political refugees into U.S. land. Refugees from Mexico and Central and South America suffered exclusion as a result, because their reasons for asylum strategically figured as economic.[75] In response to this antirefugitivity (another variation of *refugitive* spoken by Mosquito), North American churches "sacraliz[ed] . . . the border," Golden and McConnell explain, by declaring their religious space sanctuaries for political refugees, sacred spaces of noncompliance.[76] With the sacralization of the border, religious and spiritual officials declared any attempt by law enforcement to trespass church property and capture fugitives an automatic violation of sacred law. As Golden and McConnell write,

> More than seventy thousand U.S. citizens have actively participated in breaking U.S. law, as interpreted by the government, in order to "feed the hungry and shelter the homeless." Most sanctuary churches knew from the beginning that it was insufficient to merely bind up the wounds of the victims without trying to stop the cause of those wounds. Welcoming services for refugee families at sanctuary sites became occasions for decrying U.S. foreign policy and mobilizing the community at large to stop the flow of arms from the U.S.A. to Central America. Telling the truth was coupled with putting an end to the horror of that truth. Inspiration for such action came from the rich and heroic tradition of sanctuary but also from the example of the Central American church itself.[77]

Mosquito rides in the direction of that mission school and sanctuary with the hope that it might provide a safe house for Maria. When Mosquito arrives, a nun greets her: "[She] ask[ed] me whether I come there to apply for one of them housekeeping jobs that they done advertised."[78] Mosquito corrects the nun, but she is not convinced: "She look at me like she want to see my registration papers, or maybe my citizenship papers."[79] Like her namesake Sojourner Truth, Mosquito is *read* as excessive in her comportment. As Mosquito observes, the nun looks at her suspiciously "like I ain't no citizen."[80] Interestingly, race, class, and sexuality shove Mosquito outside the movement, consigning her to the potentially forgotten, putatively transparent, and immobile terrain of the (already) read and misheard.

Though the nun eventually gives Mosquito the number of a sanctuary priest, "she still looking like what concern the Sanctuary movement is of mines."[81] Like Truth, people question Mosquito's political value. Perhaps this has something to do with the intersections of blackness, femaleness, and accent; Mosquito's philosophical interventions are silenced by racist, classist, and sexist narratives of articulacy and enlightened self-presentation: "And she straighten that hood she wearing, what they call a wimple. And she looking at me like she think I'm one of them elementary school childrens too, though like I told you I'm a big one. And she a kinda smallish one. She remind me of one of them pilgrims in the storybook."[82]

Despite the fact that the nun could not read Mosquito beyond a set of specific scripts and tones, Mosquito's movement exceeds those constraints. For example, even as the nun (who resembles a pilgrim) presumes an enlightened positionality with respect to Mosquito, repeating her words "like she was talking to one them elementary school childrens," Mosquito improvises within and against the nun's attempts at instruction. Mosquito's mental ruminations on the sound of her voice and the attractiveness of the "hand-carved door you got there" circumvent the nun's endeavors in intellectual and economic tutelage.[83] Through rambling and a promiscuous change and improvisation of subject, Mosquito resists the potential scene of racialized economic enlightenment. And outside the purview of both the nun and the reader, Mosquito returns to her own "road map, backs the truck up, and pulls off."[84]

As Mosquito rides between stops and encounters, she writes and sounds out new beginnings. The encounter with Ray, a half–African American, half-Filipino sanctuary priest with "hieroglyphic eyes," for example, opens another portal of rumination, a new beginning.[85] Swayed by his hieroglyphic eyes, Mosquito muses that Ray is "of the attractive persuasion."[86] Mosquito also learns that he is a social psychologist who works with Chicano, Native American, and African American communities. At a point, in Delgadina's bar, she contemplates her roaming conversation with Ray and their mutual journeying through the idea of America as experiment, human rights abuses, the Tuskegee nightmare, and environmental racism. These reveries shift as Mosquito considers the diversity of the bar's patrons—Chicanos, Mexicans, and Native Americans—and remembers her encounter with the "one man that frequents the bar who say he a combination of Comanche, Kiowa, Kiowa-Apache, Osage, Cheyenne, and Apache Apache."[87] His name is Saturna.

Listening to Saturna, Mosquito begins to daydream again. She "moves without moving" into the Chihuahua desert surrounded by birds.[88] Saturna sits with her in the dream, pointing out "hawks and falcons, a red-tailed hawk and a prairie falcon, a golden eagle, some orchard orioles, some red cardinals, a yellow chat, a mountain bluebird, [and] a red flycatcher."[89] As they watch the birds' spectacular flight, Saturna paints Mosquito's face with red mud. It is at this moment of tribal initiation that Mosquito surfaces, "feeling like I's been resanctified."[90]

The peripatetic descent into the space of tribal initiation resanctifies Mosquito where resanctification (like the daydream) is another occasion for movement, another beginning at the middle. For the perfectibility Baptists, the follower who commits acts in accordance with moral law enjoys resanctification. From there, the follower receives "a second blessing" for those "additional convictional steps," Douglas M. Strong explains.[91] Taking these convictional steps, Mosquito returns to the daydream. She finds herself this time in the Baptist Church of Memphis, listening to Reverend Wolf and his choir singing a song about resanctification, "Hold on to de Big Truck."[92]

The Art of Telling a True Jazz Story

In this dream Mosquito listens to the deep connection between taking sacred steps and her big truck. With this knowledge, she awakens again at the bar, contemplating whether or not "it be possible to tell a true jazz story."[93] At another time, it is a scene of erotic desire—meeting Ray—that engenders such musings, even as beginnings, middles, and ends are undecidable here. As discussed earlier, Mosquito's questioning of jazz stories' truth or verifiability largely emerges out of desire's decompositional drive and the ways that truth constitutes a moving site of improvisation. Jones writes, "This is not chaos but a 'jamming' session: by forcing the personalities, images, time periods, references, situations, events into this stanzaic space, by jamming them, the poet actually extends their 'possibility, combination, and diversity'—their territory, 'suggesting new arrangements of human essentials'; they break the 'narrow borders' of time, space, and definition through the poet's memory and creative investment. The personal and historical are magnificently superimposed."[94]

Jazz stories make worlds as much as they unmake them. This is because they wander. Wandering describes the condition of possibility of their (de)composition as wandering is enacted by writers and storytellers and readers and listeners. Moreover, by offering what Jones describes as "a metaphor for freedom of movement—spatial, temporal, and imaginative," jazz shows the storyteller how to tell a story that choreographs new arrangements of time, space, landscape, and history.[95] For Mosquito, these new arrangements present possibilities for the story to transgress and trespass arbitrary and invented limits while preventing the external regulation of such possibilities. Her improvisatory digressions (a feature inherited from jazz) create the grounds for new beginnings as well as strategies for resisting state compliance and preventing capture. As we have seen, because the event of digression loses some readers and critics (not to mention throwing off border patrol), it sustains the fact of freedom as the truth of this story. What is more, new formations of liberatory subjectivity form and deform in performance, what Jones calls a "writing between the lines, and even between the words"—wanderings on other terrain.[96]

The digression, sidenote, secret, sidetrack, daydream, and critical roaming are not only inheritances from an African American aesthetic tradition but essential dimensions of Gayl Jones's storytelling. They are not only styles but actual ways of moving through the world safely. Inasmuch as this story tells itself through driving on, off, and beneath the ancient (rail) roads of this country, it refuses to tell itself, and in that way, it becomes noncompliant through the very same means. It may have been a story about a black female truck driver and it might not have been. It might have been a story with allegorical ties to the ex-slave narrative, but it might have been a whole other kind of story with ties to another genre, not yet heard of. As Jones-as-novel reminds us, jazz stories are places where the personal and the historical are superimposed as well as places where what is meant by the personal and historical exceeds what the listener-reader thinks the personal and historical are.

In other words, the world created by the novel thrives on freedom's moving line. This is its jazz foundation. In this world beginnings compose differently at the hands of storyteller and listener, and this difference in composition emerges from the singularity of wandering, as opposed to the totality of trespass. For the storyteller and the listener, freedom's moving line is a place of improvisation. These are improvisations that gather together possibilities and speculations, pasts and futures, places, moments, roads and railroads, names and acts, tales and secrets (the private combination of "new human essentials"). These are improvisations that create the foundation and the gravity necessary for "de big truck" to ride, hide, go off course, and arrive safely.[97] For Jones-as-novel, this means that even though "they [the state] come in wearing iron suits[,] . . . she won't let them touch her."[98]

CONCLUSION

"Before I Was Straightened Out"

You know, they straightened out the Mississippi River in places to make room for houses & livable acreage. Occasionally the river floods these places. "Floods" is the word they use, but in fact it is not flooding; it is remembering. Remembering where it used to be. All water has a perfect memory and is forever trying to get back to where it was. Writers are like that. . . . Like water, I remember where I was before I was straightened out.

TONI MORRISON, "THE SITE OF MEMORY"

Toni Morrison, in her beautiful meditation on the work of memory, describes being "straightened" out as a modality of (historical) forgetting. Along with the capitalist development of the Mississippi River, Morrison too has been straightened out by others' desires.[1] Still, as she powerfully observes, water doesn't obey the logic of capitalism. It flows and moves unpredictably, roaming back to the forgotten place where the river used to be.

What this insight about water reveals is an understanding that the life evicted does return and does so against restraint. In many ways wandering facilitates this return, a kind of kinesthetic homecoming, by forging modalities of embodiment for what critic M. Jacqui Alexander describes as "errant spirits, teeming with yearning not easily satisfied in towering buildings or in slabs of concrete."[2] This is life straightened out by the vertical reach of economic desire—life that knows that concrete hides a river somewhere. To wander is to renounce the limits imposed on one's movement, to live and act in excess of the moorings of someone else's desire. To make and unmake one's own way.

Still, as Alexander theorizes, making one's own way continues to be associated with and constrained by the limits of secular citizenship. In

Pedagogies of Crossing: Meditations on Feminism, Sexual Politics, Memory, and the Sacred (2005), Alexander critiques a tendency within social movements, particularly feminism, to secularize experience, justice, and survival. Such a move presumes a teleological path of freedom that begins with "external loss . . . having to prove perpetual injury as the quid pro quo to secure ephemeral rights," and ends at recognizable gain—visible as the acquisition of rights and capital.[3] On the one hand, Alexander problematizes the state's role in sanctioning legitimate routes toward freedom. On the other, she cautions against presuming safe travel despite such cartographic legitimization, asking: "So what does possession mean after all at this time of empire in the United States? . . . What is democracy to mean when its association with the perils of empire has rendered it so thoroughly corrupt that it seems disingenuous and perilous even to employ the term. Freedom is a similar hegemonic term, especially when associated with the imperial freedom to abrogate the self-determination of a people. . . . And while dispossession and betrayal provide powerful grounds from which to stage political mobilizations, they are not sufficiently expansive to the task of becoming more fully human."[4] Put another way, what does liberal personhood matter if one can't stroll home or daydream on a bus unharmed?

As I have argued, such strolls and daydreams are a luxury for bodies whose abstract, secularized rights don't extend to late-night wanderings. This is to say that even though legal emancipation promised the end of the state's violent "accounting" procedures—the recording, owning, and arresting of black movement—an ethos against black wandering persists in law after slavery's formal end.[5] The maps, flags, and captain logs of the eighteenth and nineteenth centuries are joined now by everything from forced sterilization to stop-and-frisk practices. Tragically, the endless policing of black desire—racial, sexual, kinetic—not only suggests an anxiety around unrestrained black movement but also the persistence of an antebellum fear of black "affectability" (a reckless unguidedness).[6]

Given these violences, what does it mean to resist such policing when any imagined affectable movement can get you killed? What if a desire for freedom moves beyond the secularized terrains of the physical and the agentic, surpassing the "minimal transport" afforded by the state's assessment of rights and permissions?[7] While there's no real answer or end to these questions, wandering moves by way of open musings. These are musings that roam somewhere else—somewhere past the bullet, the law, the lonely street, and the wayward gaze. In this way and in the spirit of philosophy undertaken by figures like Sojourner Truth, I dedicate these remaining pages to wandering's open musing on freedom—a musing that troubles the arbitrary distinctions between the sacred and secular, the visible and invisible, and life and death itself.

Indeed, wandering, in its engagement with actual and phantasmatic terrain, queries the complexity, range, and meaning of freedom as movement. For example, even while the state temporarily interrupted Edward Lawson's visible roaming, it could never fully contain his movement. To presume such a stoppage, in fact, implies that all life begins and ends in linear "clock time" and that its philosophical drive is "available and accessible for our consumption."[8] For critics such as Alexander, Talal Asad, and Avery Gordon, these assumptions emerge out of a desacralized notion of the secular—a hypervisible and hypermaterialistic (transparent) terrain unshaped by the elusive ambulations of otherworldly movement.

According to Asad, the desacralized secular expresses the lingering trace of the eighteenth- and nineteenth-century imperialist Enlightenment. More specifically, during the nineteenth century, white European Enlightenment philosophers radically retheorized the secular and sacred as opposing social categories.[9] In fact, the recognized Enlightenment's very justification depended on the fictitious distinction between the rational and moral secular subject and its purported opposite, the "primitive," eccentric, deluded, and hopelessly enchanted object. Moreover, these distinctions facilitated the emergence of the secular as guarantor of civilizational progress. By positing such rigid distinctions, European philosophers at once figured the domain of "false things" as the sacred, the secular's radical opposite.[10] In so doing, the enactment of secular freedom required the renunciation of such false things and the errant movement they otherwise engender.

However, even though the conditions of possibility for self-same Enlightenment identity involved "successfully unmasking pretended power," in Asad's words, the consolidation of such identity required its illusory enactment.[11] As I've argued after Johannes Fabian, European explorers often moved outside the constraints of their "rationalized frames" (including the secular) in their performative engagement with difference.[12] In other words, the conditions of possibility for becoming enlightened often involved violent games of imaginative pretense. As Saidiya Hartman argues, in the context of chattel slavery, "the fungibility of the commodity, specifically its abstractness and immateriality, enabled the black body or blackface mask to serve as the vehicle for white self-exploration, renunciation, and enjoyment."[13]

This means that even while the idealized post-Enlightenment subject can move errantly—along the crooked grooves of false things—in the interest of its definition, the bodies figured as the disposable ground of such wanderings endure immobilization and trespass. Put another way, Alexander argues that the post-Enlightenment state sanctions its idealized subject's "lapses outside the bounds of rationality" and encounters with "pretended power" as expressions of keeping order.[14] On February 26, 2012, a black teen en route back to his father's fiancée's house after buying a snack at a convenience store was gunned down by the antiblack wandering patrol, historically known as the neighborhood watch. While the state, through Florida's "Stand Your Ground" legislation, sanctioned the gunman's recklessness, the perceived recklessness of Trayvon Martin figured as grounds for punishment. Here recklessness that works in the service of the state becomes a matter of standing one's ground. Myisha Cherry writes, "Stand Your Ground is not just a bad law, an irresponsible law, or perhaps even the absence or erasure of law, insofar as it gives armed wannabes the right to live out their twisted fantasies of vigilantism and act as judge, jury, and executioner."[15]

But what about those who lack a relationship with the ground and, with it, the right to wander along the "twisted fantasies," the private longings and pretendings, such a relationship allows? How does one recover a ground without the forcible evacuation of others, the violent straightening out of rivers? Finally, how might wandering shift the idea of the ground itself, dislodging its secularized, imperialist connotations of governability and ownership and resacralizing its shape-shifting potential? The artists Adrian Piper, Carrie Mae Weems, and William Pope.L create art that philosophically enacts these ethical musings and, more specifically, reimagines freedom in wandering's shifting ground.

Following Alexander and José Esteban Muñoz, part of what these new relations to ground involve is the creative resistance to being straightened out, a refusal to abide by the political and ethical groundings imposed by the violence of a hypersecularized "straight time."[16] Akin to Alexander's discussion of the sacred, Muñoz argues for the potential of a "queer temporality," a utopic standing "out of time together, [a resistance to] the stultifying temporality and time that is not ours, that is saturated with violence both visceral and emotional, a time that is not queerness."[17] This time and, with it, space, might be the place where antistraight (and anti-straightened out) philosophies flourish, and where black philosophers move unharmed—where stories of freedom are (un)written in the private glimmer that surrounds pavement, as energies "of a dangerous memory, a second's glimpse of an entire life, of a dream or sequence of dreams."[18]

In some ways, then, I'm ending where I began, with the unnarrated wisdom enacted in daydreams, mental drifts, meditations, material renunciations, and stares at the sea. Stories forged in wandering. As I've argued throughout this book, for bodies subject to the most vicious of constraints and surveillances, physical wandering is often subject to external policing and arrest. But for the artists-philosophers I discuss, there are other modalities of wandering and unrestrained rumination possible even if the state decides you don't get to walk freely. And these modalities of wandering privately subvert the post-Enlightenment's secularized protocols of rationality, composure, and upright and upstanding comportment. For example, in 1978, in *Thunderbird Immolation*, Pope.L enjoyed freedom while sitting on the sidewalk. Just outside the famed New York City galleries of Sonnabend and Castelli, Pope.L meditated while covered in cheap alcohol and surrounded by matches. Even though he was encircled by the material (immobilizing) desire of black destruction, there was no sacrifice. Pope.L remained unmoved in a cross-legged "yoga-like pose," as Kristine Stiles describes, spiritually traveling into other realms of free black movement.[19]

Like Pope.L, Piper philosophizes other dimensions of livability and movability against the oppressive formations of interior and exterior (racist, sexist, xenophobic) desire. This becomes possible through her philosophical commitments to yogic practice and her simultaneously straight and errant Kantian-inspired concept of "transpersonal rationality."[20] Her *Everything* series, originating in 2003, expresses those commitments through the phantasmatic enactment of the claim "Everything will be taken away." This mantra appeared in various contexts, from sandwich boards to foreheads to images of Hurricane Katrina, assassinated political leaders, and the heartbreaking story of the "racially charged kidnapping, torture, and sexual assault of Megan Williams in Rural West Virginia."[21]

In the use of yogic practice and philosophy as an aesthetic and philosophical meditation on white-supremacist patriarchy, violence, and loss, Pope.L and Piper theorize an intense relation between material renunciation and otherworldly movement. Their spiritually inspired renunciation of the "minimal transport" offered by a desacralized secular opens up other portals for free, unsurveilled, unscripted, and unmappable movement.[22] And this renunciation requires not simply the relinquishment of ties to this world but rather new ways of moving upon and beyond its devastated terrain. While Piper's philosophical difference from Pope.L manifests in her written works as an investment in a straightened-out notion of Kantian rationalism, her artistic practice embraces unrestrained, phantasmatic travelings as method. I query these contradictions within Piper's philosophy later, but it is important to recognize that her art making, along with Pope.L's, rephilosophizes the abundance on the other side of secular renunciation as the "ungovernable" ground for the inviolable ambulations of freedom.[23]

Moreover, while the sacred moves as spiritual practice in Piper's and Pope.L's art, Weems's work extends its terrain in another direction. Regarding her 2006 Roaming series, in particular, the sublime sacralizes a space around bodies crawling down the street. To begin, Weems argues that the work at once attends to the various ways architecture sometimes embodies state formations, phenomenologically and symbolically making the roaming body feel like a "minion" or literally a "lower subject" in relation to power.[24] The series consists of photos of Weems in a black dress— walking, sometimes crawling, and standing in proximity to larger-than-life churches, unnamed pillars and pyramids, and other presumably important state institutions. Yet in some of these same images, the roaming body moves in excess of the scene—that is, the word *roaming* also frames images of Weems gazing out at the ocean, the city, and the world below. This indicates another potential movement, one that courses outside the recesses of the visual.

In her interview with *Art21*, Weems describes this duality of movement as a duality of desires—a desire to challenge the artifice of state domination and an investment in the sublime qualities of domineering edifices. This dual interest achieves a resistance to domination in ways that exceed a secular, visible challenge. More specifically, the sublime itself offers a movement outside of state time, outside of "straight time."[25] As with the art of Piper and Pope.L, Weems's sublime engenders an otherworldly movement— an errant kinesis that exceeds the locomotive constraints at the heart of secular freedom. Put another way, the roaming and ruminating made possible by the sublime arguably enlarges and unstraightens while remobilizing the arrested body down below.

In the end, these artists "move without moving," agitating against the straightening-out processes of post-Enlightenment, white-supremacist, capitalist, ableist, and heteronormative patriarchal modernity.[26] Their roaming and meditation potentializes another terrain; one where free movement is disaggregated from what can be seen, touched, known, and materially valued. As open musings, Pope.L's, Piper's, and Weems's artworks query (and enact) freedom in a world that criminalizes their wandering. For these reasons, their art concludes this book if only to suggest another beginning.

William Pope.L

For William Pope.L, beginnings paradoxically move at the end, in the expansive terrain engendered by material loss. More specifically, Pope.L dangerously muses upon blackness as a lack worth having. Such philosophical inquiry errantly moves in threatening his own sacrifice (*Thunderbird Immolation*); covering his entire body in mayonnaise and ingesting the *Wall Street Journal* (*Eating the Wall Street Journal*, 2000); writing, sleeping, and living outside on the American flag (*Writing/Sleeping/Living on the Flag*, 1990–91); attaching a pole to his groin in *Schlong Journey* (1996); and crawling here, there, and everywhere in his Crawl pieces and standing naked (save a skirt composed of dollar bills) outside a Chase ATM distributing dollars and sausages to bank customers (*ATM Piece*, 1997). On the one hand, by producing works that traffic in overcited images of black homelessness, racial and sexual abjection, and exoticism, Pope.L travels the uncertain terrain where the value of blackness (de)forms in its figuration as the means for another's ends. Here the lack of blackness refers to its essential though renounced relationship to a racist and sexist social order, and to histories of subjection whereby, Lindon Barrett writes, "African American presence is initially premised on ruthlessly extracted labor."[27]

> In a phrase, the New World arena of value, in both its materialist and idealist transactions, depends upon the expenditure of Blackness. To expend the "humanity" of Africans in the profitable cultivation of staple crops (or other commodities) as well as the political and psychological contours of a privileged whiteness (defined foremost as Anglo or Western European) remains a fundamental element and an enduring legacy of the New World arena of value. Forcibly, Blackness

is positioned as excess in relation to a more "legitimate" and significant presence known as whiteness, a more legitimate presence invariably revising its promiscuous interests in (re)situating the black Other.[28]

Further, in the postbellum era, black identity continues to be the (de)valued site of excess and expenditure, over and over again used to bolster white, civic, and moral order. Ailsa Chang writes, "WNYC mapped the exact coordinates of every recorded stop of a teenager in 2011. It turns out the densest hot spot for stop and frisks of teenagers last year was along a four-block section of Brownsville, next to Teachers Preparatory High School, near the Marcus Garvey public housing projects."[29] Barrett might say that these kinetic assaults—the arrests and expenditures of black humanity—are demanded by white value's dialectical force. According to Barrett, value always holds a "promiscuous interest in an underprivileged and displaced other."[30] By endlessly arresting, expending, and trespassing upon black life, white supremacy renders blackness as the straightened-out site of lack. For the kids prevented from walking a certain four blocks, this lack is felt as the absence of a roamable ground.

In a revolutionary move, however, Pope.L's art suggests the possibility of movement despite such topographical seizures. By creating art that associates blackness with lack, excess, nonsense (sometimes madness), and an impossible expenditure and consumption, Pope.L illustrates how an exercise of will at the end of visible—material and rational—topographies might radically reveal an alternative route, and, with it, other kinds of movement toward freedom. If blackness cannot be spent, incorporated, interpreted, made sense of, used, consumed, stolen from, or straightened out, it cannot serve the epistemic and economic ends of whiteness. By implication, then, lack is worth having when it inaugurates safer passages toward freedom.

Still, how can not having something pave the way for a "movement of freedom"?[31] If Pope.L engages in practices designed to willfully expend and evict himself from materiality, he preempts a white-supremacist structure of expenditure that predicates its identity on the very same process. Moreover, to be a willful black subject who self-objectifies and expends is to suggest an errancy within and against subjection. In Pope.L's art such errancy forms in an undisclosed place beyond value, a place on the other side of stolen lives and streets—a place once described by Immanuel Kant as dignity itself. For Kant, "that which is related to general human inclinations and needs has a *market price*. That which, without presupposing any need, accords with a certain taste, i.e., with pleasure in the mere purposeless play of our faculties has an *affective price*. But that which constitutes the condition under which alone something can be an end in itself does not have mere relative worth, i.e., a price, but an intrinsic worth, i.e., dignity."[32]

In Kant's "realm of ends," that which "can be replaced by something else" has value and that which is "above all price" and "admits of no equivalents" has dignity.[33] At the time of Kant's writing, black people were enslaved and, by definition, alienable, movable, and replaceable as commodities. In essence, a law of equivalents circumscribed their humanity. However, Hartman argues that resistance to enslavement, as a set of "simple exercises of any claims to the self, however restricted, challenged the figuration of the captive body as devoid of will."[34] These exercises in will occasioned illegal movements outside the principles of equivalence and replacability. Such resistances forged dignity.

In the spirit of postbellum dignity, Pope.L errantly travels the roads on the other side of lack. While working within the economic and epistemic logics of blackness as expenditure and valuelessness, Pope.L asks what new forms of movement might emerge if the public (visible, readable) exercise of will and freedom illuminates their absence? What does dignity have to do with the essentially vulnerable occupation of lack? In many ways, by self-consciously becoming the hallowed-out terrain whose lack constitutes the contours of his subjectivity and the very definition of nonreplacability, Pope.L breaks with his positioning in materiality and, with that, "remembers where [he] was before [being] straightened out."[35] Put another way, by renouncing the material as a terrain and path toward freedom and by embracing lack itself, Pope.L makes other kinds of movement possible. That is, wandering becomes possible in refusals of attachment—identitarian, topographical, material, and otherwise. In a performance undertaken in 1978, the artist experiments with this modality of movement while seated in stillness on the ground.

Sitting in repose and meditation outside the galleries Castelli and Sonnabend, Pope.L performed *Thunderbird Immolation* (see figure C.1). *Thunderbird Immolation* consisted of Pope.L's threatened self-immolation by a lethal combination of the cheap fortified wines Thunderbird and Wild Irish Rose and the strike of any of the several kitchen matches encircling him. Sitting in "yoga-like pose" on a blanket decorated with liquor, Coca-Cola, and matches, the artist, "having established for himself this atmosphere of meditative wisdom, from time to time. . . . mixed the alcohol

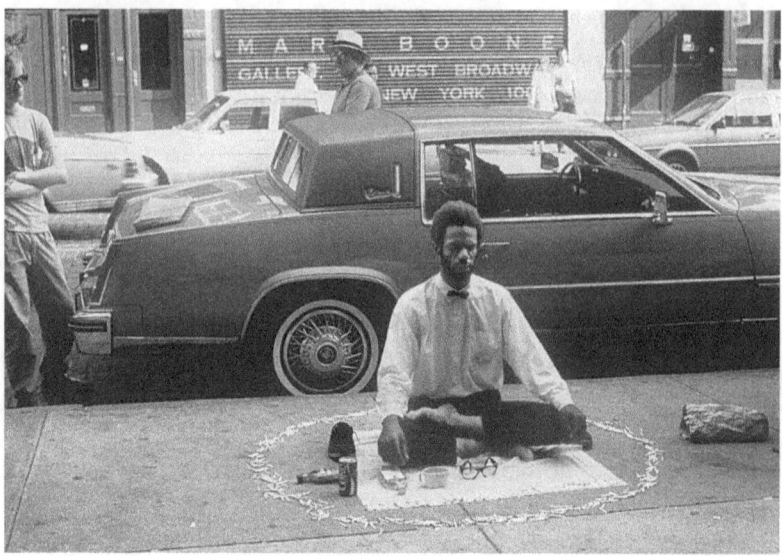

C.I William Pope.L, *Thunderbird Immolation*, street performance, New York (1978–80). Photo by Ellen LaForge, courtesy of William Pope.L.

and Coke together, never drinking a drop, and poured the mixture over himself," explains Stiles.[36] While the threat of self-immolation hovered, it never occurred. A museum administrator asked Pope.L to leave the premises before the decision concerning his self-destruction was made.

In *Thunderbird Immolation*, Pope.L makes the art world look at the racist apparatus designed to consummate the equation of lack (not having, absence) with black. Lack, in the context of *Thunderbird Immolation*, lingers and resolves at the bottom of Thunderbird, the cheap wine Ernest Gallo funneled into inner-city neighborhoods during the 1970s.[37] As Pope.L reveals in the memories of his childhood and the men with whom he shared worlds, "violence, drugs and alcohol, crime, lies, different forms of abdication, and estrangement" only exacerbated the lack in black.[38] The exacerbation and extension of black lack rendered the absence and invisibility of black people the means for Gallo's economic end. In *Thunderbird Immolation*, Pope.L makes this life script visible, but with a difference. He neither drinks nor dies. Instead he threatens self-immolation.

Self-immolation, as defined by the *Merriam-Webster Online*, is the "deliberate and willing sacrifice of oneself often by fire."[39] Labeling his performance an immolation, Pope.L brilliantly enlists the energies of "the negative" in the enactment of an unconstrained life beyond the secular.

Michael Taussig writes, "When the human body, a nation's flag, money, or a public statue is defaced, a strange surplus of negative energy is likely to be aroused from within the defaced thing itself. It is now in a state of desecration, the closest many of us are going to get to the sacred in this modern world."[40] But in *Thunderbird Immolation*, the sacred remained despite the absence of desecration. By juxtaposing impending bodily violation with meditative transcendence, Pope.L demonstrates the ways that this "strange surplus of negative energy" opens up other ways of moving through and against a hypersecularized world.

Describing the event, Pope.L reflects,

> What is difficult to see from photos are the pourings. Every once in a while I'd pour wine over myself. Then go back to sitting. For the people on the street, perhaps for some, they were waiting for me to light myself up. Maybe, probably not since reconstituted wine isn't flammable. Maybe I was waiting for a light in them or a light inside myself. Drinking yourself to death and burning yourself to death are both modes of seeking. Seeking attention, seeking the ethereal, seeking absolution, seeking oblivion. No one ever says: he burned himself to oblivion. We do say: he drank himself into oblivion. Samadhi is not oblivion; it is a lively death that can be a kind of activism.[41]

Engaged in the Buddhist meditative practice of samadhi, Pope.L seeks a liveliness in (and beyond) social death. More specifically, *Thunderbird Immolation*'s sacred restaging of value allows the black body to move beyond the murderous wanderings of others' desires. In this way, Pope.L roams even while nervous officials contemplate his arrest and a certain four blocks remain a perilous passage.

Somewhere within the "strange surplus of negative energy" other pathways for movement coalesce.[42] For Pope.L, a proximity to lack, death, and desecration suggests not the end of movement but rather its new beginning. A seeking. A way of moving through the world unbound by attachment. Similarly, Piper's Everything series proposes that devastation might potentiate other ways of ambling through the world. More nearly, Piper queries the status of life and identity after everything has been taken away. What remains? How might devastated life recover in the only movement left? If it's the case that wandering describes the kind of movement possible when material and geographical attachments are gone, how might it restore the very life broken by those attachments in the first place? As with

Pope.L, Piper's Everything poses these questions at the intersection of life's devastation and the new ambulatory possibilities engendered by loss.

Adrian Piper's Everything

To begin, in its only showing at the Elizabeth Dee Gallery in New York City and from the gallery website view, the Everything series appears sparse and almost empty. Looking at the images of post-Katrina New Orleans, *Everything #9.1* (see figure C.2), on the gallery's website, for example, one can paradoxically discern the particulars of that racialized and classed devastation as nonparticular, scrubbed-down, and hard-to-see photographs. Granted, the difficulty in seeing is partially a function of experiencing an exhibit, outside of its time and immediacy, via the World Wide Web. Still, the artist's scrubbing down of the images with "steel and foam rubber sponges" indicates the way that loss corrodes one's relationship to everyday life. In her artist statement, Piper writes,

> The *Everything* series originated in my need to come to terms intuitively with the loss of my illusions about the United States, both personally and politically. The penetration of illusion through analysis and perceptual discrimination, and the management of desire, satisfaction, and loss through meditation form part of my yogic practice. The defining task that unites all of the work in all media that constitute this open-ended series is to situate the text, Everything will be taken away, in a wide variety of contexts, in a wide variety of media and in conjunction with a wide variety of images, in order to examine how these different visual contexts change its meaning.[43]

The corrosive power of loss, which manifests as (though is not reducible to) the violent repudiation of desire, emerges in another set of representations in Piper's Everything series, this time concerning the case of Megan Williams. Williams was a twenty-one-year-old black woman from West Virginia who was brutally raped, tortured, and held in captivity by six white people in September 2007. Using text from the *International Herald Tribune*'s article "More Charges Filed in Black Woman's Torture Case" (September 19, 2007), Piper created a sheet of wallpaper. Covering an entire gallery wall (152 by 198 inches) in gray scale with 10 percent saturation of text (barely legible), Piper printed out the details of Williams's story (*Everything #19.1*; see figure C.3). Centered in the middle of that wall was a small oval mirror, with the words "Everything Will Be Taken Away" printed in gold leaf on top of Plexiglas (*Everything #4*).[44]

From the story of that incomprehensible crime—the set of brutalizing acts of violence driven by the criminally racist, sexist, and economic desire to "finish" Williams off—Piper creates a negative imprint.[45] On one level, the negativity of the imprint indexes a crisis in understanding, where the faintness of the text's color joins the unknowable violence of the crime. On another level, the secondary negativity moves through the yogic rhetoric of renunciation; the question concerning who one is after everything's been taken away shifts from being hypothetical to heartbreakingly real. What happened to Williams shoves this inquiry to the end of philosophy.

Still, Piper's Everything suggests the plenitude of the negative, the fullness of movement beyond the realms of material and moral scarcity. This might be what Pope.L refers to as a liveliness in death or, more nearly, a liveliness after loss. Indeed, after what happened to Williams, Piper created another kind of life in the negative, the inverse, and the other side and beyond, naming it Everything. For Piper, the critic Fred Moten explains, "here is an abundance—in abundance—of the present—in abundance of affirmation in abundance of the negative, in abundance of disappearance."[46] In his discussion on the (im)possibly utopic audiovisuality of Emmett Till (the crime and the famous picture of his violated body), Moten describes the other side of loss. On the other side of what's there—the visual, concrete fact of Till's murder by white supremacists—exists a performative domain constituted by the cries, moans, and whistles of desire and pain. The sound moves before and after the photo, the "inappropriable ecstatics that goes along with this aesthetics."[47] This sound of Till and those who listened to the abundance of life beneath the visual fact of his violation holds utopic promise. What's beneath the visual, the "inappropriable" domain of what can't be harmed, is the place where Piper's Everything too bears utopic potential. The "inappropriable," what can't be taken away, is where Piper's Everything, and perhaps also Williams, can roam privately.

For Piper, as with Pope.L, the open terrain of meditation, at the intersection of performance and philosophy, provides the unsurveillable ground for querying "the lives we want for ourselves."[48] In particular, a performative and philosophical engagement with yoga facilitates the material detachment essential to such inquiry. Further, as a brahmacharin yogi who is also a Kantian philosopher, Piper believes in the kinetic possi-

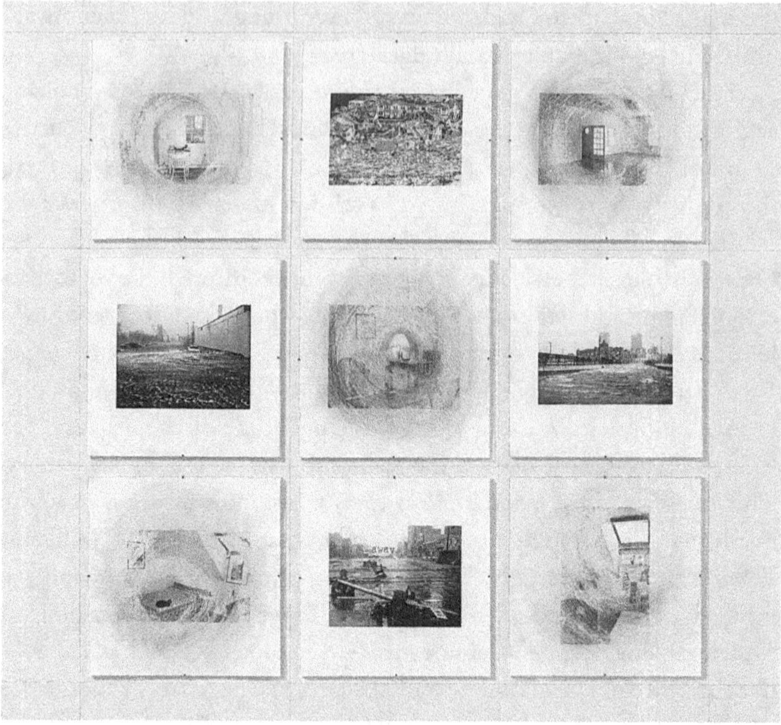

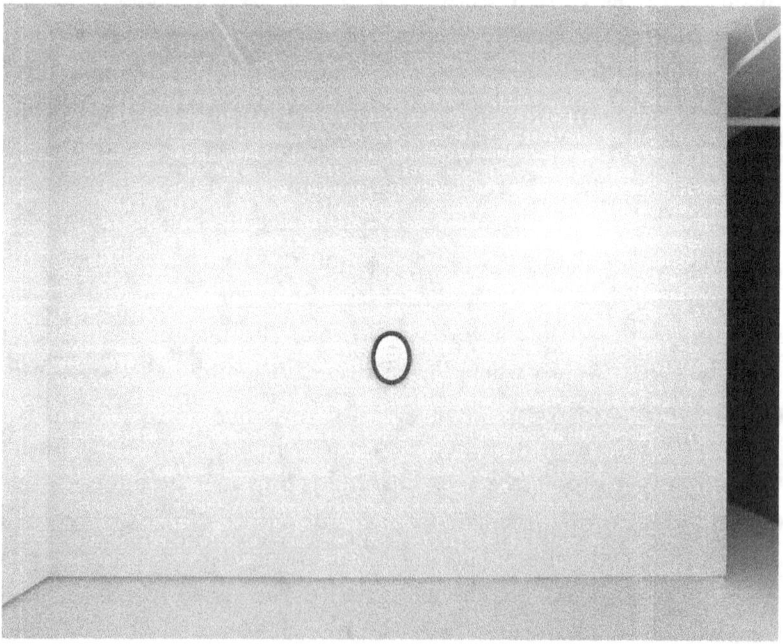

bilities offered by bodily and egoic transcendence. She believes that there are movements and paths toward freedom engendered by a regenerative relinquishing of secular ground, or roads that still glimmer even after everything's been taken away. Writing about her yogic practice, Piper argues,

> In yogic meditation (samyama) our aim is to be able to regard the attributes and experiences of the ego-self from the perspective of a transpersonal witness-consciousness (or atman in Vedanta, the philosophical view that, together with yogic practice, is first described in the Upanishads). This perspective has many benefits—among them a sense of detached amusement and compassion about one's own flaws and failures, and a keener and more pervasive sense of the tragicomic aspects of the human condition. It is also extremely useful in approaching and using for expressive or didactic purposes certain subject matter that others might regard as overtly personal or private—specifically that which concerns race or gender identity. One result of my meditation practice is that those attributes that do not seem all that personal or private to me. To me they are extremely superficial and generalized aspects of my external self-presentation that do not define at a deep level the person I am. . . . So the injunction to practice brahmacharya requires us to make a choice: either to affirm certain of our deeply instilled Western values and simply reject this one yogic prescription as incompatible with the lives we want for ourselves; or else to reexamine and revise those values in order to make room for it.[49]

For Piper, "the Western standards of power, achievement, acquisition, health, beauty or personal charisma" keep the secular self bound to the world of the senses.[50] Though such a world yields pleasure, it also carries the poten-

---

c.2 (*opposite above*) Adrian Piper, *Everything #9.1*, 2005–7. Nine ink-jet photo prints: five wash-scrubbed with steel and foam rubber sponges, four overprinted with text. Dimensions variable. Collection of the Adrian Piper Research Archive Foundation Berlin. © APRA Foundation Berlin.

c.3 (*opposite below*) Adrian Piper, *Everything #19.1*, 2008. Wall installation, light-gray painted wall with white wall text. Dimensions variable. Collection of the Adrian Piper Research Foundation Berlin. © APRA Foundation Berlin. Adrian Piper, *Everything #4*, 2004. Oval looking glass overlaid with oval Plexiglas with gold-leaf-engraved text in traditional oval mahogany frame, edition of eight. 15.125 by 10.125 inches (38.4 by 25.7 cm) oval. Collection of the Adrian Piper Research Archive Foundation Berlin. © APRA Foundation Berlin.

tial of disappointment and dissatisfaction. Instead of a worldly existence governed by secular desire, Piper argues that a renunciation of such attachments allows one to "move through and beyond the world of the senses[,] . . . to put that world to the use for which it is meant: to deepen our insight into the nature of ultimate reality, and prepare ourselves for final union with it."[51] The movement described here is a wandering, an unbound movement untethered to the constraints of external maps and scripts.

Interestingly, Piper's devotion to this open, unbound movement and the "transpersonal" Vedic ethical system that supports it—one that renders the "clarity, intricacy, and vibrational depth of each person and thing . . . an object of fascination, astonishment, and unique and inestimable value"— also connects with her Kantianism.[52] In the introduction to the first volume of her *Rationality and the Structure of the Self* (2013), Piper idealizes a Kantian mode of rationality also named as transpersonalism. She "describe[s] these principles as transpersonal because they direct our attention beyond the preoccupations and interests of the ego-self, including its particular, defining set of moral and theoretical convictions; and apply in equal measure to oneself and others. Transpersonal principles thus often require us to transcend considerations—even principled considerations— of personal comfort, convenience, profit, or gratification, whether acting on our behalf or on behalf of another."[53]

Instructively, Piper's engagement with Kant partially emerges out of her yogic practice, brahmacharya. For Piper, brahmacharya, translated as "walking with god," becomes possible in the rejection of secularized, egoic, and material interests along with an ethical refusal to exploit others as the grounds for one's own movement.[54] Further, more generally speaking, the renunciative gesture at the heart of yogic mediation dislocates freedom's path from the secular's kinetic constraints. Put another way, if the secular grounds of "power [and] achievement" no longer anchor and straighten out one's movement, then freedom itself is formed on another terrain and through another philosophically performative engagement.[55] Indeed, this might be precisely where and how Pope.L anticipated that light—the light in himself and others—to emerge.

Returning to Piper, the resistance to secular straightening is achieved through a simultaneously open and disciplined movement. Piper's walks with God are inherently subject to errancy. In a formative meditative experience engendered by brahmacharya, for example, Piper recalls, "Kinesthetically, there was no 'place' where 'I' was 'sitting' 'upright,' because all those spatial indices of location and orientation ceased to exist."[56] By walking with God, Piper seems to cede directional and self-control to another force, allowing herself to wander into the unpredictable lines of otherworldly guidance. Profoundly, this mode of philosophical performance resonates with Sojourner Truth's own method—where truth itself coalesces in and as the divinely guided sojourn. In this way, and in the philosophical tradition instantiated by Truth, Piper's reason forms in wandering.

At the same time, however, an antiwandering ethos also moves in Piper's philosophical performances. Even as her idealization of restraint in the contexts of yoga and Kantian rationalism engenders other forms and terrains of movement, the nature of that movement is often circumscribed. In particular, Piper's writings on Kantian and Humean rationalisms advance her critique of Hume's waywardness in favor of Kant's fundamentally upright ethical practice.[57] For Piper, the chief difference between Kant's and Hume's enactments of rationality consists in their relation to desire: "Whereas Hume regarded the canons of theoretical reason as mere propositional objects of calculation and computation for maximizing the satisfaction of desire, Kant maintained that the principles of theoretical reason structure the self by supplying necessary conditions for its unity."[58] Put another way, Hume deployed reason instrumentally to serve his private desire, while Kant critiqued the fundamental irrationality of such a move. Moreover, according to Piper, Kant vigilantly guarded reason's inherent straight, upright course against desire's attempts to pull it astray.

Nevertheless, I maintain that Kant's wandering with desire and private interest formed (his notion of) reason's condition of possibility. In fact, Kant's representation of reason as simultaneously knowable island and unknowable sea juts against Piper's own figuration of reason as "buoyant device."[59] Further, Piper's critique of egocentric rationality's sometimes complicity with xenophobic practice unintentionally moves Kant away from the transpersonal rationalism that he's otherwise said to embody. As I argue in chapter 1, Kant betrays the transpersonal in his wayward musings on blackness, specifically, and racial Otherness, more broadly. In fact, his indictment of the alleged reckless impulsivity of racialized, gendered bodies depends on impulsivity as its very condition. What is more, Kant's support of reason's oceanic movement in his *Critique of Pure Reason* suggests that the condition of possibility of reason (and the ethics of transpersonalism it instantiates) requires that it be left back on the shore.

Returning to Piper, even though I'm not interested in resolving this contradiction and further believe that such resolution might enact a certain straightening that this book otherwise avoids, the contradiction itself is important. The dialectic between wandering and straightness in Piper's philosophy queries whether and how the Enlightenment can offer paths for freedom that are neither trespassive nor governable by secular desire. Generally speaking, this inquiry forms a recurrent tide of the book, rising and falling with every philosophical act and innovation, every wandering. Even though Piper's writings on Kantian rationalism ascribe to the notion that the tide itself can be governed, the philosophy enacted in her art series Everything dreams of a sea beyond the current.

Put another way, while a certain level of restraint moves in her yogic philosophy, the simultaneous openness engendered by self-discipline suggests restraint's errant potential. More precisely, the movement beyond self and material desire made possible by a certain kind of spiritualized ethical performance at once releases the body from its entrenchment within the egoic paths of others while enlarging the kinesthetic possibilities of the self beyond the body. Such corporeal transgressions within the straightened-out world are wanderings—unrestrained movements that sacrally replenish what the secularized trespasses of others have taken away.

What is more, wandering enlarges the "free state" in ways that are private and invisible, unpredictable and holy.[60] Pope.L's living death. Piper's walks with God. Weems's stares at the sea. Even as these artists publically record their meditative acts using writing and photography, the very act of meditative reflection evades capture. This isn't to say that the act can't be interrupted and called something else. In fact, as I've argued with respect to Adrienne Kennedy, such private drifts figure as psychotic, inefficient, and unproductive for post-Enlightenment-minded spectators. But as processes, though, reveries, meditations, and daydreams constitute forms of movement that survive even if interrupted or if the wanderer's physical action suffers arrest. Moreover, for all three artists, an interior kinesis, what remains unseen in the visual documentation of the performance, might just provide, following Pope.L, the light they were waiting for. Concerning Weems, such (interior and exterior) kinesis became essential for her own psychic survival. Speaking with the critic Dawoud Bey about her 2006 Roaming project, she recalls: "When I first decided to return to Rome, I wanted to relax a little bit because I was working very hard and I knew that I needed a mental *break* before I had a mental *breakdown*. I decided to leave the country and come to a place that I knew and felt comfortable in."[61]

Weems's interest in architecture and power motivates the Roaming series. But, at the same time, an openness to the sublime moves alongside these secularized meditations. This openness, which arguably could be tied to Weems's understanding of self as a "woman who yearns," and as someone who needs a mental break, enlarges the roaming at work in the series.[62] Indeed, given the interplay between scenes of walking and crawling, staring and stillness, Weems's Roaming suggests a powerful movement beyond the physical. A domain constituted by phantasmatic wanderings into a world just beyond this one. A kind of movement that might just provide that light and the break she was waiting for.

Carrie Mae Weems

Significantly, the light and the break exist as potential and invisible experience. For Weems, the trip to Italy constituted a mental break, of which Roaming was a part; the nature and shape of this break, however, resists documentation. Indeed, there is a kind of cool contradiction in Roaming, the paradoxical absence of visible motion. While Roaming includes photographs that suggest physical ambulation, the body's kinesis remains fixed by the circumstances of form. There are also other photographs that indicate a still body, one that gazes out at windows and at the sea. But this isn't to argue for roaming's absence. Rather, following Moten, there's an abundance of life that surrounds the pictures. An abundance of movement, the "inappropriable ecstatics," at the heart of unseen roamings.[63] Such roaming might be before and ahead of the physical act, particularly in images where the photographed body seems to stand still.

What is more, the identity of the roamer also errantly moves into and out of the visible scene. She is Weems and not Weems at the same time:

> I call her my muse—but it's safe to say that she's more than one thing. She's an alter-ego. *My* alter-ego, yes . . . this woman can stand in for me and for you; she can stand in for the audience, she leads you into history. She's a witness and a guide. . . . She's shown me a great deal about the world and about myself, and I'm grateful to her. Carrying a tremendous burden, she is a black woman leading me through the trauma of history. I think it's very important that as a black woman she's engaged with the world around her; she's engaged with history, she's engaged with looking, with *being*. She's a guide into circumstances seldom seen.[64]

The wanderer Weems describes, Roaming's lone black woman in a black dress, is an inherently multiple self. Along with the characters of Kennedy's plays, these black women wanderers shape-shift, guiding themselves and others into "circumstances seldom seen." While the enactment of multiplicity subverts and discredits the post-Enlightenment idealization of a self-same (undifferentiated, transparent, singular) subject, the refiguration of guidance itself performs a similar labor. On the one hand, this internal movement—the private wanderings of various desires, spirits, and selves—guides the broken down traveler out of harm's way. On the other hand, the muse's ability to lead people into history potentiates another modality of healing. This is to say, even as leading itself suggests a linear, followable movement, the leader's endless shape-shifting undermines such followability. More specifically, in Weems's musings on the alter ego, she is simultaneously witness and guide, standing in for herself and others. As with Piper's renunciation of a discrete "I" in her walks with God, Weems's roaming figure moves between and beyond selves, stories, and places. Despite the photographic form's empirical seduction, who and where she is moves outside an arrestable range.

Such resistance to kinetic constraint also meanders in the muse's engagement with the state. In Roaming, just as the body in the photos figures as a "lesser subject" by the state, other unsurveillable movements—private roaming visions and meditations—seemingly enlarge the terrain of living. For example, in one image the roamer stands in front of Rome's Palazzo dei Congressi (see figure C.4). Her back is toward the viewer and her long black dress flows behind her, almost entirely hiding her legs. Casting a tiny shadow to her left, the muse looks tremendously small in front of the larger-than-life institution. The building itself fills the entire width of the photo, its pillars running past the image's frame. The striking disparity between opposites—light and dark, small and large—attends to Weems's interest in the phenomenological (in addition to the ideological) reduction of the citizen's size by the state. Elsewhere in the series we see the same traveling figure climbing aged staircases (see figure C.5), ambling near the Pyramid of Cestius and the tomb of Remus (see figure C.6), and strolling down pillared hallways (see figure C.7).

At the same time, however, the standing in front of and strolling alongside and within these architectures visualizes much more than the violent distinction between subject and monument. Weems remarks, "I've been standing in front of all of these monuments and palazzos, thinking about questions of power."[65] The standing body is also a roaming, musing body; this philosophically performative statement by Weems makes that clear. What this also suggests is a realm of phantasmatic movement inside an oppressive state; stillness and contemplation arguably disrupt the fetish of capitalist productivity at the heart of "straight time."[66] Someone who's looking at the building or sitting on the sidewalk, in Pope.L's case, isn't working. In fact, according to some interpretations of law, that person is in danger of committing an offense.

Moreover, what might be figured by the state as disruptive or nonproductive is differently meaningful for the meditating subject. To be clear, this is not an attempt to know what the subject of these photographs is thinking. The ethical interests of this project agitate against that kind of musing and the long histories of imperial violence that sanctioned such a maneuver. Still, even while it remains impossible for me to "know" the extent or limits of the roaming undertaken in the series, I cannot presume its absence when the body seemingly stands still. As I've argued throughout this book, for bodies under severe constraint, wandering offers other phantasmatic possibilities for unsurveillable movement.

In that spirit, I end with two images from the series. The first is of the muse studying a wall in Niki de Saint Phalle's sculpture *Kitchen in the Empress* (see figure C.8). The room, made of beveled glass, creates the illusion that the muse moves within a large mirror. However, this doesn't mean that she is projected, reproduced, and represented from a million different angles; if there are reflections, they are partial, muted, and blurred. Instead, the only one really able to enter into the cut glass and gaze at his or her own reflection is the muse herself. In this way, what the mirror holds and what it opens up—the relevance of this room to roaming—belongs to the woman gazing in glass and not the one glancing at the photo.

Similarly, the second image of the same woman staring at the sea evokes only to render impossible any understanding of this image's relation to the series (see figure C.9). In many ways this second image is the (in)visible accompaniment to the book itself. In it the roamer stands on the beach, her body turned away from the viewer. In scale, as with the other images, the roaming body is dwarfed by the world around her; in this particular image, the shore and ocean loom large while the woman who stands and stares seems tiny in relation. Historically speaking, this image tells many stories—stories of oceans and shores, stories of black life made to hover in between. Reason and unreason, sand and sea, presence and

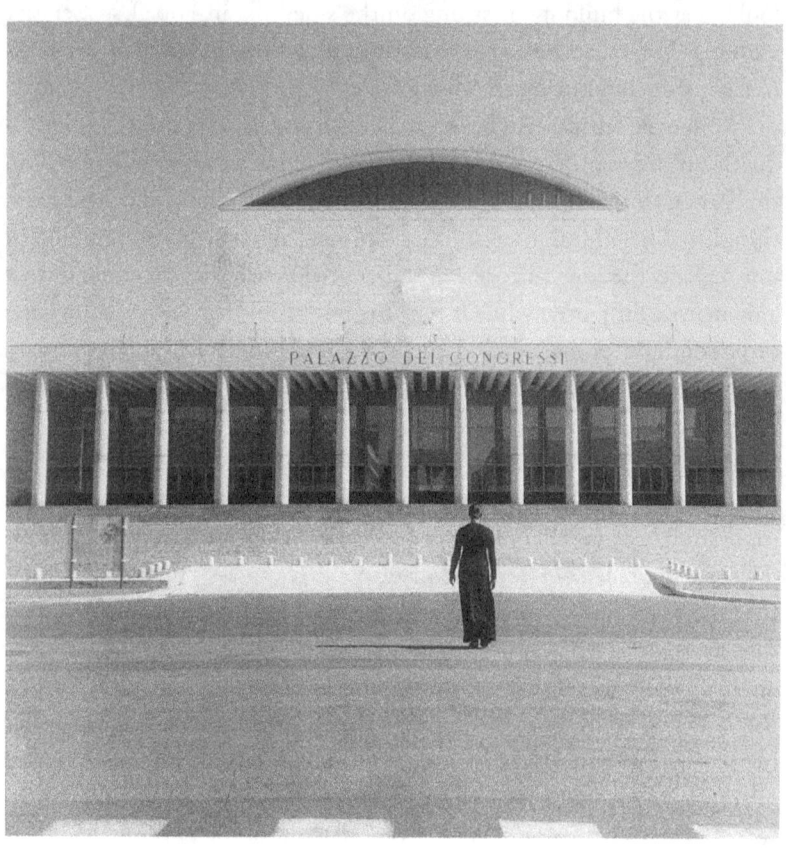

c.4 Carrie Mae Weems,
Palazzo dei Congressi—
Mussolini's Rome, 2006.
From the series Roaming.
© Carrie Mae Weems.
Image courtesy of
Carrie Mae Weems and
Jack Shainman Gallery,
New York.

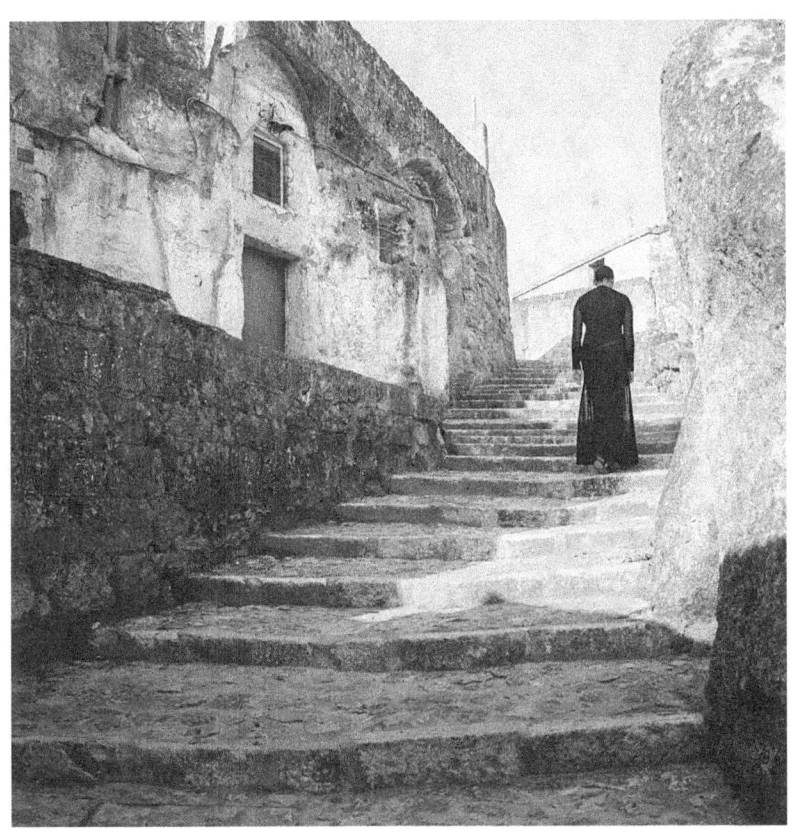

c.5 Carrie Mae Weems,
*The Rock of Ages—Ancient
Rome*, 2006. From the series
Roaming. © Carrie Mae
Weems. Image courtesy
of Carrie Mae Weems and
Jack Shainman Gallery,
New York.

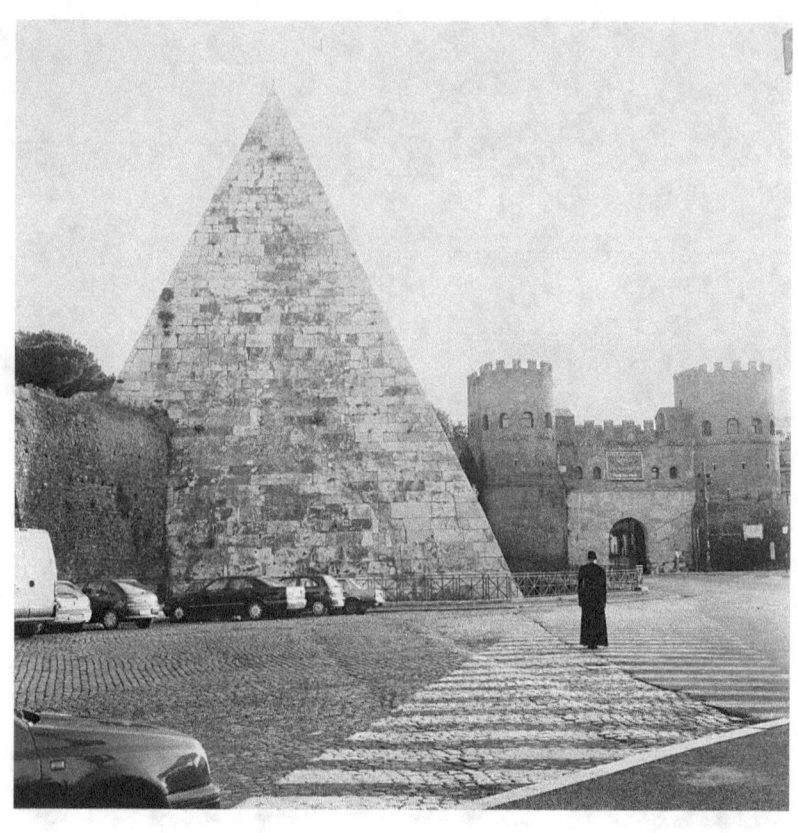

c.6 Carrie Mae Weems,
*Pyramids of Rome—Ancient
Rome*, 2006. From the series
Roaming. © Carrie Mae
Weems. Image courtesy
of Carrie Mae Weems and
Jack Shainman Gallery,
New York.

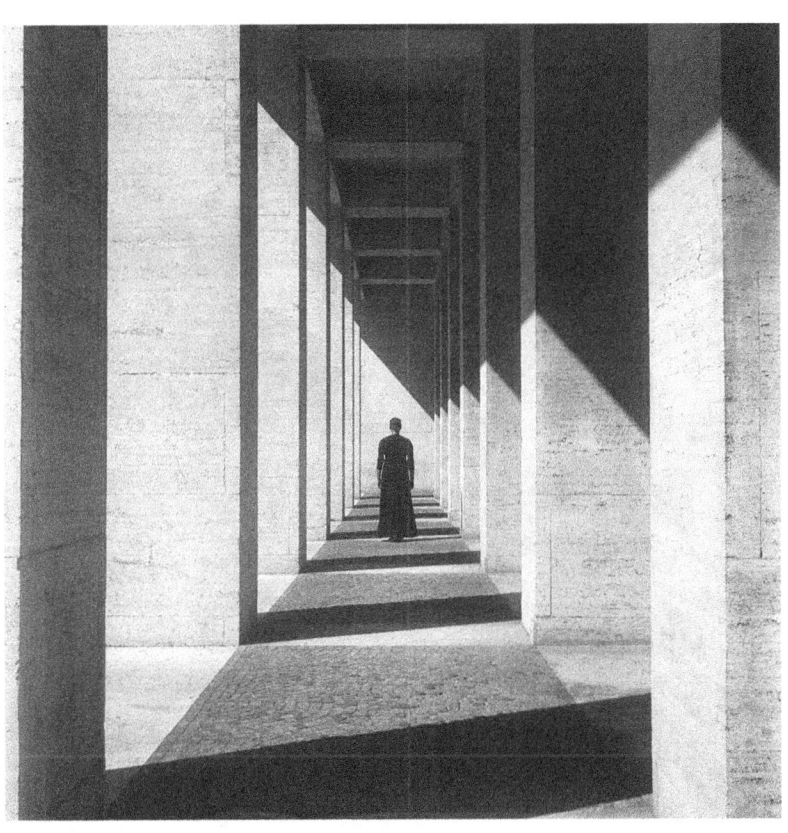

c.7 Carrie Mae Weems,
Modernism—EUR1—
Mussolini's Rome, 2006.
From the series Roaming.
© Carrie Mae Weems.
Image courtesy of
Carrie Mae Weems and
Jack Shainman Gallery,
New York.

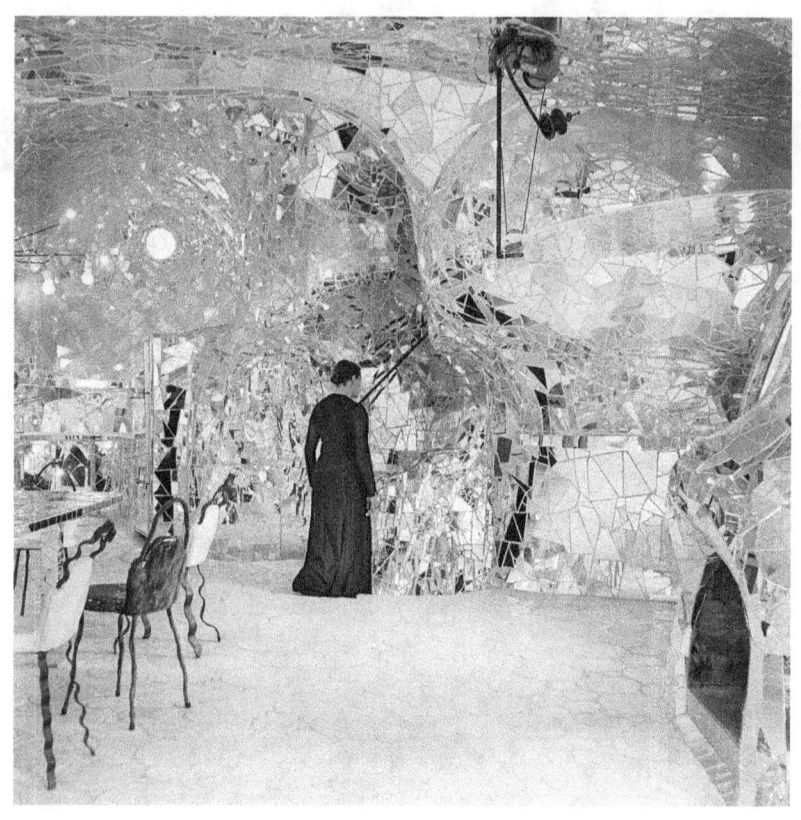

c.8 Carrie Mae Weems,
*Nikki's Place—Mussolini's
Rome*, 2006. From the series
Roaming. © Carrie Mae
Weems. Image courtesy
of Carrie Mae Weems and
Jack Shainman Gallery,
New York.

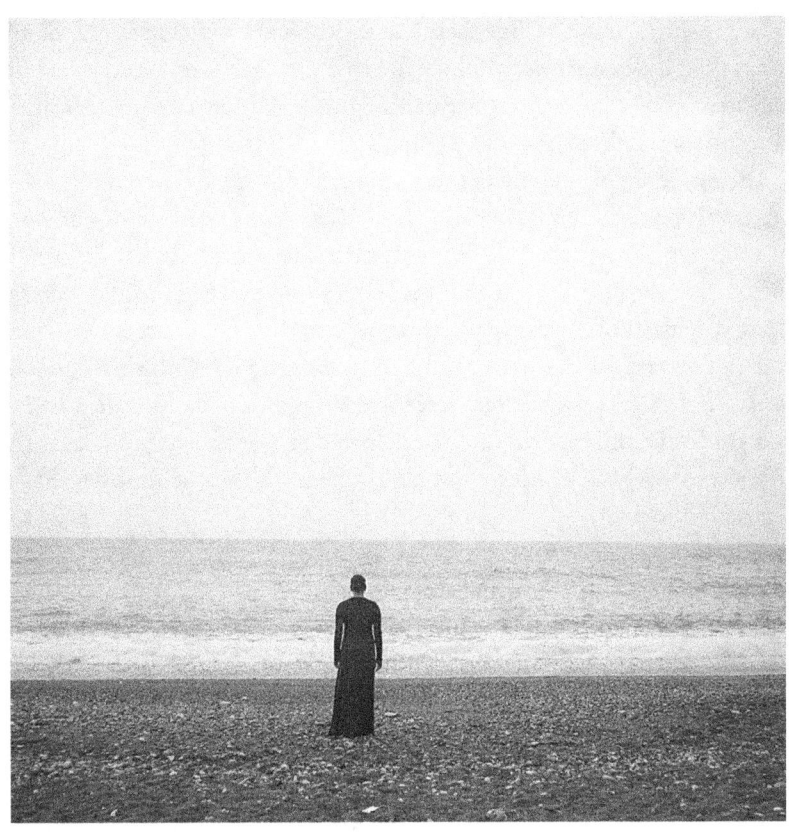

C.9 Carrie Mae Weems,
*A Broad and Expansive
Sky—Ancient Rome*, 2006.
From the series Roaming.
© Carrie Mae Weems.
Image courtesy of
Carrie Mae Weems and
Jack Shainman Gallery,
New York.

absence, life and death. But these stories aren't the only ones, and, more than that, life doesn't easily follow the course of one story or even several stories. Further, even though stories might be written, composed on the sea and on the shore, that doesn't imply their readability.

Once more, the nature of the roaming in this scene is not available to external understanding. However, this resistance to understanding doesn't preclude its possibility. If there is a world made during stares at the sea, it belongs to the one who gazes. If there is a world made in the glimmering haze produced by beveled glass, it belongs to the one who sees herself in the mirror and not the one prohibited from entering. With regard to the artist herself, it's possible that Weems recovered from her private exhaustion in Rome and that roaming participated in that recovery. But, as with the wanderer of her photos, the philosophization of such movement is better left to her.

In the end, all of these artists theorize the potential of another world, moving underneath, above, and around this one. Through roaming and mediation—sacred and sublime drifts elsewhere—their art potentiates other terrains where black life can amble unharmed. These are terrains where bodies are no longer the grounds for others' becomings, others' vicious expressions of neoimperial, homophobic, transphobic, racist, sexist, classist, and ableist desire. Importantly, in all of their art, making one's way enacts alternative, unsurveillable paths, providing safer ground for an unarrestable movement—a movement that persists even if the violences of a post-Enlightenment secular state decide that those four blocks remain off-limits.

As a mode of resistance, wandering is a philosophical performance that becomes itself outside of surveillance, outside the four-block restrictions of others' visions and fears of "dangerous dancing." Put another way, on the other side of stop and frisk, untravelable blocks, violent stares, and vicious (mis)readings, wandering still might get you home. This isn't to say that we should stop agitating against the secularized, post-Enlightenment criminalization of black wandering. Rather, we ought not presume that the arrested roamer hasn't already initiated that critique. In that person's roaming, rambling, communing with the invisible, and musing on a piece of glass, philosophies of freedom are innovated and reimagined. Somewhere in between the roamer's eyes and the ocean, some kind of undisclosed movement might very well save her life.

NOTES

Introduction

1. Gayl Jones, *Corregidora* (Boston: Beacon Press, 1975), 132.
2. G. Jones, *Corregidora*, 132.
3. Richard Schechner, *Performance Studies: An Introduction* (New York: Routledge, 2002), 5.
4. Joseph Roach and Janelle Reinelt, "Introduction," in *Critical Theory and Performance*. (Ann Arbor: University of Michigan Press, 2007), 5.
5. André Lepecki, "Mutant Enunciations," *TDR* 50, no. 4 (Winter 2006): 19.
6. G. Jones, *Corregidora*, 61.
7. Michel de Certeau, *The Practice of Everyday Life* (Berkeley: University of California Press, 1988), 97–98; E. Beneviste, *Problèmes de linquistique générale* (Paris: Seiul Points, 1974), 11, 79–88.
8. Susan Leigh Foster, "Walking and Other Choreographic Tactics: Danced Inventions of Theatricality and Performativity," *SubStance* 31, nos. 2 and 3 (2002): 129.
9. Talal Asad, *Formations of the Secular: Christianity, Islam, Modernity* (Stanford, CA: Stanford University Press, 2003), 78–79; de Certeau, *The Practice of Everyday Life*.
10. Jayna Brown, *Babylon Girls: Black Women Performers and the Shaping of the Modern* (Durham, NC: Duke University Press, 2008), 60.
11. Kolender v. Lawson, 461 U.S. 352 (1983). See the transcribed ruling of this Supreme Court case at the Legal Institute Information Institute, Cornell University Law School, http://www.law.cornell.edu/supremecourt/text/461/352.
12. Denise Ferreira da Silva, *Toward a Global Theory of Race* (Minneapolis: University of Minnesota Press, 2007), xxxix.
13. André Lepecki, *Exhausting Dance: Performance and the Politics of Movement* (New York: Routledge, 2006), 13.
14. Da Silva's work is crucial in my thinking about the racialized figurations of the post-Enlightenment subject and the ways that these figurations index kinetic investments: "Although the white female subject has been written in domesticity (as wife and mother) in the patriarchal (moral) domain, which has kept her outside the public (male) domain, the female racial subaltern has consistently been written to inhabit the *public* (non-European

or non-white) place produced by scientific strategies where her body is immediately made available to a transparent male desire but where her desire (passion, love, consent) is always already mediated by her double affectability. The result is that she is constructed as the subject of lust; hers is a dangerously unproductive will because it is guided by nothing but that which human beings possess as being ruled not even by the 'laws of [divine] nature, the preservation of life.'" Da Silva, *Toward a Global Theory of Race*, 266 (brackets in the original).

15. Dan Stormer and Paul Bernstein, "The Impact of *Kolender v. Lawson* on Law Enforcement and Minority Groups," *Hastings Constitutional Law Quarterly* 12 (1984): 105.

16. Stormer and Bernstein, "The Impact of *Kolender v. Lawson* on Law Enforcement and Minority Groups," 115.

17. Lepecki, *Exhausting Dance*, 14; my emphasis.

18. Lepecki, *Exhausting Dance*, 14.

19. Johannes Fabian, *Out of Our Minds: Reason and Madness in the Exploration of Central Africa* (Berkeley: University of California Press, 2000), 8.

20. Sankhar Muthu, *Enlightenment against Empire* (Princeton, NJ: Princeton University Press, 2003), 85.

21. Michel Foucault, *The Order of Things: An Archaeology of the Human Sciences* (New York: Vintage, 1994), 342.

22. Sylvia Wynter, "The Pope Must Have Been Drunk, the King of Castile a Madman: Culture as Actuality, and the Caribbean Rethinking Modernity," in *The Reordering of Culture: Latin America, the Caribbean, and Canada; In the Hood*, ed. Alvina Ruprecht and Cecilia Taiana (Ontario: Carleton University Press, 1995), 17.

23. Alexander G. Weheliye, "After Man," *American Literary History* 20, nos. 1–2 (Spring/Summer 2008): 322.

24. Da Silva, *Toward a Global Theory of Race*, 266.

25. This is a reference to a chapter name in Harriet Jacobs's *Incidents in the Life of a Slave Girl* (Orlando, FL: Harcourt Brace Jovanovich Publishers, 1973). The full title of the chapter is "A Perilous Passage in a Slave Girl's Life."

26. Wynter quoted in David Scott, "The Re-enchantment of Humanism: An Interview with Sylvia Wynter," *Small Axe* (September 2000): 165.

27. Hortense Spillers, "Mama's Baby, Papa's Maybe: An American Grammar Book," special issue, "Culture and Countermemory: The 'American' Connection," *Diacritics* 17, no. 2 (Summer 1987): 67.

28. Spillers, "Mama's Baby, Papa's Maybe," 78. Spillers is referring to a study by William Goodell discussed in Angela Davis's *Women, Race, and Class* (New York: Random House, 1981).

29. Saidiya V. Hartman, *Scenes of Subjection: Terror, Slavery, and Self-Making in Nineteenth-Century America* (Oxford: Oxford University Press, 1999), 26.

30. Wynter quoted in Scott, "The Re-enchantment of Humanism," 165.

31. Weheliye, "After Man," 323.

32. Hartman, *Scenes of Subjection*, 63.

33. Deborah Garfield, "Earwitness: Female Abolitionism, Sexuality, and *Incidents in the Life of a Slave Girl*," in *Harriet Jacobs and Incidents in the Life of a Slave Girl: New Critical Essays*, ed. Deborah Garfield and Rafia Zafar (Cambridge, UK: Cambridge University Press, 1996), 100.

34. Da Silva, *Toward a Global Theory of Race*, 110.

35. See Barbara Christian, "The Race for Theory," in *The Black Feminist Reader*, ed. Joy James and T. Denean Sharpley-Whiting (Oxford: Blackwell Publishing, 2000); and Audre Lorde, "Uses of the Erotic: The Erotic as Power," in *Sister Outsider: Essays and Speeches by Audre Lorde* (Berkeley, CA: The Crossing Press, 1984).

36. See Lorde's "Uses of the Erotic" and "Age, Race, Class, and Sex: Women Redefining Difference," in *Sister Outsider: Essays and Speeches by Audre Lorde* (Berkeley, CA: The Crossing Press, 1984).

37. Lorde, "Uses of the Erotic," 58.

38. Sharon Patricia Holland, *The Erotic Life of Racism* (Durham, NC: Duke University Press, 2012), 50.

39. Holland, *The Erotic Life of Racism*, 57.

40. Farah Jasmine Griffin, "That the Mothers May Soar and the Daughters May Know Their Names: A Retrospective of Black Feminist Literary Criticism," *Signs* 32, no. 2 (2007): 499; and Mae Henderson, "Speaking in Tongues: Dialogics and Dialectics and the Black Woman Writer's Literary Tradition," *African American Literary Theory: A Reader*, ed. Winston Napier (New York: New York University Press, 2000), 353.

41. M. Jacqui Alexander, *Pedagogies of Crossing: Meditations on Feminism, Sexual Politics, Memory, and the Sacred* (Durham, NC: Duke University Press, 2005), 320.

42. Katherine McKittrick, *Demonic Grounds: Black Women and the Cartographies of Struggle* (Minneapolis: University of Minnesota Press, 2006), 43.

43. Fred Moten, *In the Break: The Aesthetics of the Black Radical Tradition* (Minneapolis: University of Minnesota Press, 2003), 5.

44. Daphne Brooks, *Bodies in Dissent: Spectacular Performances of Race and Freedom, 1850–1910* (Durham, NC: Duke University Press, 2006), 8.

45. Willi Goetschel, "Epilogue: 'Land of Truth—Enchanting Name!' Kant's Journey at Home," in *The Imperialist Imagination: German Colonialism and Its Legacy*, ed. Sara Friedrichsmeyer, Sara Lennox, and Susanne Zantop (Ann Arbor: University of Michigan Press, 1998), 329.

46. Robert Bernasconi, "Who Invented the Enlightenment Concept of Race? Kant's Role in Enlightenment Construction of Race," in *Race: Blackwell Readings in Continental Philosophy*, ed. Robert Bernasconi (Malden, MA: Blackwell Publishers, 2001), 14.

47. Wynter quoted in Scott, "The Re-enchantment of Humanism," 120.

48. Fred Moten, "Knowledge of Freedom," *CR: The New Centennial Review* 4, no. 2 (2004): 274.

49. Hartman, *Scenes of Subjection*, 175.

50. David Kazanjian uses the term *black enlightenment* and connects its use to Seth Moglen, who deploys the term in his current work in progress. See David Kazanjian, *The Colonizing Trick: National Culture and Imperial Citizenship in Early America* (Minneapolis: University of Minnesota Press, 2003), 23.

Fred Moten describes appositional Enlightenment within the context of black radicalism. He writes, "The black radical tradition is in apposition to enlightenment. Appositional enlightenment is remixed, expanded, distilled, and radically faithful to the forces its encounters carry, break, and constitute. It's (the effect of) critique or rationalization unopposed to the deep revelation instantiated by a rupturing event of dis/appropriation, or the rapturous advent of an implicit but unprecedented freedom. It's the performance of something like a detour of Kant onto a Heideggerian path, a push toward a critical rhythm in which *Aufklärung* and *Lichtung* animate one another, in which the improvisation through their opposition is enacted in (interruptions of) passage, tone, pulse, phrase, silence. But the dark matter that is and that animates this tradition *sounds*, and so sounds *another* light that for both Kant and Heidegger, in the one's advocacy and in the other's avoidance, would remain unheard." Moten, "Knowledge of Freedom," 274–75.

51. Wynter quoted in Scott, "The Re-enchantment of Humanism," 165.

52. McKittrick, *Demonic Grounds*, x.

53. Weheliye, "After Man," 323.

54. Weheliye, "After Man," 323.

55. Sylvia Wynter, "Beyond Miranda's Meanings: Un/silencing the 'Demonic Ground' of Caliban's Woman," in *Out of the Kumbla: Caribbean Women and Literature*, ed. Carole Boyce Davies and Elaine Savory Fido (Trenton, NJ: Africa World Press, 1994), 356.

56. McKittrick, *Demonic Grounds*, xxiii.

57. De Certeau, *The Practice of Everyday Life*, 107.

58. De Certeau, *The Practice of Everyday Life*, 107.

59. De Certeau, *The Practice of Everyday Life*, 107.

60. Adrienne Kennedy, *Funnyhouse of a Negro*, in *Adrienne Kennedy: In One Act* (Minneapolis: University of Minnesota Press, Kennedy, 1988), 5.

61. Brooks, *Bodies in Dissent*, 135.

62. Kennedy, *Funnyhouse of a Negro*, 6.

63. Donna Haraway, "Ecce Homo, Ain't (Ar'n't) I a Woman, and Inappropriate/d Others: The Human in a Posthumanist Landscape," in *Feminists Theorize the Political*, ed. Joan Scott and Judith Butler (New York: Routledge, 1992), 87.

64. Fabian, *Out of Our Minds*, 8.

65. Da Silva, *Toward a Global Theory of Race*, 29.

66. Sharon Patricia Holland, *Raising the Dead: Readings of Death and (Black) Subjectivity* (Durham, NC: Duke University Press, 2000), 171.

67. Holland, *Raising the Dead*, 5.

68. Da Silva, *Toward a Global Theory of Race*, 30.

69. For example, according to Arun Saldanha, in his study of drugs, dance, and trance culture in Goa (in the late 1990s to the early 2000s), white participation in music, drug, and trance tourism (all variations of wandering) was motivated by a desire for transcendence. This desire for transcendence not only reinstantiated whiteness but also was accompanied by a figuration of Goa as unlivable. See Arun Saldanha, *Psychedelic Whiteness: Goa Trance and the Viscosity of Race* (Minneapolis: University of Minnesota Press, 2007).

70. McKittrick, *Demonic Grounds*, xxiii.

71. Eric Stanley, "Near Life, Queer Death: Overkill and Ontological Capture," *Social Text* 29, no. 2 (2011): 2.

One. Losing Their Heads

1. Rachel Kent, *Yinka Shonibare, MBE*, curator notes, Museum of African Art, Washington DC, November 10, 2009–March 7, 2010.

2. Denise Ferreira da Silva, *Toward a Global Theory of Race* (Minneapolis: University of Minnesota Press, 2007), xiv.

3. Da Silva, *Toward a Global Theory of Race*, xiii.

4. Da Silva, *Toward a Global Theory of Race*, 44.

5. Robert McRuer, "Composing Bodies; Or, De-composition: Queer Theory, Disability Studies, and Alternative Corporealities," *JAC* 24, no. 1 (2004): 51.

6. McRuer's discussion of the creative process, its relation to queerness and disability, is useful for my discussion of Enlightenment as a straightening project. See McRuer, "Composing Bodies," 57–58.

7. Joan Dayan, "Codes of Law and Bodies of Color," *New Literary History* 26, no. 2 (1995): 285. Dayan quotes from René Descartes, *Meditations on First Philosophy: With Selections from the Objections and Replies*, ed. John Cottingham, with an introduction by Bernard Williams (Cambridge, UK: Cambridge University Press, 1996), 59.

8. Dayan, "Codes of Law and Bodies of Color," 287.

9. The Code Noir emerged during the reign of Louis XIV in 1685. The Code Noir was a veritable instructional manual for the institutionalization of slavery in the colonies.

10. Dayan, "Codes of Law and Bodies of Color," 287.

11. This definition is from *The Oxford English Dictionary Online*, accessed February 11, 2014.

12. See C. L. R. James, *The Black Jacobins: Toussaint L'Ouverture and the San Domingo Revolution* (New York: Vintage, 1989); Paul Miller, *Elusive Origins: The Enlightenment in the Modern Caribbean Historical Imagination* (Charlottesville: University of Virginia Press, 2010); and David Scott, "Antinomies of Slavery, Enlightenment, and Universal History," *Small Axe* 14, no. 3 (2010): 152–62.

13. Scott, "Antinomies of Slavery," 153.

14. Robert Bernasconi, "Who Invented the Enlightenment Concept of Race? Kant's Role in the Enlightenment Construction of Race," in *Race: Blackwell Readings in Continental Philosophy*, ed. Robert Bernasconi (Malden, MA: Blackwell Publishers, 2001), 14.

15. Kant quoted in Pauline Kleingeld, "Kant's Second Thoughts on Race," *The Philosophical Quarterly* 57, no. 229 (2007): 573.

16. Gilles Deleuze, *Kant's Critical Philosophy: The Doctrine of the Faculties*, trans. Hugh Tomlinson (London: The Athlone Press, 1984), xii.

17. Deleuze, *Kant's Critical Philosophy*, 24.

18. Deleuze, *Kant's Critical Philosophy*, 24–25.

19. Deleuze, *Kant's Critical Philosophy*, 13.

20. Deleuze, *Kant's Critical Philosophy*, 14.

21. Deleuze, *Kant's Critical Philosophy*, 14.

22. Willi Goetschel, "Epilogue: 'Land of Truth—Enchanting Name!' Kant's Journey At Home," in *The Imperialist Imagination: German Colonialism and Its Legacy*, ed. Sara Friedrichsmeyer, Sara Lennox, and Susanne Zantop (Ann Arbor: University of Michigan Press, 1998), 329.

23. Miller, *Elusive Origins*, 163.

24. Miller, *Elusive Origins*, 132; Scott, "Antinomies of Slavery," 156.

25. Curtis Bowman, "Kant and the Project of Enlightenment," unpublished manuscript, University of Pennsylvania, 2001, accessed April 15, 2012. http://www.alphasolutionsgrp.com/Kant%20and%20the%20Project%20of%20Enlightenment.pdf, 2–3.

26. Bowman, "Kant and the Project of Enlightenment," 6.

27. Immanuel Kant, *Observations on the Feeling of the Beautiful and Sublime*, trans. John T. Goldthwait (Berkeley: University of California Press, 1960), 75.

28. Da Silva, *Toward a Global Theory of Race*, xxxix.

29. Jean-Jacques Rousseau, *The Social Contract*, trans. Maurice Cranston (New York: Penguin, 1968), 49.

30. Susan Buck-Morss, "Hegel and Haiti," *Critical Inquiry* 26, no. 4 (Summer 2000): 830. See also Charles Mills, *The Racial Contract* (Ithaca, NY: Cornell University Press).

31. Rousseau, *The Social Contract*, 50. The internal contradictions, of which he is aware, begin to show up in Rousseau's writings on the family: "Man's first law is to watch over his own preservation; his first care he owes to himself; and as soon as he reaches the age of reason, he becomes the only judge of the best means to preserve himself; he becomes his own master. The family may therefore perhaps be seen as the first model of political societies: the head of the state bears the image of the father, the people the image of his children, and all, being born free and equal, surrender their freedom only when they see advantage in doing so. The only difference is that in the family, a father's love for his children repays him for the care he bestows on them, while in the state, where the ruler can have no such feeling for his people, the pleasure of commanding must take the place of love" (50–51).

32. Rousseau, *The Social Contract*, 55.

33. Rousseau, *The Social Contract*, 62.

34. Rousseau, *The Social Contract*, 60.

35. Immanuel Kant, *Critique of Pure Reason*, trans. Norman Kent Smith (New York: Macmillan and Co., 1965), 411.

36. Fred Moten's "Knowledge of Freedom" has helped my thinking about the anxiety around lawlessness in the Enlightenment. Fred Moten, "Knowledge of Freedom," CR: *The New Centennial Review* 4, no. 2 (2004).

37. Rousseau, *The Social Contract*, 32.

38. Maurice Cranston, translator's introduction to Rousseau, *The Social Contract*, 32.

39. Mills, *The Racial Contract*, 47.

40. Rousseau, *The Social Contract*, 82.

41. Buck-Morss, "Hegel and Haiti," 822.

42. Jean-Jacques Rousseau, *The Confessions*, trans. J. M. Cohen (New York: Penguin, 1953), 50–51.

43. Rousseau, *The Confessions*, 52.

44. Rousseau, *The Confessions*, 71–73.

45. Rousseau, *The Confessions*, 75.

46. Gayatri Spivak, *A Critique of Postcolonial Reason: Toward a History of the Vanishing Present* (Cambridge, MA: Harvard University Press, 1999), 21.

47. Rousseau, *The Confessions*, 113.

48. Rousseau, *The Confessions*, 113.

49. Jean-Jacques Rousseau, *Reveries of a Solitary Walker*, trans. Peter France (New York: Penguin Books, 1979), 30.

50. Rousseau, *Reveries of a Solitary Walker*, 37.

51. Rousseau, *Reveries of a Solitary Walker*, 38–39.

52. Gilles Deleuze and Félix Guattari, *A Thousand Plateaus: Capitalism and Schizophrenia*, trans. Brian Massumi (Minneapolis: University of Minnesota Press, 1987), 259.

53. Akira Lippitt, *Electric Animal: Toward a Rhetoric of Wildlife* (Minneapolis: University of Minnesota Press, 2000), 40.

54. Rousseau, *The Confessions*, 71–73.

55. Deleuze, *Kant's Critical Philosophy*, 25.

56. Martin Schönfield, *The Philosophy of the Young Kant: The Precritical Project* (New York: Oxford University Press, 2000), 8.

57. Kant, *Observations on the Feeling of the Beautiful and Sublime*, 123n5.

58. John Zammito, *Kant, Herder, and the Birth of Anthropology* (Chicago: University of Chicago Press, 2002), 109.

59. Susan Shell, "Kant as Propagator: Reflections on 'Observations on the Feeling of the Beautiful and the Sublime,'" *Eighteenth-Century Studies*, 35 no. 3 (Spring 2002), 456.

60. Kant, *Observations on the Feeling of the Beautiful and Sublime*, 15–16.

61. Kant, *Observations on the Feeling of the Beautiful and Sublime*, 4.

62. Kant, *Observations on the Feeling of the Beautiful and Sublime*, 57.

63. Kant, *Observations on the Feeling of the Beautiful and Sublime*, 68.

64. Kant, *Observations on the Feeling of the Beautiful and Sublime*, 68.

65. Kant, *Observations on the Feeling of the Beautiful and Sublime*, 68.

66. Kant, *Observations on the Feeling of the Beautiful and Sublime*, 75; my emphasis.

67. Rousseau, *The Confessions*, 73.

68. Kant, *Observations on the Feeling of the Beautiful and Sublime*, 77.

69. Kant, *Observations on the Feeling of the Beautiful and Sublime*, 77.

70. Kant, *Observations on the Feeling of the Beautiful and Sublime*, 76, 89.

71. Kant, *Observations on the Feeling of the Beautiful and Sublime*, 85.

72. Spivak, *A Critique of Postcolonial Reason*, 25.

73. Kant, *Observations on the Feeling of the Beautiful and Sublime*, 98. I also want to acknowledge here that Kant's references to the terrifying potential of the sublime yield the possibility of a critique of Western imperialism, but the explicit calculation of this relationship remains unimagined by Kant.

74. Kant, *Observations on the Feeling of the Beautiful and Sublime*, 109.

75. Kant, *Observations on the Feeling of the Beautiful and Sublime*, 109–10.

76. Kant, *Observations on the Feeling of the Beautiful and Sublime*, 110.

77. Kant, *Observations on the Feeling of the Beautiful and Sublime*, 109.

78. Kant, *Observations on the Feeling of the Beautiful and Sublime*, 110–13; my emphasis.

79. Charles Mills, *Blackness Visible: Essays on Philosophy and Race* (Ithaca, NY: Cornell University Press, 1998), 73.

80. Kant, *Observations on the Feeling of the Beautiful and Sublime*, 69.

81. Rousseau, *The Confessions*, 113.

82. Theodor W. Adorno, *Kant's "Critique of Pure Reason,"* ed. Rolf Tiedemann, trans. Rodney Livingstone (Stanford, CA: Stanford University Press, 2002), 9.

83. Jill Vance Buroker, *Kant's Critique of Pure Reason: An Introduction* (Cambridge, UK: Cambridge University Press, 2006), 7.

84. Deleuze, *Kant's Critical Philosophy*, 3.

85. Kant, *Critique of Pure Reason*, 71.

86. Kant, *Critique of Pure Reason*, 76.

87. Kant, *Critique of Pure Reason*, 77.

88. Kant, *Critique of Pure Reason*, 77.

89. Deleuze, *Kant's Critical Philosophy*, ix.

90. Adorno, *Kant's "Critique of Pure Reason,"* 2.

91. Kant, *Critique of Pure Reason*, 118, 121–22.

92. Kant, *Critique of Pure Reason*, 165.

93. Kant, *Critique of Pure Reason*, 144.

94. Kant, *Critique of Pure Reason*, 123.

95. Deleuze, *Kant's Critical Philosophy*, 24.

96. Deleuze, *Kant's Critical Philosophy*, 25.

97. Kant, *Critique of Pure Reason*, 257.

98. Sigmund Freud, *Civilization and Its Discontents*, trans. James Strachey (New York: W. W. Norton, 1961), 10.

99. Sigmund Freud, *Civilization and Its Discontents*, 10–11, my emphasis.

100. Hortense Spillers, "Mama's Baby, Papa's Maybe: An American Grammar Book," special issue, "Culture and Countermemory: The 'American' Connection," *Diacritics* 17, no. 2 (Summer 1987): 72.

101. Spillers, "Mama's Baby, Papa's Maybe," 67.

102. Kant, *Critique of Pure Reason*, 257.

103. Rousseau, *The Confessions*, 73.

104. Immanuel Kant, "On the Use of Teleological Principles in Philosophy," in *Race*, Blackwell Readings in Continental Philosophy, ed. Robert Bernasconi (Malden, MA: Blackwell, 2001), 51; Kant, "On the Use of Teleological Principles in Philosophy," 51.

105. Immanuel Kant, *The Critique of Judgment*, trans. James Creed Meredith (Oxford: Oxford University Press, 1952), 8.

106. Kant, *The Critique of Judgment*, 18.

107. Schönfield, *The Philosophy of the Young Kant*, 8.

108. Howard Caygill, *A Kant Dictionary* (Malden, MA: Blackwell, 1995), 389.

109. Bernasconi, "Who Invented the Enlightenment Concept of Race?," 23.

110. Kant, "On the Use of Teleological Principles in Philosophy," 39.

111. Kant, "On the Use of Teleological Principles in Philosophy," 43, 51.

112. Kant, *The Critique of Judgment*, Part II, 5.

113. Kant, "On the Use of Teleological Principles in Philosophy," 50.

114. Bernasconi, "Who Invented the Enlightenment Concept of Race?," 25; Kant, "On the Use of Teleological Principles in Philosophy," 48.

115. Bernasconi, "Who Invented the Enlightenment Concept of Race?," 26.

116. Kant, "On the Use of Teleological Principles in Philosophy," 51.

117. Kant, "On the Use of Teleological Principles in Philosophy," 48.

118. Freud, *Civilization and Its Discontents*, 10.

119. Charles Mills, "Kant's *Untermenschen*," in *Race and Racism in Modern Philosophy*, ed. Andrew Valls (Ithaca, NY: Cornell University Press, 2005), 183.

120. Kant, *Critique of Pure Reason*, 327; Harriet Jacobs, *Incidents in the Life of a Slave Girl*, ed. Lydia Maria Child (Orlando, FL: Harcourt Brace Jovanovich Publishers, 1973), 55.

Two. Crooked Ways and Weak Pens

1. Paul Miller, *Elusive Origins: The Enlightenment in the Modern Caribbean Historical Imagination* (Charlottesville: University of Virginia Press, 2010), 9; Louis Sala-Molins, *Dark Side of the Light: Slavery and the French Enlightenment* (Minneapolis: University of Minnesota Press, 2006), 8.

2. Hillary McD. Beckles, "Capitalism, Slavery, and Caribbean Modernity," *Callaloo* 20, no. 4 (1997): 781.

3. Fred Moten, "Knowledge of Freedom," *CR: The New Centennial Review* 4, no. 2 (2004): 274.

4. Alexander G. Weheliye, "After Man," *American Literary History* 20, nos. 1–2 (Spring/Summer 2008): 323.

5. Sylvia Wynter, "Beyond the Word of Man: Glissant and the New Discourse of the Antilles," *World Literature Today* 63, no. 4 (Autumn 1989): 641, 645.

6. Wynter quoted in David Scott, "The Re-enchantment of Humanism: An Interview with Sylvia Wynter," *Small Axe* 8 (September 2000): 120.

7. Wynter quoted in Scott, "The Re-enchantment of Humanism," 165.

8. Katherine McKittrick, *Demonic Grounds: Black Women and the Cartographies of Struggle* (Minneapolis: University of Minnesota Press, 2006), xiii.

9. Christopher Castiglia, "Abolition's Racial Interiors and the Making of White Civic Depth," *American Literary History* 14, no. 1 (Spring 2002): 33.

10. See Marc Arkin, "The Federalist Trope: Power and Passion in Abolitionist Rhetoric," *Journal of American Literary History* 88 (June 2001); Christopher Castiglia, "Abolition's Racial Interiors and the Making of White Civic Depth"; and Carol Lasser, "Voyeuristic Abolitionism: Sex, Gender, and the Transformation of Antislavery Rhetoric," *Journal of the Early Republic* 28, no. 1 (2008).

11. Karla FC Holloway, *Codes of Conduct: Race, Ethics, and the Color of Our Character* (New Brunswick, NJ: Rutgers University Press, 1996), 29.

12. Fred Moten, *In the Break: The Aesthetics of the Black Radical Tradition* (Minneapolis: University of Minnesota Press, 2003), 131.

13. David Kazanjian, *The Colonizing Trick: National Culture and Imperial Citizenship in Early America* (Minneapolis: University of Minnesota Press, 2003), 9.

14. Kazanjian, *The Colonizing Trick*, 10.

15. Kazanjian, *The Colonizing Trick*, 10.

16. Kazanjian, *The Colonizing Trick*, 115.

17. W. E. B. Du Bois, *The Souls of Black Folk* (New York: Penguin, 1989), 135.

18. Gayl Jones, *Corregidora* (Boston: Beacon Press, 1975), 108.

19. See Nancy F. Cott, "Passionlessness: An Interpretation of Victorian Sexual Ideology," *Signs* 4, no. 2 (Winter 1978); Louise Newman, *White Women's Rights: The Racial Origins of Feminism in the United States* (New York: Oxford University Press, 1999); Margaret Washington, "'From Motives of Delicacy': Sexuality and Morality in the Narratives of Sojourner Truth and Harriet Jacobs," special issue, "Women, Slavery, and Historical Research," ed. Brenda E. Stevenson, *Journal of African American History* 92, no. 1 (Winter 2007).

20. Cott argues, "The positive contribution of passionlessness was to replace that sexual/carnal characterization of women with a spiritual/moral one, allowing women to develop their human faculties and their self-esteem. The belief that women lacked carnal motivation was the cornerstone of the argument for women's moral superiority, used to enhance women's status and widen their opportunities in the nineteenth century." Cott, "Passionlessness," 233.

21. Cott, "Passionlessness," 234.

22. Washington, "From Motives of Delicacy," 66.

23. Harriet Jacobs, *Incidents in the Life of a Slave Girl*, ed. Lydia Maria Child (Orlando, FL: Harcourt Brace Jovanovich Publishers, 1973), 54.

24. Lasser, "Voyeuristic Abolitionism," 96.

25. Washington, "From Motives of Delicacy," 69.

26. Christina Sharpe, *Monstrous Intimacies: Making Post-slavery Subjects* (Durham, NC: Duke University Press, 2010).

27. Jacobs, *Incidents in the Life of a Slave Girl*, 55.

28. Jacobs, *Incidents in the Life of a Slave Girl*, 3, 18.

29. Jacobs, *Incidents in the Life of a Slave Girl*, 27.

30. Jacobs, *Incidents in the Life of a Slave Girl*, 53.

31. Jacobs, *Incidents in the Life of a Slave Girl*, 58.

32. Saidiya V. Hartman, *Scenes of Subjection: Terror, Slavery, and Self-Making in Nineteenth-Century America* (Oxford: Oxford University Press, 1999), 106.

33. Jacobs, *Incidents in the Life of a Slave Girl*, 57.

34. Hartman, *Scenes of Subjection*, 106.

35. Jacobs, *Incidents in the Life of a Slave Girl*, 58.

36. Deborah Garfield, "Earwitness: Female Abolitionism, Sexuality, and *Incidents in the Life of a Slave Girl*," in *Harriet Jacobs and Incidents in the Life of a Slave Girl: New Critical Essays*, ed. Deborah Garfield and Rafia Zafar (Cambridge, UK: Cambridge University Press, 1996), 100.

37. Jacobs, *Incidents in the Life of a Slave Girl*, 92–93.

38. Jacobs, *Incidents in the Life of a Slave Girl*, 92–93.

39. *Oxford English Dictionary Online*, s.v. "awe." Accessed February 10, 2014.

40. Gayatri Spivak, *A Critique of Postcolonial Reason: Toward a History of the Vanishing Present* (Cambridge, MA: Harvard University Press, 1999), 10–11; my emphasis.

41. David Scott, *Conscripts of Modernity: The Tragedy of Colonial Enlightenment* (Durham, NC: Duke University Press, 2004), 192.

42. Jacobs, *Incidents in the Life of a Slave Girl*, 93.

43. Jacobs, *Incidents in the Life of a Slave Girl*, 93.

44. Jacobs, *Incidents in the Life of a Slave Girl*, 98.

45. Houston A. Baker comments on the "penal protocols" of the plantation when he writes: "From the *Oxford English Dictionary* I sample these meanings of 'plantation': 'transplanting'; 'laying out of wealth'; 'settlement of persons in some locality, especially the planting of a colony'; 'colonization'; 'to send prisoners, etc. to the plantations, i.e., to penal service or indentured labor in the colonies'; 'method of treating criminals of all kinds much in favor during the 17th century; 'plantation-Negro'; 'plantation slave.'" He continues, "The sign 'plantation' moves in its connotations and denotations from active verb to nominal resultant. Transplantation of peoples from one locale to another, or establishment of a colony in 'conquered' territory, results always in *penal* service and plantation slavery." Houston A. Baker, *Turning South Again: Re-thinking Modernism/Re-thinking Booker T.* (Durham, NC: Duke University Press, 2001), 84.

46. Jacobs, *Incidents in the Life of a Slave Girl*, 98.

47. Jacobs, *Incidents in the Life of a Slave Girl*, 103.

48. Jacobs, *Incidents in the Life of a Slave Girl*, 103.

49. Hartman, *Scenes of Subjection*, 105.

50. Hartman, *Scenes of Subjection*, 107; Jacobs, *Incidents in the Life of a Slave Girl*, 103.

51. Hartman, *Scenes of Subjection*, 105.

52. Jacobs, *Incidents in the Life of a Slave Girl*, 117.

53. Donald Gibson, "Harriet Jacobs, Frederick Douglass, and the Slavery Debate: Bondage, Family, and the Discourse of Domesticity," in *Harriet Jacobs and Incidents in the Life of a Slave Girl: New Critical Essays*, ed. Deborah Garfield and Rafia Zafar (Cambridge, UK: Cambridge University Press, 1996), 170.

54. Mary Titus, "Carnival Laughter: Resistance in Incidents," in *Harriet Jacobs and Incidents in the Life of a Slave Girl: New Critical Essays*, ed. Deborah Garfield and Rafia Zafar (Cambridge, UK: Cambridge University Press, 1996), 225.

55. Jacobs, *Incidents in the Life of a Slave Girl*, 136.

56. Gloria T. Randle, "Between the Rock and the Hard Place: Mediating Spaces in Harriet Jacobs's 'Incidents in the Life of a Slave Girl,'" *African American Review* 33, no. 1 (1999): 53.

57. McKittrick, *Demonic Grounds*, 45.

58. McKittrick, *Demonic Grounds*, 40.

59. Jacobs, *Incidents in the Life of a Slave Girl*, 171.

60. McKittrick, *Demonic Grounds*, 41.

61. Jacobs, *Incidents in the Life of a Slave Girl*, 58.

62. Peter Hinks, *To Awaken My Afflicted Brethren: David Walker and the Problem of Antebellum Slave Resistance* (University Park: Pennsylvania State University Press, 1997), 86.

63. Floyd J. Miller, "Introduction," in Martin R. Delany, *Blake; Or, the Huts of America*, ed. Floyd J. Miller (Boston: Beacon Press, 1970), xiii.

64. Martin R. Delany, "Political Destiny of the Colored Race on the American Continent," in *Martin Delany: A Documentary Reader*, ed. Robert S. Levine (Chapel Hill: University of North Carolina Press, 2003), 264.

65. Baker, *Turning South Again*, 86.

66. Baker, *Turning South Again*, 26.

67. Baker, *Turning South Again*, 15.

68. Delany, *Blake*, 16–17.

69. Delany, *Blake*, 101.

70. Baker, *Turning South Again*, 15.

71. Scott, *Conscripts of Modernity*, 195, 170.

72. Delany, *Blake*, 31.

73. Delany, *Blake*, 69; my emphasis.

74. Delany, *Blake*, 105.

75. Delany, *Blake*, 101.

76. Delany, *Blake*, 101.

77. Paul Gilroy, *The Black Atlantic: Modernity and Double Consciousness* (Cambridge, MA: Harvard University Press, 1993), 28.

78. Delany, *Blake*, 101.

79. Baker, *Turning South Again*, 33; Spivak, *A Critique of Postcolonial Reason*, 10–11.

80. Delany, *Blake*, 154.

81. Delany, *Blake*, 197.

82. Delany, *Blake*, 292.

83. Robert Levine, *Martin Delany, Frederick Douglass, and the Politics of Representative Identity* (Chapel Hill: University of North Carolina Press, 1997), 183; Delany to J. H. Kagi, letter of August 16, 1858, in "John Brown Insurrection," 291–92; Delany to M. H. Freeman, *Weekly Anglo African*, February 1, 1862, 2; M. R. Delany, Official Report of the Niger Valley Exploring Party (1861), rpt. in *Search for a Place: Black Separatism and Africa, 1860*, ed.

Howard H. Bell (Ann Arbor: University of Michigan Press, 1969), 38; Delany to Henry Ward Beecher, letter of June 17, 1858, cited in Floyd J. Miller, *The Search for a Black Nationality: Black Emigration and Colonization, 1787–1863* (Urbana: University of Illinois Press, 1975), 178.

84. Delany, *Blake*, 292.

85. Delany, *Blake*, 292.

86. Jacobs, *Incidents in the Life of a Slave Girl*, 136.

87. Hinks, *To Awaken My Afflicted Brethren*, 86.

88. David Walker and Henry Highland Garnet, *Walker's Appeal and Garnet's Address to the Slaves of the United States of America* (Nashville, TN: Winston Publishing Company, 1994), v.

89. Hinks, *To Awaken My Afflicted Brethren*, 20.

90. Walker and Garnet, *Walker's Appeal and Garnet's Address to the Slaves of the United States of America*, 11.

91. Thomas Jefferson, "The Difference Is Fixed in Nature/Notes on the State of Virginia," in *Race and the Enlightenment: A Reader*, ed. Emmanuel Eze (Malden, MA: Blackwell, 1997), 100.

92. Jefferson, "The Difference Is Fixed in Nature/Notes on The State of Virginia," 97.

93. Immanuel Kant, *Observations on the Feeling of the Beautiful and Sublime*, trans. John T. Goldthwait (Berkeley: University of California Press, 1960), 77.

94. In Jefferson, "The Difference Is Fixed in Nature/Notes on the State of Virginia," it is black men who are the objects of Jefferson's racist vision.

95. Walker and Garnet, *Walker's Appeal and Garnet's Address to the Slaves of the United States of America*, 13.

96. Walker and Garnet, *Walker's Appeal and Garnet's Address to the Slaves of the United States of America*, 13.

97. Walker and Garnet, *Walker's Appeal and Garnet's Address to the Slaves of the United States of America*, 13.

98. Kazanjian, *The Colonizing Trick*, 17.

99. Jacobs, *Incidents in the Life of a Slave Girl*, 171.

100. Hartman, *Scenes of Subjection*, 179.

101. Hinks, *To Awaken My Afflicted Brethren*, 93.

102. Hinks, *To Awaken My Afflicted Brethren*, 256.

103. Hartman, *Scenes of Subjection*, 121; my emphasis.

104. Walker and Garnet, *Walker's Appeal and Garnet's Address to the Slaves of the United States of America*, 32–33; my emphasis.

105. Kant, *Observations on the Feeling of the Beautiful and Sublime*, 75.

106. Walker and Garnet, *Walker's Appeal and Garnet's Address to the Slaves of the United States of America*, 33.

107. Walker and Garnet, *Walker's Appeal and Garnet's Address to the Slaves of the United States of America*, 42.

108. Walker and Garnet, *Walker's Appeal and Garnet's Address to the Slaves of the United States of America*, 40.

109. Walker and Garnet, *Walker's Appeal and Garnet's Address to the Slaves of the United States of America*, 40.

110. Walker and Garnet, *Walker's Appeal and Garnet's Address to the Slaves of the United States of America*, v.

111. Walker and Garnet, *Walker's Appeal and Garnet's Address to the Slaves of the United States of America*, v.

112. Hinks, *To Awaken My Afflicted Brethren*, 86; Walker and Garnet, *Walker's Appeal and Garnet's Address to the Slaves of the United States of America*, 40.

113. Hinks, *To Awaken My Afflicted Brethren*, 31.

114. Hortense Spillers, "Mama's Baby, Papa's Maybe: An American Grammar Book," special issue, "Culture and Countermemory: The 'American' Connection," *Diacritics* 17, no. 2 (Summer 1987): 80.

115. Spillers, "Mama's Baby, Papa's Maybe," 80.

116. Newman, *White Women's Rights*, 60–61.

117. Hartman brilliantly argues the ways that black subjection was achieved through its endlessly coerced occupation and theatricalization. Hartman writes, "Antebellum formations of pleasure, even those of the North, need to be considered in relation to the affective dimensions of chattel slavery since enjoyment is virtually unimaginable without recourse to the black body and the subjection of the captive, the diversions engendered by the dispossession of the enslaved, or the fantasies launched by the myriad uses of the black body. For this reason the formal features of this economy of pleasure and the politics of enjoyment are considered in regard to the literal and figurative occupation and possession of the body." Hartman, *Scenes of Subjection*, 26.

118. Donna Haraway. "Ecce Homo, Ain't (Ar'n't) I a Woman, and Inappropriate/d Others: The Human in a Posthumanist Landscape," in *Feminists Theorize the Political*, ed. Joan Scott and Judith Butler (New York: Routledge, 1992), 92.

119. Nell Painter, *Sojourner Truth: A Life, a Symbol* (New York: W. W. Norton, 1996), 11–12.

120. Sojourner Truth, Olive Gilbert, and Frances Titus, *Narrative of Sojourner Truth: A Bondswoman of Olden Time Emancipated by the New York Legislature in the Early Part of the Present Century; With a History of Her Labors and Correspondence Drawn from Her "Book of Life"* (Battle Creek, MI: published by the author, 1881), xxxvii.

121. Truth, Gilbert, and Titus, *Narrative of Sojourner Truth*, xxxvii, xliv.

122. Painter, *Sojourner Truth*, 25.

123. Truth, Gilbert, and Titus, *Narrative of Sojourner Truth*, 42.

124. Truth, Gilbert, and Titus, *Narrative of Sojourner Truth*, 66.

125. Truth, Gilbert, and Titus, *Narrative of Sojourner Truth*, 66.

126. Truth, Gilbert, and Titus, *Narrative of Sojourner Truth*, 60.

127. Naiomi Greyser, "Affective Geographies: Sojourner Truth's Narrative, Feminism, and the Ethical Bind of Sentimentalism," *American Literature* 79, no. 2 (2007): 278.

128. This account is described in Margaret Washington, *Sojourner Truth's America* (Urbana: University of Illinois Press, 2009), 56.

129. Painter, *Sojourner Truth*, 30.

130. Painter, *Sojourner Truth*, 40.

131. Painter, *Sojourner Truth*, 41.

132. Washington, *Sojourner Truth's America*, 92.

133. Painter, *Sojourner Truth*, 71. Painter further observes, "Delany and other up-and-coming young men ached to see the race exert its manhood by going into business and becoming

financially independent. Here, they thought, lay the route to respect from a wider American population, so busily persecuting them in every conceivable manner. Although later in life Isabella would, in a sense, go into business and become more or less financially independent, her ways out of humiliation were not those of Martin Delany or other leading black men." She continues, "Mental orientation as well as ideals of gender divided leading African Americans from Isabella. They took their cues from the public realm, from politics and business, where she headed the voice of the Holy Spirit. As men, they moved earlier into the larger world. In the 1830s and 1840s, the imperatives of politics drove educated, urban black men—later they would call themselves 'representative men'—and the upstanding, middle-class black women lecturers who would join them on the antislavery lecture circuit. For this majority of urban black people most noted in historical accounts, public life held much attraction. History, however, ignored an untold number of women for whom the politics of race did not supply meaning to life" (72).

134. Painter, *Sojourner Truth*, 72.
135. Painter, *Sojourner Truth*, 72.
136. According to Painter, Isabella became Sojourner Truth in 1843. Painter, *Sojourner Truth*, 73.
137. Painter, *Sojourner Truth*, 97–98; my emphasis.
138. See Gayatri Spivak's *The Critique of Postcolonial Reason*, 10–11.
139. Frederick Douglass, "What I Found at the Northampton Association," in *History of Florence, Massachusetts, Including a Complete Account of the Northampton Association of Education and Industry*, ed., Charles A. Sheffield (Florence, MA: Charles A. Sheffield, 1895), 131–32. Quoted in Painter, *Sojourner Truth*, 98. Brackets appear in original quote.
140. Painter, *Sojourner Truth*, 98.
141. Haraway, "Ecce Homo, Ain't (Ar'n't) I A Woman, and Inappropriate/d Others," 97.
142. Marius Robinson quoted in Painter, *Sojourner Truth*, 125; attributed to *Anti-Slavery Bugle* (Salem, OH), June 7, 1851.
143. Frances Dana Gage quoted in Painter, *Sojourner Truth*, 167–68.
144. Painter, *Sojourner Truth*, 171; Erlene Stetson, *Glorifying in Tribulation: The Lifework of Sojourner Truth* (East Lansing: Michigan State University Press, 1994), 112.
145. Stetson, *Glorifying in Tribulation*, 112.
146. Walker and Garnet, *Walker's Appeal and Garnet's Address to the Slaves of the United States of America*, 29.
147. Gage quoted in Painter, *Sojourner Truth*, 168.
148. Haraway, "Ecce Homo, Ain't (Aren't) I a Woman, and Inappropriate/d Others," 98.
149. Walker and Garnet, *Walker's Appeal and Garnet's Address to the Slaves of the United States of America*, 50.
150. Scott, *Conscripts of Modernity*, 204.
151. Moten, "Knowledge of Freedom," 274.
152. Hartman, *Scenes of Subjection*, 36.
153. Truth, Gilbert, and Titus, *Narrative of Sojourner Truth*, xliv.

Three. Writing under a Spell

1. Alisa Solomon, "Sojourner's Truths," *Village Voice*, October 1, 1995, 98.
2. According to Joni L. Jones, Adrienne Kennedy "earned her reputation in the avant-garde theatre world while other black artists (mostly men with decidedly nationalist politics)

were solidifying what a 'black play' was and what 'playing black' might be." Jones continues, "Similarly, the artists I mention here [Laurie Carlos, apprentices Daniel Alexander
Jones, Sharon Bridgforth, Grisha Coleman, Erik Ehn, and the next generation of Walter
Kitundu, Zell Miller III, and Florinda Bryant] have often found homeplace more com-
fortably in so-called experimental or avant-garde theatre communities. Few have been embraced by black theatres or large black audiences. Kennedy and the jazz aesthetic artists I
discuss here share an unapologetic emphasis on the subjective experience of one character,
a memory-laden sense of time and place, a keen attention to the visual/physical/imagistic
aspects of their work, and polyrhythmic musically driven language; they also share in their
exclusion from the generally accepted understanding of black theatre which tends toward
linear realism." Joni L. Jones, "Cast a Wide Net," *Theatre Journal* 57, no. 4 (December
2005): 598.

3. Denise Ferreira da Silva, *Toward a Global Theory of Race* (Minneapolis: University of
Minnesota Press, 2007), xxxviii.

4. Françoise Vergès, "To Cure and to Free: The Fanonian Project of 'Decolonized Psychiatry,'" in *Fanon: A Critical Reader*, ed. Lewis R. Gordon, T. Denean Sharpley-Whiting, and
Renée T. White (Oxford: Wiley-Blackwell, 1996), 88.

5. Ian Hacking, *Mad Travelers: Reflections on the Reality of Transient Mental Illnesses* (Charlottesville: University of Virginia Press, 1998), 27.

6. Vergès, "To Cure and to Free," 90.

7. Fred Moten, "Music against the Law of Reading the Future and 'Rodney King,'" special
issue, "The Future of the Profession," *Journal of the Midwest Modern Language Association*
27, no. 1 (Spring 1994): 53.

8. Michel Foucault, *Madness and Civilization: A History of Insanity in the Age of Reason*,
trans. Richard Howard (New York: Random House, 1965), 100.

9. Solomon, "Sojourner's Truths," 98.

10. Robert Scanlan, "Surrealism as Mimesis: A Director's Guide to Adrienne Kennedy's *Funnyhouse of a Negro*," in *Intersecting Boundaries: The Theater of Adrienne Kennedy*, ed. Paul
K. Bryant-Jackson and Lois More Overbeck (Minneapolis: University of Minnesota Press,
1992), 95.

11. Adrienne Kennedy, "Preface," in *Adrienne Kennedy: In One Act* (Minneapolis: University
of Minnesota Press, 1988), ix.

12. Kennedy, "Preface," ix.

13. José Gil, *Metamorphosis of the Body*, trans. Stephen Muecke (Minneapolis: University of
Minnesota Press, 1998), 84.

14. Franklin Rosemont, "Introduction," in *Black, Brown, and Beige: Surrealist Writings from
Africa and the Diaspora*, ed. Franklin Rosemont and Robin D. G. Kelley (Austin: University of Texas Press, 2010), 3.

15. Scanlan, "Surrealism as Mimesis," 94.

16. Even though Allen, who plays the lead character in *Funnyhouse*, finds fault with critics'
misreadings of Kennedy's plays and her purported internalized racism, she nonetheless describes Sarah as "psychotically" angry. See Paul K. Bryant-Jackson, "Interview with Billie
Allen," in *Intersecting Boundaries: The Theater of Adrienne Kennedy*, ed. Paul K. Bryant-
Jackson and Lois More Overbeck (Minneapolis: University of Minnesota Press, 1992), 219.

17. Philip Kolin, *Understanding Adrienne Kennedy* (Columbia: University of South Carolina
Press, 2005), 32, 38.

18. Kolin, *Understanding Adrienne Kennedy*, 36; Gaetano Benedetti, quoted in Margit Sichert, "The Staging of Excessive Emotions: Adrienne Kennedy's *Funnyhouse of a Negro*," *REAL: The Yearbook of Research in English and American Literature* 16 (2000): 231.

19. João Biehl, *Vita: Life in a Zone of Social Abandonment* (Berkeley: University of California Press, 2005), 18.

20. Biehl, *Vita*, 8.

21. Biehl, *Vita*, 4.

22. Hortense Spillers, "Mama's Baby, Papa's Maybe: An American Grammar Book," special issue, "Culture and Countermemory: The 'American' Connection," *Diacritics* 17, no. 2 (Summer 1987): 68.

23. J. Jones, "Cast a Wide Net," 598.

24. Adrienne Kennedy, lecture, Brown University, October 1, 1987.

25. Jacques Derrida, *Resistances of Psychoanalysis*, trans. Peggy Kamuf (Stanford, CA: Stanford University Press, 1998), 5.

26. Sigmund Freud, *New Introductory Lectures on Psychoanalysis*, trans. James Strachey (New York: W. W. Norton, 1962), 9.

27. Freud, *New Introductory Lectures on Psychoanalysis*, 20; my emphasis.

28. Adrienne Kennedy, *Funnyhouse of a Negro*, in *Adrienne Kennedy: In One Act* (Minneapolis: University of Minnesota Press, 1988), 3.

29. Frantz Fanon, *Black Skin, White Masks*, trans. Richard Philcox (New York: Grove Press, 1967), 116.

30. Fanon, *Black Skin, White Masks*, 116.

31. Kennedy, *Funnyhouse of a Negro*, 3.

32. Kennedy, *Funnyhouse of a Negro*, 2, 7.

33. Frances Bartkowski, *Travelers, Immigrants, Inmates: Essays in Estrangement* (Minneapolis: University of Minnesota Press, 1995), 85, 88.

34. Bartkowski, *Travelers, Immigrants, Inmates*, 85.

35. Bartkowski, *Travelers, Immigrants, Inmates*, xvi.

36. Howard Stein, "An Interview with Michael Kahn," in *Intersecting Boundaries: The Theater of Adrienne Kennedy*, ed. Paul K. Bryant-Jackson and Lois More Overbeck (Minneapolis: University of Minnesota Press, 1992), 192.

37. Paul Carter Harrison, "The Crisis of Black Theater Identity," *African American Review* 31, no. 4 (1997): 572.

38. Kennedy, *Funnyhouse of a Negro*, 5.

39. Kimberly Benston, "Locating Adrienne Kennedy: Prefacing the Subject," in *Intersecting Boundaries: The Theater of Adrienne Kennedy*, ed. Paul K. Bryant-Jackson and Lois More Overbeck (Minneapolis: University of Minnesota Press, 1992), 115.

40. Biehl, *Vita*, 11.

41. Kennedy, *Funnyhouse of a Negro*, 5.

42. Paul K. Bryant-Jackson, "Kennedy's Travelers in the American and African Continuum," in *Intersecting Boundaries: The Theater of Adrienne Kennedy*, ed. Paul K. Bryant-Jackson and Lois More Overbeck (Minneapolis: University of Minnesota Press, 1992), 45.

43. Stein, "An Interview with Michael Kahn," 192.

44. Fanon, *Black Skin, White Masks*, 116; Stein, "An Interview with Michael Kahn," 192.

45. Fanon, *Black Skin, White Masks*, 115.

46. Kennedy, *Funnyhouse of a Negro*, 5.

47. Kennedy, *Funnyhouse of a Negro*, 5.
48. Spillers, "Mama's Baby, Papa's Maybe," 69.
49. Gilles Deleuze and Félix Guattari, *A Thousand Plateaus: Capitalism and Schizophrenia*, trans. Brian Massumi (Minneapolis: University of Minnesota Press, 1987), 249; my emphasis.
50. Solomon, "Sojourner's Truths."
51. Fred Moten, *In the Break: The Aesthetics of the Black Radical Tradition* (Minneapolis: University of Minnesota Press, 2003), 5.
52. Adrienne Kennedy, *People Who Led to My Plays* (New York: Theater Communications Group, 1988), 116.
53. Kennedy, *People Who Led to My Plays*, 116.
54. See Spillers, "Mama's Baby, Papa's Maybe," 67.
55. Foucault, *Madness and Civilization*, 12.
56. Foucault, *Madness and Civilization*, 8.
57. Foucault, *Madness and Civilization*, 11..
58. Kennedy, *Funnyhouse of a Negro*, 6.
59. Kennedy, *Funnyhouse of a Negro*, 6.
60. Spillers, "Mama's Baby, Papa's Maybe," 72.
61. Moten, *In the Break*, 36.
62. Kennedy, *Funnyhouse of a Negro*, 8.
63. Patrice Lumumba, "Dawn in the Heart of Africa," in *Africa: Selected Readings*, ed. F. G. Burke (New York: Houghton Mifflin, 1973), 206.
64. Kennedy, *People Who Led to My Plays*, 119.
65. Kennedy, *Funnyhouse of a Negro*, 8.
66. Kennedy, *Funnyhouse of a Negro*, 9.
67. Kennedy, *Funnyhouse of a Negro*, 11.
68. Kennedy, *Funnyhouse of a Negro*, 18.
69. Moten, *In the Break*, 26.
70. Kennedy, *Funnyhouse of a Negro*, 20; my emphasis.
71. Kennedy, *Funnyhouse of a Negro*, 20.
72. Deleuze and Guattari, *A Thousand Plateaus*, 254.
73. Kennedy, *Funnyhouse of a Negro*, 20.
74. Kennedy, *Funnyhouse of a Negro*, 20.
75. Kennedy, *Funnyhouse of a Negro*, 22.
76. Adrienne Kennedy, *The Owl Answers*, in *Adrienne Kennedy: In One Act* (Minneapolis: University of Minnesota Press, 1988), 25.
77. Benston, "Locating Adrienne Kennedy," 117.
78. I am referring to Rhonda Ross's 1991 production of *The Owl Answers* (video reproduction courtesy of the Henry Ransom Research Center at the University of Texas, Austin).
79. Kolin, *Understanding Adrienne Kennedy*, 20.
80. See also Claudia Barnett, "This Fundamental Challenge to Identity: Reproduction and Representation in the Drama of Adrienne Kennedy," *Theatre Journal* 48, no. 2 (May 1996): 144.
81. Claudia Barnett, "This Fundamental Challenge to Identity," 144.
82. Plato, *The Republic*, trans. Desmond Lee (New York: Penguin Books, 2003), 242.
83. Plato, *The Republic*, 247.

84. Plato, *The Republic*, 242.

85. Barnett, "This Fundamental Challenge to Identity," 153.

86. Kolin, *Understanding Adrienne Kennedy*, 21.

87. Kennedy, *The Owl Answers*, 27.

88. Kennedy, *The Owl Answers*, 27.

89. Kennedy, *The Owl Answers*, 27.

90. Houston A. Baker, *Turning South Again: Re-thinking Modernism/Re-thinking Booker T.* (Durham, NC: Duke University Press, 2001), 69.

91. Kennedy, *The Owl Answers*, 27.

92. Johannes Fabian, *Out of Our Minds: Reason and Madness in the Exploration of Central Africa* (Berkeley: University of California Press, 2000), 8; Kennedy, *The Owl Answers*, 30.

93. Kennedy, *The Owl Answers*, 28.

94. Kennedy, *People Who Led to My Plays*, 18.

95. Gilles Deleuze and Félix Guattari, *Anti-Oedipus: Capitalism and Schizophrenia*, trans. Robert Hurley (Minneapolis: University of Minnesota Press, 1983), 105.

96. Kennedy, *The Owl Answers*, 30, 43.

97. Akira Mizuta Lippitt, *Electric Animal: Toward a Rhetoric of Wildlife* (Minneapolis: University of Minnesota Press, 2000), 8.

98. Lippitt, *Electric Animal*, 8.

99. Jeanie Forte, "Kennedy's Body Politic: The Mulatta, Menses, and the Medusa," in *Intersecting Boundaries: The Theater of Adrienne Kennedy*, ed. Paul K. Bryant-Jackson and Lois More Overbeck (Minneapolis: University of Minnesota Press, 1992), 160.

100. Forte, "Kennedy's Body Politic," 163.

101. Kennedy, *The Owl Answers*, 30.

102. Kennedy, *The Owl Answers*, 33–34.

103. Kennedy, *The Owl Answers*, 38.

104. Kennedy, *The Owl Answers*, 45.

105. Kennedy, *The Owl Answers*, 45.

106. Christina Sharpe, *Monstrous Intimacies: Making Post-slavery Subjects* (Durham, NC: Duke University Press, 2010), 88.

107. Psychologist Jonathan Schooler quoted in Josie Glausiusz, "Living in a Dream World: The Role of Daydreaming in Problem Solving and Creativity," *Scientific American Mind* 22, no. 1 (March/April 2011). Accessed November 15, 2012. http://www.scientificamerican.com /article/living-in-a-dream-world/.

108. Psychologist M. J. Kane quoted in Gluasiusz, "Living in a Dream World."

109. American Psychiatric Association, *Diagnostic and Statistical Manual of Mental Disorders: DSM-IV* (Washington, DC: American Psychiatric Publication, 2000), 519.

110. See the website for the American Civil Liberties Union for statistics regarding the disciplinary practices responsible for the new colloquialism *walking while black*. "Racial Profiling: Definition," American Civil Liberties Union, November 23, 2005, accessed November 1, 2012. https://www.aclu.org/racial-justice/racial-profiling-definition.

Four. "I Am an African American Novel"

1. Sally Eckhoff, "The Terrible Mystery of Gayl Jones," February 26, 1998, accessed January 1, 2005. http://web.archive.org/web/19991201112700/http://www.salon.com/media/1998 /02/26media.html.

2. Gayl Jones, "From *The Quest for Wholeness*: Re-Imagining the African-American Novel; An Essay on Third World Aesthetics," *Callaloo* 17, no. 2 (Spring 1994): 510.

3. G. Jones, "From *The Quest for Wholeness*," 507.

4. G. Jones, "From *The Quest for Wholeness*," 509.

5. Eckhoff, "The Terrible Mystery of Gayl Jones."

6. G. Jones, "From *The Quest for Wholeness*," 511.

7. Srikanth Reddy, "Changing the Sjuzet: Lyn Hejinian's Digressive Narratologies," *Contemporary Literature* 50 no. 1 (2009): 56.

8. G. Jones, "From *The Quest for Wholeness*," 508.

9. Hent de Vries, *Minimal Theologies: Critiques of Secular Reason in Adorno and Levinas* (Baltimore, MD: Johns Hopkins University Press, 2005), 197.

10. Gilles Deleuze and Félix Guattari, *A Thousand Plateaus: Capitalism and Schizophrenia* (Minneapolis: University of Minnesota Press, 1987), 11.

11. Deleuze and Guattari, *A Thousand Plateaus*, 11.

12. Deleuze and Guattari, *A Thousand Plateaus*, 11.

13. G. Jones, "From *The Quest for Wholeness*," 508.

14. Hortense Spillers, "Mama's Baby, Papa's Maybe: An American Grammar Book," special issue, "Culture and Countermemory: The 'American' Connection," *Diacritics* 17, no. 2 (Summer 1987): 65.

15. Denise Ferreira da Silva, *Toward a Global Theory of Race* (Minneapolis: University of Minnesota Press, 2007), 50; Candace Jenkins, *Private Lives, Proper Relations: Regulating Black Intimacy* (Minneapolis: University of Minnesota Press, 2007), 24.

16. Gayl Jones, *Eva's Man* (Boston: Beacon Press, 1976), 122.

17. G. Jones, "From *The Quest for Wholeness*," 510.

18. G. Jones, "From *The Quest for Wholeness*," 509.

19. Claudia C. Tate, "An Interview with Gayl Jones," *Black American Literature Forum* 13, no. 4 (Winter 1979): 143.

20. Trudier Harris, "Foreword," in *After the Pain: Critical Essays on Gayl Jones*, ed. Fiona Mills and Keith B. Mitchell (New York: Peter Lang, 2006), xi.

21. Jenkins, *Private Lives, Proper Relations*, 183.

22. Spillers, "Mama's Baby, Papa's Maybe," 67.

23. Avery Gordon, *Ghostly Matters: Haunting and the Sociological Imagination* (Minneapolis: University of Minnesota Press, 1997), 16.

24. Gayl Jones, *Mosquito* (Boston: Beacon Press, 1999).

25. Henry Louis Gates, "'Sanctuary, Rev. of Mosquito' by Gayl Jones," *New York Times*, November 14, 1999, section 7 (Books), 14.

26. Tamala M. Edwards. "*Mosquito*," Short Takes, *Time*, February 8, 2009, accessed November 1, 2004. http://www.time.com/time/magazine/shorttakes/0,9485,1101990208,00.html.

27. Tom LeClair, "Mosquito," Salon.com, January 12, 2009, accessed November 15, 2004. http://www.salon.com/1999/01/12/sneaks_54/.

28. Here is the information about the scene of McDonald's discipline: "McDonald was walking past a local bar on June 5, 2011 when an altercation between her and Schmitz, in addition to other patrons, erupted on the sidewalk outside. According to various reports, McDonald—who was transitioning at the time—said she pulled out a pair of scissors in an attempt to defend herself after the group hurled a glass at her face, and taunted her and her friends with both anti-gay and racist epithets, including 'faggots,' 'niggers' and 'chicks with d*cks.'" "CeCe McDonald, Minnesota Transgender Woman, Pleads Guilty

In Manslaughter Case Despite Supporters' Defense," posted May 2, 2012, at 4:04 p.m., updated May 2, 2012, at 11:53 p.m., Huffingtonpost.com, accessed November 15, 2012. http://www.huffingtonpost.com/2012/05/02/cece-mcdonald-minnesota-transgender -woman-manslaughter_n_1472078.html.

29. Robert McRuer, "Composing Bodies; Or, Decomposition: Queer Theory, Disability Studies, and Alternative Corporealities," *JAC* 24, no. 1 (2004): 53.

30. McRuer, "Composing Bodies."

31. McRuer, "Composing Bodies."

32. Greg Tate, "Going Underground, Review of Mosquito by Gayl Jones," *VLS: Voice Literary Supplement* 44, no. 6 (16 February 1999): 127; my emphasis.

33. Eckhoff, "The Terrible Mystery of Gayl Jones."

34. Fred Moten, *In the Break: The Aesthetics of the Black Radical Tradition* (Minneapolis: University of Minnesota Press, 2003), 41.

35. Gayl Jones, *Liberating Voices: Oral Tradition in African American Literature* (New York: Penguin, 1991), 200–201.

36. Maurice Blanchot, *The Infinite Conversation*, trans. Susan Hanson (Minneapolis: University of Minnesota Press, 1993), 403; my emphasis.

37. Nathaniel Mackey, "Other: From Noun to Verb," in *The Jazz Cadence of American Culture*, ed. Robert O'Mealley (New York: Columbia University Press, 1998), 518.

38. Gayl Jones, *Mosquito*, 601.

39. Gayl Jones, "The Siege," *Callaloo*, no. 16 (1982): 92.

40. G. Jones, *Mosquito*, 93.

41. G. Jones, *Mosquito*, 1.

42. G. Jones, *Mosquito*, 36.

43. G. Jones, *Mosquito*, 3.

44. Deleuze and Guattari, *A Thousand Plateaus*, 11.

45. Reddy, "Changing the Sjuzet," 54–55.

46. Reddy, "Changing the Sjuzet," 59.

47. G. Jones, *Mosquito*, 38.

48. G. Jones, *Mosquito*, 4.

49. G. Jones, *Mosquito*, 6.

50. Charles H. Rowell, "An Interview with Gayl Jones," *Callaloo*, no. 16 (October 1982): 39.

51. Edwards, "*Mosquito*."

52. Gilles Deleuze and Félix Guattari, *Kafka: Toward a Minor Literature* (Minneapolis: University of Minnesota Press, 1986), 3.

53. G. Jones, *Mosquito*, 7.

54. Renny Golden and Michael McConnell, *Sanctuary: The New Underground Railroad* (Maryknoll, NY: Orbis Books, 1986), 58.

55. G. Jones, *Mosquito*, 9.

56. G. Jones, *Mosquito*, 14.

57. G. Tate, "Going Underground, Review of Mosquito by Gayl Jones."

58. G. Jones, *Mosquito*, 14.

59. Gilles Deleuze and Félix Guattari, *Anti-Oedipus: Capitalism and Schizophrenia* (Minneapolis: University of Minnesota Press, 1983), 105.

60. G. Jones, *Mosquito*, 14.

61. G. Jones, *Mosquito*, 28.

62. G. Jones, *Mosquito*, 29.

63. G. Jones, *Mosquito*, 34.

64. G. Jones, *Mosquito*, 35.

65. G. Jones, *Mosquito*, 37.

66. G. Jones, *Mosquito*, 42–43.

67. Frances Bartkowski, *Travelers, Immigrants, Inmates: Essays in Estrangement* (Minneapolis: University of Minnesota Press, 1995), xxv.

68. Nell Painter, *Sojourner Truth: A Life, a Symbol* (New York: W. W. Norton, 1996), 109.

69. Sojourner Truth, Frances Titus, and Olive Gilbert, *Narrative of Sojourner Truth: A Bondswoman of Olden Time Emancipated by the New York Legislature in the Early Part of the Present Century; With a History of Her Labors and Correspondence Drawn from Her "Book of Life"* (Battle Creek, MI: published by the author, 1881), xliv.

70. Donna Haraway, "Ecce Homo, Ain't (Ar'n't) I a Woman, and Inappropriate/d Others: The Human in a Posthumanist Landscape," in *Feminists Theorize the Political*, ed. Joan Scott and Judith Butler (New York: Routledge, 1992), 98.

71. Truth, Titus, and Gilbert, *Narrative of Sojourner Truth*, xliv.

72. G. Jones, *Mosquito*, 62.

73. Golden and McConnell, *Sanctuary*, 14; Numbers 35:15.

74. G. Jones, *Mosquito*, 34.

75. Gary MacEoin and Nivita Riley, *No Promised Land: American Refugee Policy and the Rule of Law* (Boston: Oxfam America, 1982).

76. Golden and McConnell, *Sanctuary*, 47.

77. Golden and McConnell, *Sanctuary*, 3.

78. G. Jones, *Mosquito*, 67.

79. G. Jones, *Mosquito*, 69.

80. G. Jones, *Mosquito*, 69.

81. G. Jones, *Mosquito*, 69.

82. G. Jones, *Mosquito*, 66–67.

83. G. Jones, *Mosquito*, 67.

84. G. Jones, *Mosquito*, 73.

85. G. Jones, *Mosquito*, 74.

86. G. Jones, *Mosquito*, 77.

87. G. Jones, *Mosquito*, 82.

88. Houston A. Baker, *Turning South Again: Re-thinking Modernism/Re-thinking Booker T.* (Durham, NC: Duke University Press, 2001), 14.

89. G. Jones, *Mosquito*, 89.

90. G. Jones, *Mosquito*, 89.

91. Douglas M. Strong, *Perfectionist Politics: Abolitionism and the Religious Tensions of American Democracy* (Syracuse, NY: Syracuse University Press, 1999), 4.

92. G. Jones, *Mosquito*, 93.

93. G. Jones, *Mosquito*, 93.

94. G. Jones, *Liberating Voices*, 49–50.

95. G. Jones, *Liberating Voices*, 121.

96. G. Jones, *Mosquito*, 94.

97. G. Jones, *Mosquito*, 93.

98. G. Jones, "The Siege," 94.

Conclusion. "Before I Was Straightened Out"

1. Toni Morrison, "The Site of Memory," in *Out There: Marginalization and Contemporary Culture*, ed. Russell Furgeson, Martha Gever, Trinh T. Minh-ha, Cornel West, and Felix Gonzales-Torres (Cambridge, MA: MIT Press, 1992), 305.

2. M. Jacqui Alexander, *Pedagogies of Crossing: Meditations on Feminism, Sexual Politics, Memory, and the Sacred* (Durham, NC: Duke University Press, 2005), 287.

3. Alexander, *Pedagogies of Crossing*, 326.

4. Alexander, *Pedagogies of Crossing*, 17.

5. Hortense Spillers, "Mama's Baby, Papa's Maybe: An American Grammar Book," special issue, "Culture and Countermemory: The 'American' Connection," *Diacritics* 17, no. 2 (Summer 1987): 72.

6. Denise Ferreira da Silva, *Toward a Global Theory of Race* (Minneapolis: University of Minnesota Press, 2007), xxxix.

7. José Esteban Muñoz, *Cruising Utopia: The Then and There of Queer Futurity* (New York: New York University Press, 2009), 1.

8. Alexander, *Pedagogies of Crossing*, 309; Avery Gordon, *Ghostly Matters: Haunting and the Sociological Imagination* (Minneapolis: University of Minnesota Press, 1997), 16.

9. In his chapter "What Might an Anthropology of Secularism Look Like?," Asad writes, "What facilitates the essentialization of the 'sacred' as an external transcendent power? My tentative answer is that new theorizations of the sacred were connected with European encounters with the non-European world, in the enlightened space and time that witnessed the construction of "religion" and "nature" as universal categories." Talal Asad, *Formations of the Secular: Christianity, Islam, Modernity* (Stanford, CA: Stanford University Press, 2003), 35.

10. Asad, *Formations of the Secular*, 35.

11. Asad, *Formations of the Secular*, 35.

12. Johannes Fabian, *Out of Our Minds: Reason and Madness in the Exploration of Central Africa* (Berkeley: University of California Press, 2000), 8.

13. Saidiya V. Hartman, *Scenes of Subjection: Terror, Slavery, and Self-Making in Nineteenth-Century America* (Oxford: Oxford University Press, 1999), 26.

14. Alexander, *Pedagogies of Crossing*, 327; Asad, *Formations of the Secular*, 35.

15. Myisha Cherry, "Young Black Philosophers Respond to the Trayvon Martin Case," Huffingtonpost.com, March 29, 2012, accessed November 31, 2012. http://www.huffington post.com/myisha-cherry/trayvon-martin_b_1378726.html.

16. Muñoz, *Cruising Utopia*, 186.

17. Muñoz, *Cruising Utopia*, 187.

18. Alexander, *Pedagogies of Crossing*, 309.

19. Kristine Stiles, "Thunderbird Immolation: Burning Racism," in *William Pope.L: The Friendliest Black Artist in America*, ed. William Pope.L and Marc H. C. Bessire (Cambridge, MA: MIT Press, 2002), 37.

20. Adrian M. S. Piper, *Rationality and the Structure of the Self*, vol. 1, *The Humean Conception*, 2nd ed. (Berlin: Adrian Piper Research Archive Foundation Berlin, 2013), 1. http://adrian piper.org/rss/docs/PiperRSSVol1HC.pdf.

21. From the artnews.org piece on Adrian Piper's Everything series, accessed October 13, 2011. "Everything will be taken away" was written on a sandwich board and worn by the curator

Jacob Fabricius in his Sandwiched series, sponsored by the Public Art Fund in New York City (2003). The mantra was written in henna on the foreheads of volunteers, as part of Creative Time's "Six Actions for New York City" (2007). Use of the mantra in relationship to images of Hurricane Katrina, the assassination of political leaders, and the evil events surrounding the Megan Williams case were part of the Everything exhibit, held at the Elizabeth Dee Gallery in New York City from March 1 to April 19, 2008.

22. Muñoz, *Cruising Utopia*, 1.

23. David Scott, *Conscripts of Modernity: The Tragedy of Colonial Enlightenment* (Durham, NC: Duke University Press, 2004), 204.

24. "Short: Carrie Mae Weems; 'Roaming,'" Art21.org, accessed November 1, 2012. http://www .art21.org/videos/short-carrie-mae-weems-roaming.

25. Muñoz, *Cruising Utopia*, 186.

26. Houston A. Baker, *Turning South Again: Re-thinking Modernism/Re-thinking Booker T.* (Durham, NC: Duke University Press, 2001), 14.

27. Lindon Barrett, *Blackness and Value: Seeing Double*, Cambridge Studies in American Literature and Value (Cambridge, UK: Cambridge University Press, 1998), 87.

28. Barrett, *Blackness and Value*, 57.

29. Ailsa Chang, "For City's Teens, Stop and Frisk Is Black and White," WNYC News, May 29, 2012, accessed November 1, 2012. http://www.wnyc.org/articles/wnyc-news/2012/may /29/city-teenagers-say-stop-and-frisk-all-about-race-and-class/.

30. Barrett, *Blackness and Value*, 28.

31. Umberto Eco, "The Frames of Comic 'Freedom,'" in *Carnival! Approaches to Semiotics*, vol. 64, ed. Thomas A. Sebeok (New York: Mouton, 1984), 7–8; cited in William Pope.L and Marc H. C. Bessire, eds., *William Pope.L: The Friendliest Black Artist in America*, ed. William Pope.L and Marc H. C. Bassire (Cambridge, MA: MIT Press, 2002), 23.

32. Immanuel Kant, *Foundations for the Metaphysics of Morals* (Indianapolis, IN: Bobbs-Merrill, 1959), 53.

33. Kant, *Foundations for the Metaphysics of Morals*, 53.

34. Hartman, *Scenes of Subjection*, 69.

35. Morrison, "The Site of Memory," 305.

36. Stiles, "Thunderbird Immolation," 37.

37. "Ernest Gallo," *Frontline*, PBS.org, accessed October 1, 2010, http://www.pbs.org/wgbh /pages/frontline/president/players/gallo.html.

38. Lowery Sims, "Interview with William Pope.L," in *William Pope.L: The Friendliest Black Artist in America*, ed. William Pope.L and Marc H. C. Bessire (Cambridge, MA: MIT Press, 2002), 62.

39. Accessed February 11, 2014.

40. Michael Taussig, *Defacement: Public Secrecy and the Labor of the Negative* (Stanford, CA: Stanford University Press, 1999), 1.

41. William Pope.L, e-mail correspondence, August 12, 2009.

42. Taussig, *Defacement*, 1.

43. Artist statement, courtesy of Dr. Constanze Von Marlin, Adrian Piper Research Archive (Berlin, Germany); February 24, 2009.

44. Tim Saltarelli, Elizabeth Dee Gallery, e-mail correspondence, March 16, 2009.

45. In an interview with the Nation of Islam's *Final Call*, Williams recalls the following: "They didn't feed me, didn't give me no water, they said when they came back they were

going to finish me off." "Final Call Exclusive: One-on-One Interview with West Virginia Race Torture Victim Megan Williams," *Final Call*, October 14, 2007, accessed October 15, 2010. http://www.finalcall.com/artman/publish/article_3997.shtml.

46. Fred Moten, *In the Break: The Aesthetics of the Black Radical Tradition* (Minneapolis: University of Minnesota Press, 2003), 200.

47. Moten, *In the Break*, 201.

48. Adrian M. S. Piper, "The Meaning of Brahmachari," in *How We Live Our Yoga: Teachers and Practitioners on How Yoga Enriches, Surprises, and Heals Us*, ed. Valerie Jeremijenko (Boston: Beacon Press, 2001), 40.

49. Piper, "The Meaning of Brahmachari," 38–39.

50. Piper, "The Meaning of Brahmachari," 43.

51. Piper, "The Meaning of Brahmachari," 46.

52. Piper, "The Meaning of Brahmachari," 38, 48.

53. Piper, *Rationality and the Structure of the Self*, vol. 2, 1–2.

54. Piper, "The Meaning of Brachmachari," 40.

55. Piper, "The Meaning of Brachmachari," 43.

56. Piper, "The Meaning of Brachmachari," 48.

57. I am referring to Piper's *Rationality and the Structure of the Self*.

58. Adrian M. S, Piper, *Rationality and the Structure of the Self*, vol. 2, *A Kantian Conception*, 2nd ed. (Berlin: Adrian Piper Research Archive Foundation Berlin, 2013), 49. http://adrian piper.org/rss/docs/PiperRSSVol2KC.pdf.

59. Piper, *Rationality and the Structure of the Self*, vol. 2, 1. In the *Critique of Pure Reason*, Kant describes reason's relationship to the ocean as follows: "This domain (reason) is an island, enclosed by nature within unalterable limits. It is the land of truth—enchanting name! Surrounded by a wide and stormy ocean, the native home of illusion, where many a fog bank and many a melting iceberg giving deceptive appearance of farther shores, deluding the adventurous seafarer ever anew with empty hopes, engaging him in enterprises which he can never abandon and yet is unable to carry to completion. Before we venture on this sea, to explore it in all directions, and to obtain assurance whether there be any ground for such hopes, it will be well to begin by casting a glance upon the map of the land which we are about to leave, and to enquire, first, whether we cannot in any case be satisfied with what it contains—are not; indeed under settle, and secondly by what title we possess even this domain, and can consider ourselves as secured against all opposing claims." Immanuel Kant, *Critique of Pure Reason*, trans. Norman Kent Smith (New York: Macmillan, 1965), 257.

60. Saidiya V. Hartman, "Venus in Two Acts," *Small Axe* 12, no. 2 (June 2008): 2.

61. Dawoud Bey, "Carrie Mae Weems," *BOMB*, Summer 2009. http://bombsite.com/issues /108/articles/3307.

62. Bey, "Carrie Mae Weems."

63. Moten, *In the Break*, 201.

64. Bey, "Carrie Mae Weems."

65. Bey, "Carrie Mae Weems."

66. Muñoz, *Cruising Utopia*, 186.

BIBLIOGRAPHY

Adorno, Theodor W. *Kant's "Critique of Pure Reason."* Ed. Rolf Tiedemann. Trans. Rodney Livingstone. Stanford, CA: Stanford University Press, 2002.

Alexander, M. Jacqui. *Pedagogies of Crossing: Meditations on Feminism, Sexual Politics, Memory, and the Sacred.* Durham, NC: Duke University Press, 2006.

American Civil Liberties Union. "Racial Profiling: Definition." November 23, 2005, accessed November 1, 2012. https://www.aclu.org/racial-justice/racial-profiling-definition.

American Psychiatric Association. *Diagnostic and Statistical Manual of Mental Disorders: DSM-IV.* Washington, DC: American Psychiatric Publication, 2000.

Arkin, Marc. "The Federalist Trope: Power and Passion in Abolitionist Rhetoric." *Journal of American Literary History* 88 (June 2001): 75–98.

Asad, Talal. *Formations of the Secular: Christianity, Islam, Modernity.* Stanford, CA: Stanford University Press, 2003.

Baker, Houston A. *Turning South Again: Re-thinking Modernism/Re-thinking Booker T.* Durham, NC: Duke University Press, 2001.

Barnett, Claudia. "This Fundamental Challenge to Identity: Reproduction and Representation in the Drama of Adrienne Kennedy." *Theatre Journal* 48, no. 2 (May 1996): 141–55.

Barrett, Lindon. *Blackness and Value: Seeing Double.* Cambridge, UK: Cambridge University Press, 1998.

Bartkowski, Frances. *Travelers, Immigrants, Inmates: Essays in Estrangement.* Minneapolis: University of Minnesota Press, 1995.

Beckles, Hillary McD. "Capitalism, Slavery, and Caribbean Modernity." *Callaloo* 20, no. 4 (Fall 1997): 777–89.

Bell, Howard, ed. *Search for a Place: Black Separatism and Africa, 1860.* Ann Arbor: University of Michigan Press, 1969.

Beneviste, E. *Problèmes de linquistique générale.* Paris: Seiul Points, 1974.

Benston, Kimberly. "Locating Adrienne Kennedy: Prefacing the Subject." In *Intersecting Boundaries: The Theater of Adrienne Kennedy*, ed. Paul K. Bryant-Jackson and Lois More Overbeck, 113–30. Minneapolis: University of Minnesota Press, 1992.

Bergson, Henri. *Matter and Memory.* Trans. N. M. Paul. Brooklyn, NY: Zone Books, 1988.

Bernasconi, Robert. "Who Invented the Concept of Race? Kant's Role in the Enlightenment Construction of Race." In *Race: Blackwell Readings in Continental Philosophy*, ed. Robert Bernasconi, 11–36. Malden, MA: Blackwell Publishers, 2001.

Bey, Dawoud. "Carrie Mae Weems." *BOMB*, 108 (Summer 2009). Accessed November 1, 2012. http://bombsite.com/issues/108/articles/3307.

Biehl, João. *Vita: Life in a Zone of Social Abandonment*. Berkeley: University of California Press, 2005.

Biehl, João, and Peter Locke. "Deleuze and the Anthropology of Becoming." *Current Anthropology* 51, no. 3 (June 2010): 317–51.

Blanchot, Maurice. *The Infinite Conversation*. Trans. Susan Hanson. Minneapolis: University of Minnesota Press, 1993.

Bowman, Curtis. "Kant and the Project of Enlightenment." Unpublished manuscript, University of Pennsylvania, 2001, accessed December 29, 2012. www.alphasolutionsgrp.com/Kant%20and%20the%20Project%20of%20Enlightenment.pdf.

Brody, Jennifer DeVere. *Impossible Purities: Blackness, Femininity, and Victorian Culture*. Durham, NC: Duke University Press, 1998.

Brooks, Daphne. *Bodies in Dissent: Spectacular Performances of Race and Freedom, 1850–1910*. Durham, NC: Duke University Press, 2006.

Brown, Jayna. *Babylon Girls: Black Women Performers and the Shaping of the Modern*. Durham, NC: Duke University Press, 2008.

Bryant-Jackson, Paul K. "Kennedy's Travelers in the American and African Continuum." In *Intersecting Boundaries: The Theater of Adrienne Kennedy*, ed. Paul K. Bryant-Jackson and Lois More Overbeck, 45–57. Minneapolis: University of Minnesota Press, 1992.

Bryant-Jackson, Paul K., and Lois M. Overbeck. "Interview with Billie Allen." In *Intersecting Boundaries: The Theater of Adrienne Kennedy*, ed. Paul K. Bryant-Jackson and Lois More Overbeck, 216–23. Minneapolis: University of Minnesota Press, 1992.

Buck-Morss, Susan. "Hegel and Haiti." *Critical Inquiry* 26, no. 4 (Summer 2000): 821–65.

Buroker, Jill Vance. *Kant's Critique of Pure Reason: An Introduction*. Cambridge, UK: Cambridge University Press, 2006.

Castiglia, Christopher. "Abolition's Racial Interiors and the Making of White Civic Depth." *American Literary History* 14, no. 1 (Spring 2002): 32–59.

Caygill, Howard. *A Kant Dictionary*. Malden, MA: Blackwell Publishers, 1995.

Champion, Laurie. "*Mosquito* by Gayl Jones." *African American Review* 34, no. 2 (Summer 2000): 366–68.

Chang, Ailsa. "For City's Teens, Stop and Frisk Is Black and White," WNYC News. May 29, 2012, accessed November 1, 2012. http://www.wnyc.org/articles/wnyc-news/2012/may/29/city-teenagers-say-stop-and-frisk-all-about-race-and-class/.

Cherry, Myisha. "Young Black Philosophers Respond to the Trayvon Martin Case." HuffingtonPost.com. March 29, 2012, accessed November 31, 2012. http://www.huffingtonpost.com/myisha-cherry/trayvon-martin_b_1378726.html.

Christian, Barbara. "The Race for Theory." In *The Black Feminist Reader*, ed. Joy James and T. Denean Sharpley-Whiting, 11–23. Oxford: Blackwell Publishing, 2000.

Cott, Nancy F. "Passionlessness: An Interpretation of Victorian Sexual Ideology." *Signs* 4, no. 2 (Winter 1978): 219–36.

Damrosch, Leo. *Jean-Jacques Rousseau: Restless Genius*. New York: Houghton Mifflin, 2005.

da Silva, Denise Ferreira. *Toward a Global Theory of Race*. Minneapolis: University of Minnesota Press, 2007.

Davis, Angela. *Women, Race, and Class*. New York: Random House, 1981.

Dayan, Joan. "Codes of Law and Bodies of Color." *New Literary History* 26, no. 2 (1995): 283–308.

de Certeau, Michel. *The Practice of Everyday Life*. Trans. Steven Randall. Berkeley: University of California Press, 1984.

Delany, Martin R. *Blake; Or, the Huts of America*. Ed. Floyd J. Miller. Boston: Beacon Press, 1970.

———. "The Condition, Elevation, Emigration, and Destiny of the Colored People of the United States." In *Martin Delany: A Documentary Reader*, ed. Robert S. Levine, 189–216. Chapel Hill: University of North Carolina Press, 2003.

———. "Political Destiny of the Colored Race on the American Continent." In *Martin Delany: A Documentary Reader*, ed. Robert S. Levine, 245–79. Chapel Hill: University of North Carolina Press, 2003.

Deleuze, Gilles. *Kant's Critical Philosophy: The Doctrine of the Faculties*. Trans. Hugh Tomlinson. London: The Athlone Press, 1984.

Deleuze, Gilles, and Félix Guattari. *Anti-Oedipus: Capitalism and Schizophrenia*. Trans. Robert Hurley. Minneapolis: University of Minnesota Press, 1983.

———. *Kafka: Toward a Minor Literature*. Trans. Dana Polan. Minneapolis: University of Minnesota Press, 1986.

———. *A Thousand Plateaus: Capitalism and Schizophrenia*. Trans. Brian Massumi. Minneapolis: University of Minnesota Press, 1987.

Derrida, Jacques. *Of Spirit: Heidegger and the Question*. Trans. Geoffrey Bennington. Chicago: University of Chicago Press, 1989.

———. *Resistances of Psychoanalysis*. Trans. Peggy Kamuf. Stanford, CA: Stanford University Press, 1998.

Descartes, René. *Meditations on First Philosophy: With Selections from the Objections and Replies*. Ed. John Cottingham. With an introduction by Bernard Williams. Cambridge, UK: Cambridge University Press, 1996.

de Vries, Hent. *Minimal Theologies: Critiques of Secular Reason in Adorno and Levinas*. Baltimore, MD: Johns Hopkins University Press, 2005.

Diamond, Elin. *Unmaking Mimesis: Essays on Feminism and Theater*. New York: Routledge, 1997.

Douglass, Frederick. "What I Found at the Northampton Association." In *History of Florence, Massachusetts, Including a Complete Account of the Northampton Association of Education and Industry*, ed. Charles A. Sheffield. Florence, MA: Charles A. Sheffield, 1895.

Dube, Saurabh. "Travelling Light: Missionary Musings, Colonial Cultures, and Anthropological Anxieties." In *Travel Worlds: Journeys in Contemporary Cultural Politics*, ed. Raminder Kuar and John Hutnyk, 29–50. London: Zed Books, 1999.

Du Bois, W. E. B. *The Souls of Black Folk*. New York: Penguin, 1989.

Eckhoff, Sally. "The Terrible Mystery of Gayl Jones." Salon.com. February 26, 1998, accessed January 1, 2005. http://web.archive.org/web/19991201112700/http://www.salon.com/media/1998/02/26media.html.

Eco, Umberto. "The Frames of Comic 'Freedom.'" In *Carnival! Approaches to Semiotics*. Vol. 64, ed. Thomas A. Sebeok. New York: Mouton, 1984.

Edwards, Tamala. "*Mosquito*." Short Takes, *Time*. February 8, 2009, accessed November 1, 2004. http://www.time.com/time/magazine/shorttakes/0,9485,1101990208,00.html.

Eze, Emmanuel Chukwudi. *Achieving Our Humanity: The Idea of a Postracial Future*. New York: Routledge, 2001.

Fabian, Johannes. *Out of Our Minds: Reason and Madness in the Exploration of Central Africa*. Berkeley: University of California Press, 2000.

Fanon, Frantz. *Black Skin, White Masks*. Trans. Richard Philcox. New York: Grove Press, 1967.

Forte, Jeanie. "Kennedy's Body Politic: The Mulatta, Menses, and the Medusa." In *Intersecting Boundaries: The Theater of Adrienne Kennedy*, ed. Paul K. Bryant-Jackson and Lois More Overbeck, 157–69. Minneapolis: University of Minnesota Press, 1992.

Foster, Susan Leigh. "Walking and Other Choreographic Tactics: Danced Inventions of Theatricality and Performativity." *SubStance* 31, nos. 2 and 3 (2002): 125–46.

Foucault, Michel. "Lives of Infamous Men." In *Power*. Trans. Robert Hurley, 157–75. New York: New Press, 2000.

———. *Madness and Civilization: A History of Insanity in the Age of Reason*. Trans. Richard Howard. New York: Random House, 1965.

———. *The Order of Things: An Archaeology of the Human Sciences*. New York: Vintage, 1994.

Freud, Sigmund. *Civilization and Its Discontents*. New York: W. W. Norton and Co., 1961.

———. *New Introductory Lectures on Psychoanalysis*. Trans. James Strachey. New York: W. W. Norton and Co., 1962.

Garfield, Deborah. "Earwitness: Female Abolitionism, Sexuality, and *Incidents in the Life of a Slave Girl*." In *Harriet Jacobs and Incidents in the Life of a Slave Girl: New Critical Essays*, ed. Deborah Garfield and Rafia Zafar, 100–30. Cambridge, UK: Cambridge University Press, 1996.

Gates, Henry Louis. "'Sanctuary, Rev. of Mosquito' by Gayl Jones." *New York Times*. November 14, 1999, section 7 (Books), 14.

Gibson, Donald. "Harriet Jacobs, Frederick Douglass, and the Slavery Debate: Bondage, Family, and the Discourse of Domesticity." In *Harriet Jacobs and Incidents in the Life of a Slave Girl: New Critical Essays*, ed. Deborah Garfield and Rafia Zafar, 156–78. Cambridge, UK: Cambridge University Press, 1996.

Gil, José. *Metamorphosis of the Body*. Trans. Stephen Muecke. Minneapolis: University of Minnesota Press, 1998.

Gilroy, Paul. *The Black Atlantic: Modernity and Double Consciousness*. Cambridge, MA: Harvard University Press, 1993.

Glausiusz, Josie. "Living in a Dream World: The Role of Daydreaming in Problem Solving and Creativity." *Scientific American Mind*, 22, no. 1 (March 2011): 24–31.

Goetschel, Willi. "Epilogue: 'Land of Truth—Enchanting Name!' Kant's Journey at Home." In *The Imperialist Imagination: German Colonialism and Its Legacy*, ed. Sara Friedrichsmeyer, Sara Lennox, and Susanne Zantop, 321–36. Ann Arbor: University of Michigan Press, 1998.

Golden, Renny, and Michael McConnell. *Sanctuary: The New Underground Railroad*. Maryknoll, NY: Orbis Books, 1986.

Gordon, Avery. *Ghostly Matters: Haunting and the Sociological Imagination*. Minneapolis: University of Minnesota Press, 1997.

Greyser, Naomi. "Affective Geographies: Sojourner Truth's Narrative, Feminism, and the Ethical Bind of Sentimentalism." *American Literature* 79, no. 2 (2007): 275–305.

Griffin, Farah Jasmine. "That the Mothers May Soar and the Daughters May Know Their Names: A Retrospective of Black Feminist Literary Criticism." *Signs* 32, no. 2 (2007): 483–507.

Guattari, Félix. *Chaosmosis: An Ethico-Aesthetic Paradigm*. Trans. Paul Bains. Bloomington: Indiana University Press, 1995.

Hacking, Ian. *Mad Travelers: Reflections on the Reality of Transient Mental Illnesses*. Charlottesville: University of Virginia Press, 1998.

Haraway, Donna. "Ecce Homo, Ain't (Ar'n't) I a Woman, and Inappropriate/d Others: The Human in a Posthumanist Landscape." In *Feminists Theorize the Political*, ed. Joan Scott and Judith Butler, 86–100. New York: Routledge, 1992.

Harper, Michael, and Robert B. Steptoe. *Chant of Saints: A Gathering of Afro-American Literature, Art, and Scholarship*. Urbana: University of Illinois Press, 1979.

Harris, Trudier. "Forward." In *After the Pain: Critical Essays on Gayl Jones*, ed. Fiona Mills and Keith B. Mitchell, ix–xiv. New York: Peter Lang, 2006.

Harrison, Paul Carter. "The Crisis of Black Theater Identity." *African American Review* 31, no. 4 (1997): 567–78.

Hartman, Saidiya V. *Scenes of Subjection: Terror, Slavery, and Self-Making in Nineteenth-Century America*. Oxford: Oxford University Press, 1999.

———. "Venus in Two Acts." *Small Axe* 12, no. 2 (June 2008): 1–14.

Henderson, Mae. "Speaking in Tongues: Dialogics and Dialectics and the Black Woman Writer's Literary Tradition." *African American Literary Theory: A Reader*, ed. Winston Napier, 348–68. New York: New York University Press, 2000.

Hinks, Peter. *To Awaken My Afflicted Brethren: David Walker and the Problem of Antebellum Slave Resistance*. University Park: Pennsylvania State University Press, 1997.

Holland, Sharon Patricia. *The Erotic Life of Racism*. Durham, NC: Duke University Press, 2012.

———. *Raising the Dead: Readings of Death and (Black) Subjectivity*. Durham, NC: Duke University Press, 2000.

Holloway, Karla FC. *Codes of Conduct: Race, Ethics, and the Color of Our Character*. New Brunswick, NJ: Rutgers University Press, 1996.

———. *Private Bodies, Public Texts: Race, Gender, and a Cultural Bioethics*. Durham, NC: Duke University Press, 2011.

Horkheimer, Max, and Theodor W. Adorno. *Dialectic of Enlightenment*. Ed. Gunzelin Schmid Noerr. Trans. Edmund Jephcott. Stanford, CA: Stanford University Press, 2007.

HuffingtonPost.com. "CeCe McDonald, Minnesota Transgender Woman, Pleads Guilty in Manslaughter Case Despite Supporters' Defense." posted May 2, 2012, at 4:04 p.m., updated May 2, 2012, at 11:53 p.m., accessed November 15, 2012. http://www.huffingtonpost.com/2012/05/02/cece-mcdonald-minnesota-transgender-woman-manslaughter_n_1472078.html.

Jacobs, Harriet. *Incidents in the Life of a Slave Girl*. Ed. Lydia Maria Child. Orlando, FL: Harcourt Brace Jovanovich Publishers, 1973.

James, C. L. R. *The Black Jacobins: Toussaint L'Ouverture and the San Domingo Revolution*. New York: Vintage, 1989.

Jefferson, Thomas. "The Difference Is Fixed in Nature/Notes on the State of Virginia." In *Race and the Enlightenment: A Reader*, ed. Emmanuel Eze, 95–103. Malden, MA: Blackwell Publishing, 1997.

Jenkins, Candice. *Private Lives, Proper Relations: Regulating Black Intimacy*. Minneapolis: University of Minnesota Press, 2007.

Jones, Gayl. *Corregidora*. Boston: Beacon Press, 1975.

———. *Eva's Man*. Boston: Beacon Press, 1976.

———. "From *The Quest for Wholeness*: Re-Imagining the African-American Novel; An Essay on Third World Aesthetics." *Callaloo* 17, no. 2 (Spring 1994): 507–18.

———. *Liberating Voices: Oral Tradition in African American Literature*. New York: Penguin, 1991.

———. *Mosquito*. Boston: Beacon Press, 1999.

———. "The Siege." *Callaloo*, no. 16 (1982): 89–94.

Jones, Joni L. "Cast a Wide Net." *Theater Journal* 57, no. 4 (2005): 598–600.

Jones, Martha. *All Bound up Together: The Woman Question in African American Public Culture, 1830–1900*. Chapel Hill: University of North Carolina Press, 2007.

Judy, R. A. T. "Kant and the Negro." *Surfaces* 1, no. 8 (1991): 1–70.

Kane, M. J., L. H. Brown, J. C. McVay, P. J. Silvia, I. Myin-Germeys, and T. R. Kwapil. "For Whom the Mind Wanders, and When: An Experience-Sampling Study of Working Memory and Executive Control in Daily Life." *Psychological Science* 18, no. 7 (July 2007): 614–21.

Kant, Immanuel. *Anthropology from a Pragmatic Point of View*. Trans. Robert B. Louden. Cambridge, UK: Cambridge University Press, 2006.

———. *The Critique of Judgment*. Trans. James Creed Meredith. Oxford: Oxford University Press, 1952.

———. *Critique of Pure Reason*. Trans. Norman Kent Smith. New York: Macmillan and Co., 1965.

———. *Foundations for the Metaphysics of Morals*. Trans. Lewis White Black. Indianapolis, IN: Bobbs-Merrill, 1959.

———. *Observations on the Feeling of the Beautiful and the Sublime*. Trans. John T. Goldthwait. Berkeley: University of California Press, 1960.

———. "On the Use of Teleological Principles in Philosophy." In *Race*, Blackwell Readings in Continental Philosophy, ed. Robert Bernasconi, 37–56. Malden, MA: Blackwell Publishers, 2001.

Kazanjian, David. *The Colonizing Trick: National Culture and Imperial Citizenship in Early America*. Minneapolis: University of Minnesota Press, 2003.

Kennedy, Adrienne. *Funnyhouse of a Negro*. In *Adrienne Kennedy: In One Act*, 1–23. Minneapolis: University of Minnesota Press, 1988.

———. *The Owl Answers*. In *Adrienne Kennedy: In One Act*, 25–45. Minneapolis: University of Minnesota Press, 1988.

———. *People Who Led to My Plays*. New York: Theater Communications Group, 1988.

———. "Preface." In *Adrienne Kennedy: In One Act*, ix. Minneapolis: University of Minnesota Press, 1988.

Kleingeld, Pauline. "Kant's Second Thoughts on Race." *Philosophical Quarterly* 57, no. 229 (2007): 573–92.

Kolin, Philip. *Understanding Adrienne Kennedy*. Columbia: University of South Carolina Press, 2005.

Lasser, Carol. "Voyeuristic Abolitionism: Sex, Gender, and the Transformation of Antislavery Rhetoric." *Journal of the Early Republic* 28, no. 1 (2008): 83–114.

LeClair, Tom. "Mosquito." Salon.com, January 12, 2009, accessed November 15, 2004. http://www.salon.com/1999/01/12/sneaks_54/.

Lepecki, André. *Exhausting Dance: Performance and the Politics of Movement*. New York: Routledge, 2006.

———. "Mutant Enunciations." *TDR* 50, no. 4 (Winter 2006): 17–20.

Levine, Robert, ed. *Martin Delany: A Documentary Reader*. Chapel Hill: University of North Carolina Press, 2003.

——. *Martin Delany, Frederick Douglass, and the Politics of Representative Identity*. Chapel Hill: University of North Carolina Press, 1997.

Lippitt, Akira Mizuta. *Electric Animal: Toward a Rhetoric of Wildlife*. Minneapolis: University of Minnesota Press, 2000.

Lorde, Audre. "Age, Race, Class, and Sex: Women Redefining Difference." In *Sister Outsider: Essays and Speeches by Audre Lorde*, 114–23. Berkeley, CA: Crossing Press, 1984.

——. "Uses of the Erotic: The Erotic as Power." In *Sister Outsider: Essays and Speeches by Audre Lorde*, 53–59. Berkeley, CA: Crossing Press, 1984.

Lumumba, Patrice. "Dawn in the Heart of Africa." In *Africa: Selected Readings*, ed. F. G. Burke, 206–7. New York: Houghton Mifflin, 1973.

MacEoin, Gary, and Nivita Riley. *No Promised Land: American Refugee Policy and the Rule of Law*. Boston: Oxfam America, 1982.

Mackey, Nathaniel. "Other: From Noun to Verb." In *The Jazz Cadence of American Culture*, ed. Robert O'Mealley, 513–32. New York: Columbia University Press, 1998.

Martin, Randy. *Critical Moves: Dance Studies in Theory and Politics*. Durham, NC: Duke University Press, 1998.

McKittrick, Katherine. *Demonic Grounds: Black Women and the Cartographies of Struggle*. Minneapolis: University of Minnesota Press, 2006.

McRuer, Robert. "Composing Bodies; Or, De-composition: Queer Theory, Disability Studies, and Alternative Corporealities." *JAC* 24, no. 1 (2004): 48–78.

Michel, Jean Claude. *The Black Surrealists*. New York: Peter Lang, 2000.

Miller, Floyd J. *The Search for a Black Nationality: Black Emigration and Colonization, 1787–1863*. Urbana: University of Illinois Press, 1975.

Miller, Paul. *Elusive Origins: The Enlightenment in the Modern Caribbean Historical Imagination*. Charlottesville: University of Virginia Press, 2010.

Mills, Charles. *Blackness Visible: Essays on Philosophy and Race*. Ithaca, NY: Cornell University Press, 1998.

——. "Kant's *Untermenschen*." In *Race and Racism in Modern Philosophy*, ed. Andrew Valls, 169–93. Ithaca, NY: Cornell University Press, 2005.

——. *The Racial Contract*. Ithaca, NY: Cornell University Press, 1997.

Morrison, Toni. "The Site of Memory." In *Out There: Marginalization and Contemporary Culture*, ed. Russell Furgeson, Martha Gever, Trinh T. Minh-ha, Cornel West, and Felix Gonzales-Torres, 299–324. Cambridge, MA: MIT Press, 1992.

Moten, Fred. *In the Break: The Aesthetics of the Black Radical Tradition*. Minneapolis: University of Minnesota Press, 2003.

——. "Knowledge of Freedom." *CR: The New Centennial Review* 4, no. 2 (2004): 269–310.

——. "Music against the Law of Reading the Future and 'Rodney King.'" Special issue, "The Future of the Profession," *The Journal of the Midwest Modern Language Association* 27, no. 1 (Spring 1994): 51–64.

Muñoz, José Esteban. *Cruising Utopia: The Then and There of Queer Futurity*. New York: New York University Press, 2009.

——. *Disidentifications: Queers of Color and the Performance of Politics*. Minneapolis: University of Minnesota Press, 1999.

Murray, Albert. "Improvisation and the Creative Process." In *The Jazz Cadence of American Culture*, ed. Robert O'Mealley, 111–13. New York: Columbia University Press, 1998.

Muthu, Sankhar. *Enlightenment against Empire*. Princeton, NJ: Princeton University Press, 2003.

Newman, Louise. *White Women's Rights: The Racial Origins of Feminism in the United States*. New York: Oxford University Press, 1999.

O'Mealley, Robert G, ed. *The Jazz Cadence of American Culture*. New York: Columbia University Press, 1998.

Overbeck, Lois More. "The Life of the Work." In *Intersecting Boundaries: The Theater of Adrienne Kennedy*, ed. Paul K. Bryant-Jackson and Lois More Overbeck, 21–41. Minneapolis: University of Minnesota Press, 1992.

Painter, Nell. *Sojourner Truth: A Life, a Symbol*. New York: W. W. Norton, 1996.

Piper, Adrian M. S. "The Meaning of Brahmachari." In *How We Live Our Yoga: Teachers and Practitioners on How Yoga Enriches, Surprises, and Heals Us*, ed. Valerie Jeremijenko, 35–56. Boston: Beacon, 2001.

———. *Rationality and the Structure of the Self*. Vol. 1, *The Humean Conception*. 2nd ed. Berlin: Adrian Piper Research Archive Foundation Berlin, 2013. http://www.adrianpiper.com/rss/docs/PiperRSSVol1HC.pdf.

———. *Rationality and the Structure of the Self*. Vol. 2, *A Kantian Conception*. 2nd ed. Berlin: Adrian Piper Research Archive Foundation Berlin, 2013. http://www.adrianpiper.com/rss/docs/PiperRSSVol2KC.pdf.

Plato. *The Republic*. Trans. Desmond Lee. New York: Penguin Books, 2003.

Pope.L, William, and Marc H. C. Bassire, eds. *William Pope.L: The Friendliest Black Artist in America*. Cambridge, MA: MIT Press, 2002.

Randle, Gloria T. "Between the Rock and the Hard Place: Mediating Spaces in Harriet Jacobs's 'Incidents in the Life of a Slave Girl.'" *African American Review* 33, no. 1 (1999): 43–56.

Reddy, Srikanth. "Changing the Sjuzet: Lyn Hejinian's Digressive Narratologies." *Contemporary Literature* 50, no. 1 (2009): 54–93.

Reid-Pharr, Robert. "Violent Ambiguity: Martin Delany, Bourgeois Sadomasochism, and the Production of a Black National Masculinity." In *Representing Black Men*, ed. Marcellus Blount and George P. Cunningham, 73–94. New York: Routledge, 1995.

Richardson, Marilyn. *Maria W. Stewart: America's First Black Woman Political Writer*. Bloomington: Indiana University Press, 1987.

Roach, Joseph, and Janelle Reinelt, eds. *Critical Theory and Performance*. Ann Arbor: University of Michigan Press, 2007.

Rosemont, Franklin. "Introduction," in *Black, Brown, and Beige: Surrealist Writings from Africa and the Diaspora*, ed. Franklin Rosemont and Robin D. G. Kelley. Austin: University of Texas Press, 2010.

Rousseau, Jean-Jacques. *The Confessions*. Trans. J. M. Cohen. New York: Penguin Books, 1953.

———. *Reveries of a Solitary Walker*. Trans. Peter France. New York: Penguin Books, 1979.

———. *The Social Contract*. Trans. Maurice Cranston. New York: Penguin, 1968.

Rowell, Charles H. "An Interview with Gayl Jones." *Callaloo*, no. 16 (October 1982): 32–53.

Sala-Molins, Louis. *Dark Side of the Light: Slavery and the French Enlightenment*. Minneapolis: University of Minnesota Press, 2006.

Saldanha, Arun. *Psychedelic Whiteness: Goa Trance and the Viscosity of Race*. Minneapolis: University of Minnesota Press, 2007.

Sanders, Leslie. *The Development of Black Theater in America: From Shadows to Selves.* Baton Rouge: Louisiana University Press, 1988.

Scanlan, Robert. "Surrealism as Mimesis: A Director's Guide to Adrienne Kennedy's *Funnyhouse of a Negro.*" In *Intersecting Boundaries: The Theater of Adrienne Kennedy,* ed. Paul K. Bryant-Jackson and Lois More Overbeck, 93–112. Minneapolis: University of Minnesota Press, 1992.

Schechner, Richard. *Performance Studies: An Introduction.* New York: Routledge, 2002.

Schönfield, Martin. *The Philosophy of the Young Kant: The Precritical Project.* New York: Oxford, 2000.

Schott, Robin. *Cognition and Eros: A Critique of the Kantian Paradigm.* Boston: Beacon Press, 1988.

Scott, David. "Antinomies of Slavery, Enlightenment, and Universal History." *Small Axe* 14, no. 3 (2010): 152–62.

———. *Conscripts of Modernity: The Tragedy of Colonial Enlightenment.* Durham, NC: Duke University Press, 2004.

——— "The Re-enchantment of Humanism: An Interview with Sylvia Wynter." *Small Axe* 8 (September 2000): 119–207.

Sedgwick, Eve. *Novel Gazing: Queer Readings in Fiction.* Durham, NC: Duke University Press, 1997.

Sharpe, Christina. *Monstrous Intimacies: Making Post-slavery Subjects.* Durham, NC: Duke University Press, 2010.

Shell, Susan. "Kant as Propagator: Reflections on *Observations on the Feeling of the Beautiful and the Sublime.*" *Eighteenth-Century Studies* 35, no. 3 (Spring 2002): 455–68.

Shonibare, Yinka, and Anthony Downey. "Setting the Stage: Yinka Shonibare MBE in Conversation with Anthony Downey." In *Yinka Shonibare, MBE,* ed. Rachel Kent, 38–45. Munich: Prestel Publishing, 2008.

Sichert, Margit. "The Staging of Excessive Emotions: Adrienne Kennedy's *Funnyhouse of a Negro.*" *REAL: The Yearbook of Research in English and American Literature* 16 (2000).

Siebert, Wilbur H. *The Underground Railroad from Slavery to Freedom.* New York: Arno Press, 1968.

Sims, Lowery. "Interview with William Pope.L." In *William Pope.L: The Friendliest Black Artist in America,* ed. William Pope.L and Marc H. C. Bessire, 62–67. Cambridge, MA: MIT Press, 2002.

Smith, Valerie. *Self-Discovery and Authority in Afro-American Narrative.* Cambridge, MA: Harvard University Press, 1987.

Sollors, Werner. "Owls and Rats in the American Funnyhouse: Adrienne Kennedy's Drama." *American Literature* 63, no. 3 (September 1991): 507–32.

Solomon, Alisa. "Sojourner's Truths." *Village Voice,* October 1, 1995.

Southgate, Martha. "Mosquito." *Essence* 29, no. 11 (1999): 80.

Spillers, Hortense. *Black, White, and in Color: Essays on American Literature and Culture.* Chicago: University of Chicago Press, 2003.

———. "Mama's Baby, Papa's Maybe: An American Grammar Book." Special issue, "Culture and Countermemory: The 'American' Connection," *Diacritics* 17, no. 2 (Summer 1987): 64–81.

Spivak, Gayatri. *A Critique of Postcolonial Reason: Toward a History of the Vanishing Present.* Cambridge, MA: Harvard University Press, 1999.

Stanley, Eric. "Near Life, Queer Death: Overkill and Ontological Capture." *Social Text* 29, no. 2 (2011): 1–19.

Stein, Howard. "An Interview with Michael Kahn." In *Intersecting Boundaries: The Theater of Adrienne Kennedy*, ed. Paul K. Bryant-Jackson and Lois More Overbeck, 189–98. Minneapolis: University of Minnesota Press, 1992.

Stetson, Erlene, and Linda David. *Glorifying in Tribulation: The Lifework of Sojourner Truth*. East Lansing: Michigan State University Press, 1994.

Stiles, Kristine. "Thunderbird Immolation: Burning Racism." In *William Pope.L: The Friendliest Black Artist in America*, ed. William Pope.L and Marc H. C. Bessire, 37–43. Cambridge, MA: MIT Press, 2002.

Stormer, Dan, and Paul Bernstein. "The Impact of *Kolender v. Lawson* on Law Enforcement and Minority Groups." *Hastings Constitutional Law Quarterly* 12 (1984): 105–25.

Strauss, Sarah. "The Master's Narrative: Swami Sivananda and the Transnational Production of Yoga." *Journal of Folklore Research* 39, no. 2 (2002): 217–41.

———. *Positioning Yoga: Balancing Acts across Cultures*. New York: Oxford University Press, 2005.

Strong, Douglas M. *Perfectionist Politics: Abolitionism and the Religious Tensions of American Democracy*. Syracuse, NY: Syracuse University Press, 1999.

Tate, Claudia C. "An Interview with Gayl Jones." *Black American Literature Forum* 13, no. 4 (Winter 1979): 142–48.

Tate, Greg. "Going Underground, Review of Mosquito by Gayl Jones." *VLS: Voice Literary Supplement* 44, no. 6 (16 February 1999): 127.

Taussig, Michael. *Defacement: Public Secrecy and the Labor of the Negative*. Stanford, CA: Stanford University Press, 1999.

Taylor, Yuval, and Charles Johnson. *I Was Born a Slave: An Anthology of Classic Slave Narratives*. Chicago: Lawrence Hill Books, 1999.

Titus, Mary. "Carnival Laughter: Resistance in Incidents." In *Harriet Jacobs and Incidents in the Life of a Slave Girl: New Critical Essays*, ed. Deborah Garfield and Rafia Zafar, 216–32. Cambridge, UK: Cambridge University Press, 1996.

Truth, Sojourner, Olive Gilbert, and Frances Titus. *Narrative of Sojourner Truth: A Bondswoman of Olden Time; Emancipated by the New York Legislature in the Early Part of the Present Century; With a History of Her Labors and Correspondence Drawn from Her "Book of Life."* Battle Creek, MI: published by the author, 1881.

Van Horne, John C., and Jean Fagan Yellin, eds. *The Abolitionist Sisterhood: Women's Political Culture in Antebellum America*. Ithaca, NY: Cornell University Press, 1994.

Vergès, Françoise. "To Cure and to Free: The Fanonian Project of 'Decolonized Psychiatry.'" In *Fanon: A Critical Reader*, ed. Lewis R. Gordon, T. Denean Sharpley-Whiting, and Renée T. White, 85–99. Oxford: Wiley-Blackwell, 1996.

———. "Theotopographies: Nancy, Hölderlin, Heidegger." *MLN* 109, no. 3 (1994): 445–77.

Walker, David, and Henry Highland Garnet. *Walker's Appeal and Garnet's Address to the Slaves of the United States of America*. Nashville, TN: Winston Publishing Company, 1994.

Ward, Jerry W. "Escape from Trublem: The Fiction of Gayl Jones." *Callaloo*, no. 16 (October 1982): 95–104.

Washington, Margaret. "'From Motives of Delicacy': Sexuality and Morality in the Narratives of Sojourner Truth and Harriet Jacobs." Special issue, "Women, Slavery, and Historical Research," ed. Brenda E. Stevenson, *The Journal of African American History* 92, no. 1 (Winter 2007): 57–73.

———. *Sojourner Truth's America*. Urbana: University of Illinois Press, 2009.

Weheliye, Alexander G. "After Man." *American Literary History* 20, nos. 1–2 (Spring/Summer 2008): 321–36.

Wynter, Sylvia. "Beyond Miranda's Meanings: Un/silencing the 'Demonic Ground' of Caliban's Woman." In *Out of the Kumbla: Caribbean Women and Literature*, ed. Carole Boyce Davies and Elaine Savory Fido, 355–72. Trenton, NJ: Africa World Press, 1994.

———. "Beyond the Word of Man: Glissant and the New Discourse of the Antilles." *World Literature Today* 63, no. 4 (Autumn 1989): 637–48.

———. "The Pope Must Have Been Drunk, the King of Castile a Madman: Culture as Actuality, and the Caribbean Rethinking Modernity." In *The Reordering of Culture: Latin America, the Caribbean, and Canada In the Hood*, ed. Alvina Ruprecht and Cecilia Taiana, 17–41. Ontario: Carleton University Press, 1995.

Zammito, John. *Kant, Herder, and the Birth of Anthropology*. Chicago: University of Chicago Press, 2002.

INDEX

abecedarian progression (Reddy), 123
able-bodiment, 25, 128
abolitionism, 10, 61, 63–64, 66, 84–85; and
the abolitionist reader, 10, 69–70, 89, 98;
in Jones's *Mosquito*, 135, 137, 139; kinetic
constraints in, 66
affectability (da Silva): in Delany's *Blake; or
the Huts of America*, 72; of imperialism, 8;
Kennedy and, 96, 111; people of color and,
5, 9, 13, 31, 96, 146; of white, Enlightenment subject, 25–26, 30, 37
agency, 6, 23; as exterior kinesis, 4; and unreadability, 4–5
Age of Enlightenment (exhibit). *See* Yinka
Shonibare
Alexander, Jacqui M.: on black feminism, 13;
on freedom, 146; on the sacred, 148; on
secular citizenship, 145–47
animality: in Kennedy's *The Owl Answers*,
117–18; in Rousseau's *Reveries of a Solitary
Walker*, 42
ante-articulate: and black enlightenment,
62–63, 68; in Jacobs's *Incidents in the Life
of a Slave Girl*, 76; in Jones's *Mosquito*, 139;
in Jones's novels, 125; in Kennedy's theater,
98; in Kennedy's *The Owl Answers*, 120;
Sojourner Truth and, 93; in Walker's
*Appeal to the Coloured Citizens of the
World*, 84
ante-composure, 128–29

anthropology, 7–8, 43–44
anticaptivity, 10, 19; in Jacobs's *Incidents
in the Life of a Slave Girl*, 68; in Jones's
Mosquito, 139; in Kennedy's theater, 98; in
Kennedy's *Funnyhouse of a Negro*, 107
antislavery, 10–11, 16–17, 20, 59–60, 94; in
Delany's *Blake; or the Huts of America*,
71, 73; in Jacobs's *Incidents in the Life of
a Slave Girl*, 64–66; in Jones's *Mosquito*,
138–39; in Walker's *Appeal to the Coloured
Citizens of the World*, 78, 81–82
antiwandering, 6, 11, 18, 43, 121; in Kant,
49; in Kant's *Critique of Pure Reason*, 52;
in Kant's *Observations on the Feeling of
the Beautiful and Sublime*, 54; in Kant's
"On the Use of Teleological Principles in
Philosophy," 54; in Kennedy's *The Owl
Answers*, 119; Piper and, 161; in Rousseau's
The Confessions, 41; in Rousseau's *The
Social Contract*, 35; in Walker's *Appeal to
the Coloured Citizens of the World*, 78
Appeal to the Coloured Citizens of the World
(Walker), 62, 78–84; on Africa, 82–83,
90; on American Enlightenment, 80;
antislavery in, 81–82; antiwandering in,
78; black enlightenment in, 79–84; and
black reform, 82; black women in, 83–84;
crookedness in (as unenlightened comportment), 81–84; desire in, 84; emotion
in, 81, 83–84; and the feminine, 83–84;